1958

CHANGING GREENLAND

Old and new rubbed shoulders on the occasion of the Royal visit of 1952. A polar-bear-hunter from Thule and a worker from the boat-building yards on the quay-side at Holtsteinsborg. The King of Denmark's yacht, *Dannebrog*, lies at anchor.

[*Frontispiece*

GEOFFREY WILLIAMSON

Changing Greenland

WITH AN INTRODUCTION BY

OLE BJØRN KRAFT
*Acting Prime Minister of Denmark, and
Minister for Foreign Affairs*

SIDGWICK AND JACKSON LIMITED
LONDON

First published in 1953

DEDICATED TO THE MEMORY OF

HANS EGEDE AND DR HENDRIK RINK

whose faith in Greenland's future
is being strikingly vindicated

Printed in Great Britain by Richard Clay and Company, Ltd.,
Bungay, Suffolk

INTRODUCTION

A NEW era for the Greenland people began in the year of 1952, when our Danish Sailor-King navigated his yacht *Dannebrog* across the Atlantic to the Greenland Coast, and thus set the seal on a development of which a new and extensive legislative work had formed the foundation.

It is true that the approach to a different life had already begun during the war, but there can be no doubt that the Royal Visit last summer heralded the opening of a new era.

Many of the elderly people in Greenland may perhaps not quite understand the meaning of the new administration and the many technical developments. Very naturally. For them the kayak and the Church, the harpoon and the seal are all that matter in life. They are a hardy race, who for many generations have proved their vitality as a nation. But the old days are gone: the new life has come to stay.

Mr. Geoffrey Williamson saw a great deal of Greenland last year, when he travelled along the west coast during the Royal Visit. He has made a comprehensive survey of a rather complex subject, and has written a fine book about Greenland, her people and the outstanding exploring of those far-off northern latitudes. I would like to congratulate Mr. Williamson on his achievement.

He knows, as all British people seem to understand, that one of the driving powers behind any great undertaking, any great expedition, any sea-going journey, any strenuous climb has been and will always be—the human curiosity: what is behind the skyline?

That curiosity has without doubt advanced our knowledge and our civilisation, as this present volume will undoubtedly advance the knowledge of Greenland and her problems.

OLE BJØRN KRAFT
Acting Prime Minister, and
Minister for Foreign Affairs.

Copenhagen,
July 14, 1953.

CONTENTS

ILLUSTRATIONS

MAPS

PART ONE

OLD ORDERS

CHAPTER I

IN GREENLAND NOW

A MODERN traveller, arriving in Greenland by air, is quite likely to imagine that he is landing upon another planet. If, by chance, he approaches westwards across the Ice Cap, to land at the mountain-girt air-base of Sondrestromfiord, just within the Arctic Circle, this illusion will almost certainly be heightened. For hundreds of miles he has seen nothing below him but a vast, desolate white waste, the accumulated mass of snow that has gone on falling through the centuries. Its very serenity is awesome. It is a frozen desert, implacable, austere, inscrutable, offering no quarter to the explorer who seeks to probe its mysteries; merciless to the flyer forced down upon its inhospitable face. Then, without warning, the plane is over the mountainous coastal fringe, and the contrast is as startling as it is perplexing. There may be a momentary feeling of relief that the Polar Sahara has been left behind; but this gives way to wonder as spectacles of unexpected splendour begin to unfold and the plane circles among fantastic peaks. Quaintly irregular in outline, and viewed through swirling eddies of mist, these peaks are revealed in subtle pastel shades, a medley of grey and green and blue and salmon-pink and terra-cotta, with here and there, perhaps, a sudden gleam of gold or silver or bronze. The effect suggests an imaginative artist's illustration to some spaceship adventure; but the illusion is lost with the touch-down, and the traveller steps from the snug comfort of the air-liner to find himself hemmed in by frowning rocks of depressing drabness, whose barren sides seem to exude the chill of ages.

His first human contact is probably with American ground-crews, some, with revolvers on their hips, wearing conspicuous armlets marked "Air Police"; for Sondre-stromfiord is one of the air-bases established by Americans during the Second World War under the code name "Bluie West 8", when, with Denmark in enemy occupation, the United States assumed responsibility for Greenland's defence.

Today no one seems to know where the "Bluie" came from. Some say there may have been an engineer named Bluie who had a hand in the early planning of the Greenland bases; others say that it may be a corruption of "Blue", and point out that opposite bases on the eastern coast of Baffin Island and Newfoundland had the code-name "Crystal". Whatever the truth, peace-time attempts to call the bases by their place-names have not proved very successful; the picturesque code-names stubbornly persist.

A new agreement, signed in Copenhagen in 1951, has renewed the war-time arrangement with certain modifications and extensions under NATO, with the result that the Americans have been left in occupation of Bluie West 8 and other bases for an indefinite term. Now, however, "Old Glory" and the Danish national flag, "Dannebrog", fly side by side at all these bases. They are raised and struck simultaneously, and when King Frederik IX and Queen Ingrid visited their Greenland people in the summer of 1952 this formality was scrupulously synchronised with the like ceremony aboard the Royal yacht.

It is unlikely that the traveller will gain more than a fleeting impression of the Sondrestromfiord base, with its straggling rows of barrack huts. With their traditional efficiency, the Americans will provide motor transport to whisk arrivals away along the "Blacktop Boulevard", which they built themselves, to the head of the fiord which gives the base its name. Motor-boats will bear the traveller to a waiting ship, and his last impression as he leaves the rough landing-stage will be of a notice-board erected by some waggish G.I. with the legend: "WELCOME TO CONEY ISLAND."

If he is lucky, the waiting ship will be one of the smart new vessels specially built for the Greenland trade, like M.S. *Umanak*, which left the shipyards at Elsinore in 1949—comfortable, fast, sturdy, and with the broad bows so necessary for nosing her way through the vast fields of drift-ice so often encountered round the coast.

During the 100-mile voyage down the long, narrow fiord he will have time in which to collect himself and to enjoy the panorama unfolding on either side. If it is summer-time, all the beauty of the rugged scenery will be enhanced, but he will scan the mountain-sides in vain for the bewitching medley of pastel tints he noticed from his circling plane. That was a phenomenon produced by sun-play on frosted upper slopes half-veiled in mist; now, seen from the boat-deck, the same peaks seem drab, though the grandeur of their outline is eternal.

Subdued brown or slate-grey provide the predominating tones, with occasional darker patches, which closer inspection would reveal as green, where mosses strive to assert themselves. But absence of colour does not make for monotony. Even the grey-green waters of the fiord seem, by some trick of wind and current, to be able to transform themselves at will.

But as Nature thus rings her changes for mile after mile with the simple materials of rock and ice and cloud and water, the traveller sees no sign of human hand or habitation. Gradually he becomes aware of the silence; an obtrusive, overmastering silence with a metallic quality to match the penetrating chill. It may seem absurd to think of silence masking sound, yet so deep is the stillness of the fiord that even the throb of the ship's motors seems to fade into a negligible hum or murmur, and then to lose itself in the void. Lost, too, seem the crew and fellow-passengers. The traveller feels alone as never before, for the silence induces such an impression of solitude that he might be voyaging through an empty world.

The silence and the solitude are real. Greenland, the world's largest island, with a total area of 840,000 square miles, has a native population of only 22,000. This is about equal to the population of the Kentish town of Ashford; less than the combined populations of Whitby and Bangor; less than the population of King's Lynn.

The Greenlanders are scattered over an extensive area in small settlements, trading-stations and outposts. God-thaab, their capital, is a community of 1,884, or 2,117 if outlying districts are included. The entire population of Greenland could be accommodated in the Wembley Stadium and still leave seats to spare for all the people of Bath or Lincoln!

But figures are not always important. Though small numerically, the Greenlanders are a people with qualities that tell. Like their native mosses which thrive and assert themselves among the barren rocks, these people have battled for generations against Nature in her least benign moods and have not only contrived to survive but, under Danish tutelage, have brought themselves to the foothills of civilisation. There are still Greenlanders living very close to Nature. There are polar-bear hunters in the Thule area who make long sledge journeys across the ice to Canada and back, finding their way by "sniffing the air"; and small children along the coast can follow mountain trails that are invisible to Western eyes. There are still seal-hunters who, with their families, lead a Stone Age existence; but they are a dwindling minority only temporarily untouched by the changes that have already transformed the lives of most of their fellows.

Until recently Greenland was a forbidden country, closed to Danes and foreigners alike. This was part of a deliberate policy designed to protect a simple people from exploitation. It was felt desirable that the Greenlanders should be allowed to grow up in their own way and at

Danish Press Photographers' Assn.

Greenland's Icy Mountains as they appear to a modern traveller when his airliner circles over the coastal belt on nearing the American-manned base of Narsarssuaq.

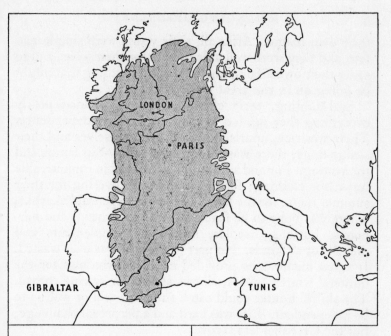

GREENLAND, with an area of 840,000 square miles, is, if we except the continent of Australia, the world's largest island. The distance from its northern fringe to its southern tip is approximately 1,600 miles, but a true idea of its vast bulk may be gained from these comparative maps, which show Greenland in relation to the continent of Europe and to the British Isles. In the former, with the northern shore level with Scotland, the southern tip reaches to the Sahara; in the latter, the map of the United Kingdom appears isolated and dwarfed in the centre of the Greenland Ice Cap.

their own tempo. After all, their wants were simple and few, and they were well able to fend for themselves and to order their own affairs, untroubled by anything that might be going on in the great world outside.

Seal-hunting, their chief occupation, yielded nearly everything they needed to ensure a happy independence. There was rich, nourishing meat for themselves and their sledge-dogs; there was oil for their tallow-dip lamps and for heating. Fur and skin could be utilised in innumerable ways: for clothing; for decoration; as covering for their summer tents; for the fabric of their indispensable kayaks. There was bone to be fashioned into spearheads and harpoons, buttons, needles, knives and implements and utensils of all kinds. No part of the seal was ever wasted. Internal membranes provided excellent windows for the hunters' winter houses; sinews served for sewing-thread. The skilful hunter could catch sufficient seal or walrus to be independent. Life was hard and a perpetual challenge; but the Greenlanders throve.

In the nineteen-twenties, however, the seal began to disappear, partly through climatic changes which drove them farther and farther north, partly because they had been thinned out by over-hunting. Deprived of his normal occupation, the Greenlander had, perforce, to turn to other pursuits. He did not have to turn far. Bounteous Nature seems to have been waiting somewhere in the wings for just this cue to enter. At about the same time that the seal began to thin out, the warming waters round the Greenland coast began to attract phenomenal shoals of cod. Thus a ready-made solution presented itself just when it was needed. Seal-hunting might be finished as a worthwhile proposition or as a means of sustenance, but now in its place there suddenly appeared this excellent prospect of indulging in large-scale fishing.

The transition from one way of life to another was not by any means simple, for the two ways could hardly have been more violently opposed. Seal-hunting is, of necessity, a solitary occupation. It is, in effect, a "one-man business", with each lone hunter seeking his prey in his home-made kayak, or stalking it behind a small white camouflage screen pushed steadily before him over the ice. In practice it becomes a communal effort *after* the catch, when womenfolk and children all lend a hand in flensing the creature and in preparing the various by-products. In practice, too, a lucky seal-hunter will always share his spoils with his less fortunate fellows, knowing that, under the unwritten law of the Arctic, any other hunter will always reciprocate should positions become reversed.

This natural instinct for neighbourly co-operation found greater scope in the change-over to big-scale cod-fishing because many hands were needed from the outset. Adaptable, resourceful and realist, the Greenlander appreciated this, and lone hunters readily sank their individualism and got used to working in teams—a matter of readjustment which might well have proved far more difficult but for the deep-seated good-neighbour instinct.

But that was not the whole answer. The cod, though undeniably valuable as a food and as a readily marketable commodity, could not furnish all those utilitarian by-products of the vanishing seal. Nor were kayaks or ordinary hunting gear of much use in the new battle that had to be fought. A completely new technique had to be mastered, and for this purpose small boats, quantities of tackle, equipment and clothing had to be obtained from somewhere.

The prolific shoals of cod solved this problem. Surplus catches were bartered for the gear required, and thus the erstwhile seal-hunters organised their new project on economic lines. Barter still obtains in some remote stations, but a monetary system has developed steadily elsewhere, and stores have been set up where the hunters and fishermen can obtain everything they need at prices that are kept low by State subsidy.

Once this transition from a primitive economy had

been successfully effected, the fishing industry developed at such amazing speed that the Danish Government realised that an all-round reform of the Colony's affairs was now desirable. It tackled its obligations with all the energy and resource shown by the seal-hunters, and always with the single aim of expanding the country's economy to ensure social and cultural standards for the Greenlander comparable to those enjoyed by the Europeans.

III

All these things the traveller learns as he chats with the Skipper of his ship. By now he will have left the friendly shelter of Sondrestromfiord and will be experiencing his first taste of Greenland summer weather as the vessel feels her way down the west coast towards Godthaab, the capital.

"Most of the world's weather is *made* in Greenland," the Skipper has said, and off the west coast, even in midsummer, the traveller may savour samples of every variety, ranging from roistering, blustering storms to dense, blanketing fog. But Greenland weather is a quick-change artist supreme: fog can vanish as rapidly as it descends; bright sunshine, warm as any June day in England, can oust the Arctic chill in a trice. At one moment the stern crags seem full of menace, like the crags in Doré's conception of the Inferno; but the next reveals them mellow and serene.

It is this, no doubt, that explains why a favourite word among the Greenlanders is *imaka*—"perhaps". With them nothing can be assured. Perhaps it will be fine; perhaps it will be stormy; perhaps it will be warm; perhaps it will be cold. Who can forecast anything with certainty when Nature herself changes her moods a dozen times a day? But if the people are thus understandably non-committal in some things, it must not be imagined that they are in any way taciturn or aloof. They are naturally friendly and cheerful, with a great gusto for life and a lively interest in all their fellows.

Whenever a ship ties up alongside the new wharf now under construction at Godthaab (literally "Good Hope") a happy crowd of adults and children is certain to assemble. One of the first things the traveller notes is that many jaws are working in rhythm, for gum-chewing came to Greenland with the Americans, as well as such things as jeeps, bulldozers, prefabricated huts and station wagons. Many Greenland girls will be seen, too, smoking cigarettes, and most of them will be in European dress, with a preference for tartan skirts and three-quarter-length swing-back coats of scarlet blanket cloth, and nylons and high-heeled shoes. Only on festival occasions are they to be seen in traditional Eskimo attire, with gaily decorated thigh-boots, sealskin trousers and broad capes of coloured beads.

Most of the men and boys will be wearing white *anoraks*—hooded blouses, reinforced in the chest and proof against the biting winds—and dark serge trousers stuffed into sealskin knee-boots.

First impressions of the immediate background may be unfavourable. The unfinished wharf is littered with baulks of timber, girders, hawsers, rope, old crates and piles of miscellaneous scrap metal. The few warehouse sheds within sight are primitive and ugly, and the brightest object to meet the eye will be a streamlined red vehicle bearing a white polar-bear emblem on its side. This is "the town bus", waiting to take passengers to the capital.

The journey of about a mile along a rough and winding road affords splendid vistas of bays and headlands on the left, but anyone who attempts to judge Godthaab itself by European standards is likely to be disappointed when the capital first sweeps into view. It appears as a sprawling, seemingly unplanned collection of wooden villas and hut-ments, many of them so obviously new that it seems hard to believe that the settlement has been in existence for more than 200 years. The first impression gained is that a handful of pioneers has lately come ashore and is trying to establish some kind of community.

But first impressions can often prove misleading. Closer acquaintance with the capital reveals much more than rough roads, open drains and plagues of mosquitoes. Godthaab's population may be less than that of many an English hamlet, but their civic consciousness is developing fast, and behind the scenes in what, at a glance, seems no more than a crude settlement, big things are happening.

IV

There is always an explanation for everything if you seek it. Natural stone abounds on every hand, and the stranger wonders why it is not being utilised. Everywhere he sees houses built of timber—timber laboriously and expensively shipped from Scandinavia. It does not seem to make sense until he begins to inquire, and learns that wooden houses, properly insulated, are warmer, healthier and easier to build. A great deal of building is going on in Godthaab today, and it is planned building to meet the needs of the new Greenland. A bigger and better hospital; a bigger and better school and very many new homes, both for the local people and for the Danish officials who keep arriving to help in the administration. These new buildings are of attractive, serviceable design, and gradually the cruder type of hutment is being swept away. Public works are going forward, too, including the construction of a big new reservoir that is being blasted out of the mountain-side by Danish engineers, who toil in green mosquito veils, and who have established a temporary colony of their own beside their work in a cluster of huts made gay with a lavish application of bright paint. To come upon this small community suddenly is startling; there are yellow huts, green huts, red huts, blue huts, standing out against the drab, rocky background like rows of dolls' houses in a child's painting-book.

The houses and public buildings of Godthaab are painted, too, but with slightly more restraint. Brick-red or dark blue predominates for roofs; buff for walls. But doors and window-frames may be picked out in white or green or blue. A feature of many of the new villas which the visitor cannot fail to notice is a small built-in conservatory; and masses of flowers may be seen blooming in the windows of nearly every home.

Rambling afoot, the visitor soon comes to realise that Godthaab, for all its haphazard appearance, has many buildings of character. There is the stone-built home of Hans Egede, who founded the town in 1721; there is the picturesque wooden church, somehow reminiscent in its architectural features of New England; there is the trim, grey-blue Residency of His Excellency the Governor of All Greenland, Mr. P. H. Lundsteen; the Chief Justice's house; a post office and a fire-station; a bakery; a radio and telegraph station and a general store.

The store is a busy centre where Godthaab folk stop to gossip in between making purchases of anything they may require. Every conceivable want seems to have been anticipated when stocks were laid in. The open shelves and counters are crammed with such a miscellaneous variety of articles that stocktaking must be quite a formidable operation. Everything, from postage stamps to shot-guns, is to be had for the asking. There are bales of cloth, with tartan well in evidence, but imported from Denmark, not Scotland. There are clothes, rubber boots, hurricane lanterns, electrical fittings, fishing-rods, books, hooks, kettles, primus stoves, cigars, pipes, cigarettes, pens and pencils, mosquito veils and toothpaste, razor-blades, cartridges, knives, tinned foods in variety, cheeses and miscellaneous groceries, tools, nails, screws, matches, petrol lighters, lamp-shades and numerous pots, pans and utensils. There are chocolates, sweets and chewing-gum, candles and toys.

The playthings on view are of a kind to gladden the

heart of any child anywhere—dolls, soldiers, building bricks, paint-boxes, motor cars and trains. The visitor will perhaps note with a smile of surprise the prominence given to juvenile Western outfits, complete with "Stetsons", cartridge belts, holsters and toy pistols; but he will not be able to wander through Godthaab's by-ways for long without coming upon little groups of young Greenlanders playing their own spirited version of "Cowboys and Indians", some of them fully accoutred with outfits from the local store and twirling pearl-handled six-shooters on their trigger fingers with the dexterity of Hopalong Cassidy himself.

More surprises await him should he stray into the offices of the local printing-works, for there he will find Greenlandic versions of *Settlers in Canada*, *Children of the New Forest* and many other favourites of his own childhood. He will be told that editions of 2,500 or 3,000 copies of these attractively printed paper-backed volumes sell without difficulty; that the Greenlanders, among whom there is no illiteracy, have become avid readers, and that the demand for something to read far exceeds the present supply. Already the Greenlanders have tasted the delights of *The Count of Monte Cristo*, *Uncle Tom's Cabin*, various works by Jules Verne, and the fairy tales of Hans Andersen—all in their own tongue. Those who acquire the Danish language—a growing band—are quick to extend their reading field, and well-stocked libraries of books in Danish are available in most centres.

Greenlanders will be seen at work in the composing-room or operating the presses; others will be encountered in the Broadcasting studios, which opened in 1942, and which provide a regular service of news, talks, plays, music and outside broadcasts. Others again will be seen at work in the telegraph station, in the power-station, in the telephone exchange, in the post-office and in various administrative departments.

Yesterday there was little choice before the young

Greenlander but to engage in hunting and fishing; today avenues of opportunity are opening up everywhere, and he is proving himself quick and resolute in following the calling of his choice. He is helping to build the New Greenland.

Although Godthaab is largely the administrative centre, what is happening there is symptomatic of all that is going on in the other settlements scattered up and down the coast.

Nearly everywhere among the 200-odd settlements and out-stations between Cape Farewell and Thule a tremendous renaissance is in evidence. The lives of Greenland's 22,000 people are being changed almost overnight as they race to take their place in a modern world, forsaking the Stone Age for the Age of Jet and Atom in circumstances which will be seen to affect us all.

CHAPTER II

ARCTIC RENAISSANCE

ONE of the first things to strike the traveller who journeys up and down the coast in search of the new Greenland now being born is the prevalence of little boats. Wherever he may happen to call, whether it be Julianehaab, Sukkertoppen or Godhavn, he cannot fail to be impressed by the swarms of small motor-boats plying round the shore. He will note that they are all manned by Greenlanders who might, to judge from their confident skill, have been handling such craft all their lives. Graceful native kayaks —those slender, buoyant canoes—may still be encountered, especially around Egedesminde and points north; but everywhere they are already outnumbered by motor-boats.

This in itself is a major revolution. In the old days, not so far distant, everything centred upon the kayak. The average Greenlander learned to handle his tricky craft in childhood, often in a miniature version specially built for him by his parents. The schooling would be thorough, and would include practice in the art of capsizing the craft sideways and, by deft use of the paddle under water, making a complete revolution and bobbing up quickly on the other side. Remaining kayak fishermen still like to show off this trick to astonish visitors, but the practical value lies in the ability to right the craft instantly should it turn turtle by accident.

The Greenlander and his kayak were inseparable. Even when it became necessary to trek across the ice in search of new hunting grounds, or to explore inland lakes, he invariably took his kayak with him, for it was light enough to be borne easily upon the head. Now, however, because of the rapid change-over to fishing and other industries, the kayak is becoming rarer, and some think it will eventually disappear except as a museum piece.

Since the close of the Second World War nearly every ship that has sailed to Greenland from Denmark has carried numbers of small motor-boats lashed to her decks. Today it is said that something like 600 Greenlanders, who formerly hunted or fished from their kayaks, now own these modern vessels, which they are able to buy from the Danish Government on easy terms. The size of these boats varies from fifteen-footers to fishing-cutters. Bigger boats may be jointly owned by two or three enterprising Greenlanders who have put their savings together and who run their boats on a co-operative basis.

With this widespread adoption of the motor-boat has come the need for adequate servicing facilities. So repair yards are now to be found at several points along the west coast, while at Holsteinsborg there is a flourishing boat-building yard with a spacious covered shop where work can be carried on without pause throughout the long winter. At most of the settlements, too, conspicuous new landmarks have sprung up. First seen from the sea, they appear as shimmering silver ghosts, which materialise on close approach into brand-new oil-storage tanks, rendered necessary to meet the ever-growing demand for motor spirit.

The significance of all this comes home when one learns that there are now some eighty landing-places where fishing harvests can be dealt with. At many of these depots are to be found the very latest plants for filleting, salting or freezing cod for export to European markets.

At Christianshaab and Narssak there are also thriving shrimp-canneries, for the world's largest shrimp-beds were discovered in Disko Bay in 1948. Modern machinery has been imported, and Greenland girls have adapted themselves to factory conditions as cheerfully and as skilfully as their menfolk have taken to motor-boat and workshop. They provide their own music while they work, and may be heard chanting their haunting Greenlandic songs as their deft fingers wash, shell and pack the shrimps.

In the milder south, where there are patches of pasture among the rocks, sheep-rearing is being tried. Setbacks in one exceptionally severe winter have not discouraged the farmers. They mean to keep on, and they are confident of ultimate success. There are some 20,000 sheep in the Julianehaab area alone; and at Narssak a huge cannery has been built for cold-storage for 2,000 carcases. Greenlanders in charge love to take inspecting visitors through the refrigerating chambers, and to chuckle as one after another complains of feeling colder there than at many points inside the Arctic Circle. At the moment there is enough local-grown mutton for home consumption, but the farmers are looking forward to the day when they will have an exportable surplus.

Greenland's most flourishing industry at the present time is the open-cast mining of cryolite, a mineral used in the manufacture of aluminium. There are only two other known deposits in the world.

There is also a long-term scheme for exploiting commercially new finds of lead, wolfram and zinc. A company has been formed for this purpose with Danish, Swedish and Canadian capital.

Coal is already mined successfully at Qutdligssat, where sufficient supplies for internal consumption are obtained.

In all these varied enterprises Greenland labour is used. There are many Danish technicians, of course, but there are Greenlandic smiths, mechanics, coopers, carpenters, electricians, engineers, masons, typists, teachers, telegraph operators and trade officials—all applying themselves with tremendous zeal to the task of creating a modernised Greenland.

II

It was always the basic policy of Danish rule that the people of Greenland should be helped to achieve a full life in accordance with their own traditions. While seal-hunting remained the chief pursuit it seemed best that the people should be left to their own way of life, and not have their simple economy disrupted by outside influences. But when Nature dictated the change-over to fishing, the tempo of development quickened so much that some reform in the administrative system also became inevitable. District Councils, which gave Greenlanders a voice in the management of local affairs, were already in being, having been set up in 1908. It was now decided to widen the scope of these bodies, and this was done in 1925.

Progress continued for twenty-five years; then, in 1950, following a comprehensive report by a Royal Commission, a National Council was created, its members being elected by all Greenland men and women above the age of twenty-three. Citizens thus went to the polling-booth for the first time in 1951.

The Greenland National Council, in turn, elects two of its members to sit on a special Parliamentary Greenland Committee in Copenhagen, and with this modern administrative machinery to meet the expanding needs of the new Greenland, a series of Acts provides legislation governing every facet of national life.

Education, formerly the responsibility of the Church, is now administered by a Board comprised of the National Commissioner, the Rural Dean and a new Director of Education.

The Greenland Church is still closely linked with the Church of Denmark, the Bishop of Copenhagen being also Bishop of Greenland.

There is a new Health Act, providing for a National Health Officer to supervise health services, which, as in the case of education, are free.

A new Trading Act divorces State trading from the Administration and makes its principal aim the safeguarding of supplies of consumer goods and occupational implements. It also provides for the purchase, processing and exportation of Greenland goods in association with commercial firms if required.

Another far-seeing Act relating to the practice of an occupation in Greenland governs the licensing of commercial hunting, fishing and shooting. Such pursuits are reserved for Danish subjects domiciled in the country, other Danish subjects being required to obtain special licences from the Prime Minister's Department. There are also special provisions to ensure that part of the proceeds from exports in boom years shall be set aside to offset the effects of possible slumps to come—a wise measure, this, for no one can guarantee that the vast shoals of cod will not vanish one day as suddenly as they came.

Supplementary to this Act is another which provides for a Greenland Commercial Loan Fund for the development of the export trade.

By these and other measures Denmark is seeking to continue realistically her original policy of promoting the spiritual and material welfare of Greenland's people and to ensure that they shall be able to keep in step with the ever-quickening pace of economic expansion. And nearly everywhere among the 200-odd settlements the fruits of this policy are to be seen.

III

Side by side with the new fields of economic endeavour, big social welfare and cultural developments are taking place. New hospitals and new sanatoria are being established and more and more doctors and nurses are being appointed in an all-out drive to eliminate the No. 1 scourge of tuberculosis.

The entire population of Greenland has been tuberculin-tested by special personnel sent out by the Danish Red Cross in co-operation with local medical officers. Nevertheless, with 70 per cent of hospital beds now occupied by T.B. patients, the authorities have a tremendous problem to combat.

Education likewise presents special problems, for 20 per cent of Greenland's total population are children under twelve. Free education for all between the ages of seven and fourteen is the rule; but in some centres teachers often have to close their schools if families wish to take their children hunting.

We have become accustomed to overcrowded schools and big classes in our own country, but would any of our most harassed teachers care to change places with Mr. and Mrs. Staermose, of Sukkertoppen, who has to supervise the schooling of 646 children under twelve out of a local population of 1,813? Old traditions die hard, and most Greenlandic children are expected to participate in hunting and fishing expeditions at the age of nine. As so much still depends on these pursuits in many centres, leave of absence from school is never withheld.

When a country is developing as rapidly as Greenland, "growing pains" must be expected; but, notwithstanding the pace and the problems, there is no trace of bewilderment or resentment among the people when things go wrong or when imperfections are revealed. A mixture of Eskimo and European blood has produced distinct traits. Battling for generations against the rigours of climate has not made these people in any way cold or callous. They have a warmth of character that is in direct contradiction to the bleak severity of their background. They are naturally musical, and love to dance and sing. They have a spontaneous sense of humour, can join in a laugh against themselves and are invariably cheerful and friendly.

In the old Eskimo tradition it was the custom to settle all personal disputes with a ceremonial drum dance. The adversaries, whatever their smouldering hatreds, would

face up to each other within a compact circle formed by
their fellows. Then they would take it in turns to recite
lampoons against each other, punctuating their taunts and
accusations with rhythmic beats upon a sealskin drum,
not unlike a tambourine. Passions might thus be worked
up to white heat, but would be vented in caustic songs in
which each singer in turn would enumerate his enemy's
failings and strive to make him appear ridiculous in the
eyes of the watching families and friends. In the end, the
one who scored the greater number of laughs at the
other's expense would be lustily acclaimed as the victor,
and the beaten man would bow to the verdict of the
majority. Even the least philosophically inclined must
find it hard to repress a wistful regret that all the
nations of the world cannot settle their disputes so
blithely.

Greenlanders today are peaceable, good-natured
fellows, though instinctively conscious that their country's
destiny is linked inexorably with a far-from-peaceable
world beyond their own frozen shores.

Perhaps the first tangible inkling of what this implies
came to them in 1941, when, in circumstances already
mentioned, the United States assumed active responsibility for Greenland's defence. The continued presence of
the American airmen and technicians, who now number
between 12,000 and 15,000, is accepted by the native
population as necessary and, happily, the very vastness of
their country permits the visiting forces to go about their
mission without occasioning the slightest inconvenience
to the Greenlanders themselves.

It was finally deemed desirable to move the little
settlement of Thule; and today the men of this most
northerly outpost pursue their normal occupation of
hunting polar bear, walrus, seal, narwhal and blue and
white fox 70 miles to the north of the great 90,000-acre
air-base, whose garrison outnumbers them by fifty to one.
The hunters are not permitted within the perimeter of the

Polar Diploma presented to the author (*inset*) on crossing the Arctic Circle. Old seafaring tradition says those who have rounded Cape Horn may place one foot on the table after dinner; those who have crossed the Arctic Circle may put up both feet.

POLAR-DIPLOM

Uvagut kúnge NEPTUNUS pilerkârneranile imarssuarnut nunanik ungaluisimangnigtunut nâlagaussugut ajugakângitsugutdlo matumûna nalunaerpugut

Geoffrey Williamson Esq.

M/S ÛMÁNAMUT ilauvdlune uvdlok mana kausuitsup kigdlekarfia kângersimagâ.

kausuitsup kigdlekarfiane anno domini 195?   uvdlok

kaldet kigssaviarssuk   túniunekarpok.

L. Coister ....,
umiarssûp nâlagâ.

kunge ocean?

Vi NEPTUNUS REX fra Tidernes Morgen det jordomsluttende Havs almægtige Behersker gøre vitterligt at
We NEPTUNUS REX since the beginning of time the whole oceans almighty rulers certify that

                    Geoffrey Williamson Esq.

under nedenstaaende Dato har passeret den nordlige Polarkreds om Bord paa
under the date mentioned below has crossed the northern polar circle
M/S UMANAK.
on board the vessel m/s Umanak.
        Givet paa Polarkredsen anno domini 1952.
        Issued on the northern polar circle at the 1?th July 1952.

Skibschef   Rex oceani
captain.

M/s „UMANAK".

base, and the Americans are not allowed within the Thule settlement.

Contacts between the Greenlanders and the Americans are few and always of a co-operative nature—as when American airmen flew two leading polar-bear hunters by Constellation from Thule to Sondrestromfiord to enable them to meet the King and Queen of Denmark; or when flyers from Narsarssuaq (Bluie West 1) picked up an SOS for penicillin from the Danish Medical Officer at Godhavn and dropped supplies there the next day.

Events like these linger in the Greenlanders' memory. They saw similar co-operation last summer, when ski-planes from Thule rescued the British flyers whose Hastings aircraft had crashed in the middle of the Ice Cap. Such things they understand and approve as being akin to their own help-your-neighbour policy practised by seal-hunters for generations.

In any case, they have long grown familiar with flying. A regular service of Catalina amphibian machines plies between the more important settlements, carrying visiting officials or distributing mail. Many Greenlanders, too, have memories of the first British Polar Air Route Expedition led by "Gino" Watkins in 1930. Though he perished mysteriously two years later, Watkins is still remembered with respect by Danes and Greenlanders alike as one of the few European explorers to master a kayak.

Others remember the visit of America's flying ace, Colonel Charles Lindbergh, in 1933, when he and his wife made numerous flights up and down the west coast and over the Ice Cap in their seaplane.

And now, just over twenty years after the Watkins expedition, another little band of British explorers has arrived in the country and is active upon the Inland Ice under the leadership of Commander C. J. W. Simpson. Its members have deliberately marooned themselves with the intention of remaining on the Ice Cap for two years,

c

during which time they intend to try out various types of new-style arctic clothing and equipment, and conduct scientific research generally.

At the close of 1952, Scandinavian Airlines System completed two very successful passenger flights from Los Angeles to Copenhagen, with an appreciable saving in time and mileage, by flying over the top of the world by way of the big new American-built base at Thule. These proving flights, completed ahead of schedule, were a prelude to a scheme for launching regular passenger services over the same route.

All these stupendous developments are brought home to the present-day visitor to Greenland. Self-contained they may be, yet they merge into one vast tapestry—the tapestry of progress. It is impossible for anyone to remain in the country for many weeks without gaining a growing impression that a common thread of Destiny may be traced through everything that is happening there today.

Nor is it merely the life of the individual Greenlander that is being affected. Triple-pronged forces are at work —forces with economic, social and strategic implications which make it impossible any longer to dismiss Greenland as a remote, frozen territory "out of this world". Already it is looming large in international affairs; already, with Russian bases no more than one jet-hour away in Franz Josef Land, it may be reckoned a factor in the cold war.

To look behind the scenes, therefore, and to study the various forces at work, is to discover much that merits serious consideration. The story, like the congested store at Godthaab, contains some things that seem incongruous and bizarre; but the deeper one probes the greater the surprises that spring to light.

CHAPTER III

VIKING VANGUARD

As one moves up and down the coast, taking in more and more details of life in Greenland today, curiosity is awakened and an inevitable question poses itself: "How did it all begin?" Local people will point to the ruins of old dwellings and old churches and tell of scientists and archæologists whose excavations have brought forth numerous implements and relics of vanished settlers and of early nomadic Eskimo tribes who flourished more than 1,000 years ago.

There was a time when the musk-ox, reindeer, polar wolf and other Arctic animals had the silence and the solitude of Greenland's icy mountains to themselves. The first men to view the majestic splendour of the coastal ranges where the present-day settlements are to be found were bands of wandering Eskimos who ventured across the frozen wastes from North America and Canada, prompted perhaps by sheer wanderlust or by the necessity of following migrating game on which they depended for their survival.

It is thought that these men may have originated somewhere north of Lake Superior, for their movements have been traced northwards to the Canadian Arctic coast between Coronation Gulf and Boothia Peninsula. Apparently they split up into two streams. One proceeded westwards along the north coast of America, then round the western and southern shores of Alaska as far as Port William Sound; the other moved eastwards across the ice to the north-west tip of Greenland, and then split again, some following the west coast down to Cape Farewell, others keeping on across the northern fringe of what is now Pearyland.

The oldest finds of Eskimo encampments to date in Greenland are in the region of Disko Bay; but traces of the wandering tribes are discernible all round the vast coastline. Of necessity, they rarely stayed very long in one place, and once hunting possibilities had been fully exploited they pushed on to fresh fields. Their way of life was the Stone Age life still followed by their descendants in some parts of Greenland to this day. Prompted by hunting techniques, they evolved weapons and implements which, though primarily utilitarian, were fashioned in forms which became traditional. Their clothing, too, though naturally designed to withstand the rigours of climate, and made from materials yielded by the sea mammals or Arctic birds and animals which fell to them in the chase, was shaped according to a traditional pattern and decorated with pleasing embroidery.

Two distinct cultures have been traced in Greenland: the high Arctic or Thule culture in the north and a sub-Arctic culture in the south. Materials at the disposal of the Eskimos were limited, but they were used with intelligence and ingenuity. Skin, fur, bone, narwhal tusks, walrus tusks, musk-ox hide, reindeer antlers, soapstone, a little driftwood, moss, peat and flint—these were the materials which had to be made to serve all purposes.

The Eskimo learned to adapt these things to his needs. He wanted heat for combatting the intense cold; he needed light through the long months of darkness; so he learned to scoop out vessels from soapstone, filled them with blubber, collected dry moss and produced tallow-dip lamps.

He needed transport, so he evolved a sledge with runners of whalebone and harnessed dogs with leather thongs. Cargoes had a way of slipping off when he travelled at speed, so he evolved "upstanders" at the rear which also proved useful for steering the sledge, and he found that reindeer antlers were just right for this purpose.

He needed bone for arrow-heads and spearheads, for tipping kayak paddles, for needles, and for scores of other purposes. So he learned to split large pieces of bone by perforating them in several places with the aid of a bow-drill, which he already used for obtaining fire.

He desired something bigger than the kayak for transporting families and goods over water, so he evolved the umiak on the same principle, first building a skeleton framework of bones and driftwood, lashed together with thongs, and then covering it with sealskins or walrus hide, sewn together with more thongs with the aid of the indispensable bone needle.

In the frozen north, when he needed shelter from the blizzards, he evolved the streamlined igloo, and perfected his own technique for building it swiftly with shaped blocks of snow cut out with long bone knives designed for just that purpose.

On the mainland in the winter he learned to build snug communal houses of stones, insulated with sods for additional warmth. To exclude draughts he evolved a passage-way to the one entrance, and made the floor of this passage lower than that of the house itself. He used flat stones to form a roof and learned to place them in layers on the cantilever principle. He used membranes for windows with small peep-holes in the centre. He made the inside comfortable by draping the walls, and a raised sleeping platform, with skins of musk ox, polar bear and seal.

All these things and many more may be seen in the Ethnological Department of the National Museum in Copenhagen, which boasts one of the most complete collections of Arctic exhibits in the world. But they may also be seen in Greenland to this day because secrets of craftsmanship have been handed down through the ages, and there are still hunters who live precisely as their ancestors lived and who find that all the old weapons and implements are perfect for their purpose. Traditional gear may be supplemented in some instances by a rifle or shotgun, and many hunters now carry primus stoves with them on their expeditions, yet the fact remains that the ancient Eskimos devised the best means of utilising the limited materials at their disposal.

Their sledges alone serve to show the thought and intelligence they applied to their problems. Runners were fitted with substantial tyres of frozen peat, and at the commencement of every day's trip these would be rubbed with water, which, freezing instantly, would provide a friction-free surface, so that a comparatively small span of huskies could pull a formidable load.

Though the museum pieces can be matched by similar articles still in daily use, their value lies in the light they throw upon Greenland's past. Gathered from countless points within the Arctic, they confirm beyond question the routes followed by the nomadic Eskimo ancestors of the present inhabitants.

The movements of the first visitors to Greenland can be pin-pointed, therefore, and their mode of life becomes apparent; nevertheless these people provide an ethnological riddle. In most of the settlements one may encounter nearly every transitional type between pure Eskimo and pure European; Mongolian features are common, but here and there, particularly among the East Greenlanders, the cast of countenance carries more than a suggestion of the Red Indian.

Some anthropologists have traced links with Mongolian tribes, and others think the Eskimos are merely a kind of North American Indian. The very name Eskimo is said to have been coined by Indians to denote a tribe which ate its food raw, and it was applied in a derogatory sense. It is thought that some 2,000 years ago the ancestors of present Eskimos were forest-dwellers somewhere north of Lake Superior; but a study of the language does not seem to help. Its source is a mystery; and it is one of the most difficult languages in the world. The declension of a single noun may involve the use of as many as 150 suffixes. It is guttural, yet melodious and expressive, being rich in hunting terms and in descriptions of animals, weapons or utensils. Place-names are always picturesque comparisons with parts of the body. Thus, Umanak is literally "heart-shaped mountain"; Akuliarussek might be translated "Root-of-the-nose-valley-between-the-eyes"; Kuvdlorssuak is "Big Thumb Mountain".

Modern Eskimos are just as ready with apt nomenclature. When Colonel Lindbergh visited Greenland in his seaplane in 1933 it was instantly christened "Tingmissartoq"—"the one who flies like a big bird".

The Eskimos count in fives, indicating fingers and toes. Thus, "the whole man" signifies twenty, and if higher figures are needed it is "The whole man and the hand of the chap on the left" or "The whole man and two hands and a foot of the chap on the left".

Today there are many variations in Eskimo dialect. That spoken in East Greenland differs from that of the West; and polar-bear hunters from Thule in their long expeditions across the ice into Canadian territory sometimes encounter Eskimo hunters whose dialect they cannot understand at all.

The first Eskimos to descend upon Greenland did not remain. After following the entire coastline they disappeared into the Polar regions as mysteriously and as suddenly as they had come; and once again the musk ox, reindeer, polar wolf and other Arctic animals had the silence and the solitude of Greenland's icy mountains to themselves.

II

The first European to sight Greenland was Gunnbjorn,* a Norwegian explorer, driven off course from Iceland in about A.D. 900. Because he saw nothing but snow-clad mountain ranges, he christened the unknown territory "White Shirt Land", and apparently let it go at that.

The next European to be associated with the country

* *See* Chronology 1935.

was an Icelander, Eric the Red, who was destined to contemplate it much more closely, being driven there in exile from his homeland, where he was "wanted" for manslaughter. Three years of the silence and the solitude failed to crush his spirit; indeed, he saw possibilities of making a fresh start and conceived an ambitious scheme for founding a new colony with himself at the head.

Someone in whom he confided asked: "What shall we call this land?"

"Call it Greenland," said Eric.

"But it is not a green land," demurred the other, taking him literally.

Eric the Red must have smiled as he answered: "It matters not. Give it a good name and people will come to it."

His psychology was sound. In A.D. 986 he induced 500 settlers to follow him from Iceland and to apply their energies to the task of transforming his dream into reality. Whether any of his fellow countrymen ever reproached him for his deception cannot be told. As the first Eskimo migration had ended by that time, they must have arrived to find themselves in an empty world, cheerless and austere, with precious little greenery about it.

But, under Eric's direction, they established settlements in the region of Godthaab and Julianehaab and started farming. Eric ordered affairs on similar lines to those prevailing in the homeland, and local assemblies, or *Tings*, were held regularly for formulating laws or passing judgments.

That his colonising efforts were successful may be judged from the fact that some 3,000 new settlers followed from Iceland after a time and, between them, established 280 farms in the region now known by American airmen as "Sunny Southern Greenland—the Miami of the North".

As they tilled the shallow soil in the rock-girt valleys near the coast, the settlers came upon many a relic of the departed Eskimos to tell them that they were not the first men to dwell in those parts. Like these unknown nomads, they hunted seal and walrus round their shores and built up a trade in skins and tusks.

Sir Ernest Shackleton used to confess that Eric the Red had been one of his boyhood's heroes; that reading of the Norseman's exploits had first fired him with the ambition of turning explorer on his own account one day.

Eric also fired his own son, Leif Ericsson, with similar ambitions, for he voyaged to and from Greenland on many a venture into the unknown, as is told in the Olaf Sagas of Snorre Sturlasson.

On at least one occasion he tried to induce his father to accompany him on a fresh voyage of exploration in a newly acquired ship with a crew of thirty-five. Eric the Red agreed, but on the way to the ship he fell from his horse and hurt his foot. He took this mishap as an omen. "It is not destined," said Eric, "that I should discover more lands than this Greenland on which we dwell and live; and now we must not run hastily into this adventure." So, ruefully reflecting, no doubt, that his venturing days were done, Eric returned to his home at Brattalid, the ruins of which lie some 5 miles from the air-base at Narsarssuaq, and left his son Leif to carry on alone.

From the Sagas, too, we learn how Leif Ericsson brought Christianity to Greenland in A.D. 1000. "Greenland Baptised", runs the heading of Chapter CIV.

"The same spring King Olaf also sent Leif Ericsson to Greenland to proclaim Christianity there, and Leif went there that summer. He . . . arrived about harvest in Greenland; and had with him for it a priest and other teachers, with whom he went to Brattalid to lodge with his father Eric."

On the voyage, Leif Ericsson rescued a number of seamen whom he found clinging to wreckage after their ship had foundered—an exploit which earned him the nickname of Leif the Lucky.

His father, however, seems to have received him churlishly because he was not in favour of Leif's religious mission. "But his father, Eric, said that his luck and ill luck balanced each other," runs the Saga. "For, if Leif had saved a wreck in the ocean he had brought a hurtful person with him to Greenland, and that was the priest."

As Eric the Red died that winter, he was unable to offer any opposition to his son, who carried out his high charge with great vigour and caused sixteen churches to be built. It is recorded that Leif prospered and became highly respected. It is also recorded that some of the early settlers who ventured more deeply inland among the icy mountains came upon a few fertile spots that were more suited for pasturage and for cultivation.

III

In 1126 a Norwegian bishop landed in Greenland and founded his see at Gardar in the district then known as Eystribyd, where the Church of St. Nicholas, patron saint of sailors, became Greenland's cathedral.

The settlers flourished to such an extent that in 1256 they felt confident enough to refuse to pay tribute to Magnus, King of Norway. This show of independence was short-lived, for at the request of Magnus, Eric, King of Denmark, equipped a fleet to show the flag in Greenland and restore authority there. This was sufficient to make the would-be rebels abandon republican dreams. As soon as the King's ships were sighted they began to sue for peace, frightened, no doubt, at the prospect of being cut off from essential supplies. The peace was ratified in 1261.

In 1348 the colonists were smitten by a "great pestilence" or plague, and those who survived were engulfed by a second migration of Eskimo tribes from the north, who swept down Greenland's west coast. It is supposed that there was a clash with the settlers, who were wiped out piecemeal. Eskimo legends, passed down verbally through the generations, seem to tell of some such encounter; but some historians think there is evidence that friendly relations were established between Eskimos and settlers, and that it is possible that the latter, already greatly reduced in numbers by pestilence and a long period of adversity, may have been absorbed by the wandering tribes.

Whatever the truth may be, there is a report of Henry, Bishop of Gardar, sailing for Denmark in 1389, while in 1406, Eskuld, Archbishop of Drontheim, is said to have sent a prelate named Andrew to Greenland as Henry's successor. That was the last heard of them both.

Christian III had an expedition fitted out with the intention of probing the mystery of the silent settlements, but it never sailed. Frederick II, his son, despatched Magnus Heignugsen on the same mission, but this mariner returned with a sensational story of his ship being stopped by some mysterious lodestone under the water. Unable to proceed, he returned home.

Sir Martin Frobisher got within sight of Greenland's coast in 1576, but did not venture ashore. He returned in the following spring, but the inhabitants fled inland at his approach. He examined their dwellings, however, and found them to be made in the form of tents and fashioned from sealskins stitched together with sinews and stretched over poles—a description which exactly fits the Greenlanders' summer tents today.

When Sir Martin and his companions landed on another part of the coast, farther north, they found the natives full of guile. Raw meat was spread upon the beach as if to lure wild beasts, but as the explorers did not take this bait, the natives carried one of their companions, who seemed to be lame, down to the shore and left him. Scenting another trap, Sir Martin ordered a shot to be fired over the man's head. The fact that he leapt up instantly and fled confirmed that he had been placed there as a decoy. These natives were armed with small bows and used arrows tipped with bone.

In 1605 King Christian IV sent for an English seaman, John Knight, and put him in command of three ships fitted out for a new Greenland expedition. Knight steered south-west to avoid the ice. A second vessel kept with him, but the third, under the Danish Admiral Godske Lindenau went north-east and reached the coast. Natives who came out to trade fox, bear and seal skins for knives, needles and mirrors, declined wine with grimaces, but drank whale oil with relish. Lindenau stayed at anchor for three days, but did not go ashore; on the fourth day he sailed away, taking two of the natives with him.

Meanwhile, Knight reached Cape Farewell, and both vessels entered the Davis Strait and coasted eastwards. He traded with the natives, discovered various harbours and bays, went ashore and made a chart. Like Lindenau, he was anxious to take back natives. Four were captured, but resisted fiercely, and in the struggle one was killed. Other companions came bravely to their aid, and were only driven off when firearms were used.

Knight's captives were taken back to Denmark and presented to the King. It is said that they were of superior physique and more civilised than those taken by Lindenau, and that they also dressed differently, spoke another dialect and affected other manners and customs. Similar differences are to be noted today between the people of East and West Greenland.

In 1606 Admiral Lindenau set forth again, departing from Copenhagen on May 8 with a fleet of five ships. He took with him three of the Eskimos captured on the previous voyage, though one died on the way. Rounding Cape Farewell, the Admiral steered for Davis Strait, but one vessel in the convoy was lost in fog, and only four made landfall. Numerous Eskimos were encountered, and they proved decidedly hostile. A fine harbour was located, but the hostility of the Eskimos forced the

Admiral to push on farther north, where he captured six fishermen and took their kayaks on board, too. When they finally cast anchor, one of Lindenau's men volunteered to go ashore as a scout. He had not gone far, however, before he was surrounded and slain, the Eskimos there being armed with swords and knives made from sharpened narwhal tusks.

On the homeward voyage one of the prisoners flung himself overboard and perished. A happier omen was the reappearance of the fifth ship of the convoy, and all reached Copenhagen safely on October 5.

IV

The King of Denmark now decided to fit out a third expedition. Two large ships were provided under Captain Karsten Rich Kordisen, of Holstein, with mixed crews of Norwegian and Icelandic seamen. They are said to have sailed in May, though the actual year is uncertain. Greenland was sighted on June 8, but the ice-belt round the coast proved an insuperable barrier, and the expedition was forced to return.

By this time there were about eight Eskimos in Denmark, and they were being well cared for. In addition to receiving their native delicacies of raw fish and raw meat and whale oil, they were given plenty of milk, butter and cheese. But they did not settle. It was often observed that they looked wistfully northwards, and on many occasions they seized small boats and put out to sea in desperate bids for freedom. After one such abortive attempt three of the prisoners pined away and died from grief.

The remaining five rallied sufficiently to give a kayak display for the entertainment of the Spanish Ambassador in Copenhagen. He rewarded them generously, and they promptly used the money to buy themselves plumed hats, knee-boots and spurs, and announced a desire to serve with the King's cavalry.

But the high spirits waned, and two of their number

made a determined attempt to get away in their kayaks. One was lost, and the other was overtaken and brought back. After ten or twelve years there was one survivor, the others having pined and died. This lone Eskimo still hungered for the north, and when an opportunity for stealing a small boat presented itself he immediately put out to sea. He was pursued, and died soon after recapture.

Greenland was next heard of in 1636, when a company of Copenhagen merchants fitted out two ships with the idea of building up a profitable trade. Both vessels returned in due course with their holds crammed with what the voyagers fondly imagined to be gold, but which experts declared to be valueless. The entire cargo was jettisoned, and this trading enterprise presumably petered out.

Two more ventures may be mentioned. In 1654 a Captain David Nelles visited Greenland and brought back three women prisoners, but what became of them or what else the trip yielded does not seem to be recorded. Then, six years later, King Christian V despatched an expedition under Captain Otto Axelson. One historian says there is "no account of its issue", and another declares that the expedition never returned.

At about this time plans for the resettlement of Greenland were frequently talked about both in Norway and Denmark. Dutch and other whalers, many from Bergen, carried on a more or less regular traffic in the Davis Strait, and frequently set parties ashore to explore the mainland. But they encountered only Eskimos, and another century was to dawn before European influence was to make itself felt in Greenland again.

CHAPTER IV

HANS EGEDE—"APOSTLE OF GREENLAND"

A CONSPICUOUS landmark in Godthaab today is a statue of a noble figure in ruff and gown, clasping a staff and gazing steadily seawards from the crest of a low hill which overlooks the broad bay. This is the statue of Hans Egede, Godthaab's founder.

It is fitting that his memory should be thus honoured, for he, more than any man, helped to reshape Greenland's destiny after the first attempts at colonisation had ended disastrously with the elimination of those early pioneers who had followed Eric the Red.

Norwegian born, in the vogtship of Sengen, on January 31, 1686, Egede studied at Copenhagen University and entered the Lutheran Church, becoming pastor of Vaagen in the Lofoten Islands.

As a young man he must have heard much talk about the mystery of the vanished Norsemen and of the wonders of Greenland. At any rate his imagination was so kindled that in his thirty-fifth year he became fired with an overmastering desire to visit Greenland and to search for the missing settlers, who were now presumed to have scattered and to be living as pagans. To find them and to Christianise them, thought Egede, would be a splendid achievement; but it was first necessary to find someone to share his own zeal, and this proved no easy matter. People listened and shook their heads. All the voyages made throughout the preceding century had borne little fruit, and there was no reason to suppose that a priest could succeed where merchants and skilled seamen had failed. Everyone seemed to think that the difficulties entailed in

37

such an undertaking as that proposed by Egede must outweigh any hypothetical advantages which might accrue.

"Year after year," writes his son-in-law in *The Story of Hans Egede*, published in London in 1864, "Egede had heard the same objections made; again and again he had petitioned the Bishops of Drontheim and of Bergen, and sent memorials to the College of Missions at Copenhagen, urging the duty of regaining the lost land, and offering himself as the first missionary there; but exhortations from some to patience, and derision from others, appeared the only result of his unwearied labours."

But Egede persevered and allowed nothing to quench his zeal. His Bishop did eventually bring the scheme to the notice of the King of Denmark, though the help and encouragement Egede had hoped for were not forthcoming. Lacking a patron, he decided to help himself, and he went to Bergen determined to form a commercial company with the idea of financing his missionary efforts from trading activities.

His perseverance paid. On hearing that he was putting in his own savings—a matter of £60—two or three Bergen merchants contributed £40 apiece. Other merchants soon followed their example, as did several ship-owners and other members of the clergy. In this way Egede raised £2,000. Finally, the King had second thoughts and decided that Egede might be worthy of support, after all. He accordingly made him a grant of £40 for his immediate needs and promised a regular allowance of £60 yearly.

It was at this stage, just as Egede was completing his preparations for departure on his great adventure, that his future son-in-law, Jans Olaf, saw him for the first time. Olaf, then a lad of fourteen, could hardly fail to be thrilled by everything connected with the planned voyage, and his impressions of that encounter always remained vividly with him.

Danish Press Photographers' Assn.

This bleak, uninviting terrain is typical of the coastal belt which skirts the Ice Cap.

The hunter prepares his harness before setting off across the ice with his sledge and dog-team.

Jette Bang

One of the many glaciers which sweep down to the water's edge in Sondrestromfiord.

Icebergs, adrift in Disko Bay, after being calved from the giant glaciers of Jakobshavn, often assume fantastic form.

"I saw him, quiet in manner, reserved in speech, slightly though strongly made, with the look of a student —which he was—rather than that of a pioneer of civilisation," is the picture he drew in later life when recording those impressions.

Egede's wife, Gertrud, he described as:

" . . . the calm and determined heroine of the undertaking; inspiring all concerned in it with some share in her own confidence; while he, firm, but not joyful, appeared chiefly conscious of the immensity of the sacrifice he had demanded of her. Madame Egede was then scarcely thirty; a gentle young mother; with blue eyes and flaxen hair, and a mild but resolute expression of countenance.

"Her eldest daughter, Anna, resembled herself; Paul, the next to her, was a clever boy with remarkable artistic talent; while Carl, who carefully led about his baby sister, Olga, looked all the time like a frolicsome elf from the pine forest; he was so full of play and fun that it made me gay to look at him."

Egede embarked on May 12, 1721, in his vessel, the *Good Hope*. His family, gathered round him, heard a prayer and a blessing from the Bishop of Bergen; their home coast faded and their venture into the unknown began.

Greenland was reached on July 3, and they dropped anchor in Balls River, 64° N. latitude. The ship's company numbered forty, and they lost no time in building a stone-and-turf house on the island of Kangek, which they promptly re-christened "Hope Island", after the vessel which had brought them from Bergen.

Even in summer the bleak austerity of their surroundings must have occasioned misgivings among that little band. Egede's own feelings on discovering that the Scandinavian settlers had not survived may well be imagined. In their place he found a primitive people

D

whose language he could not understand and whose religion and customs were strange. A lesser man might have returned home, but, notwithstanding the bleakness of the land to which he had brought his beloved family and the unpromising plight in which they found themselves, Hans Egede accepted the challenge and resolved to stay.

He stayed for fifteen years!

II

At the end of the first year young Jans Olaf managed to get to Greenland aboard a vessel taking supplies to Egede. Already the numbers had dwindled, and those who rushed wildly to greet the folk from home looked worn and haggard. They had not exhausted all the provisions they had brought with them, but a shortage of fresh meat and vegetables had undermined health, and many had been stricken with scurvy.

Now, as fresh food was unloaded from the newly arrived ship, the settlers grabbed vegetables and ate them raw; and when flour was distributed they could hardly wait for cakes or bread to be properly baked, but devoured them eagerly when half-cooked.

Olaf, with his eye for detail, has set down a full description of Egede's first Greenland home. It was built of large blocks of stone, the crevices being packed with turf and moss inside and out. The roof was supported by heavy timbers, and the hut itself was divided into two compartments, lined with dried moss and lit by small, doubly-glazed windows. One compartment, larger than the other, had an open fireplace for burning driftwood, and the smaller room was equipped with a stove they had brought with them from Norway. Egede, having some skill in carpentry, had striven to make the interior of this rough dwelling as comfortable as possible.

In addition to fresh supplies, the relief boat had brought letters from home, and among them was one from the College of Missions assuring Egede that it was the King's pleasure to continue his support of the Greenland mission.

"Thanks be to God!" exclaimed Gertrud Egede. "He is a shield to those who trust in Him."

"If you had not arrived before the end of June," said her husband, wringing Olaf's hand, "we were pledged to return to Norway, and this is the twenty-seventh."

Olaf's sharp eyes had noted that twelve months of Greenland weather had been enough to play havoc with the settlers' homes; but the damage was not exclusively the work of wind, snow and ice. A fortnight before, impatient to return, some of the sailors had started to dismantle their huts. They had had enough!

But Madame Egede would not listen when anyone urged her to return.

"We would rather, if no roof is left to us, burrow in the earth like foxes," she told Olaf, "than desert the land in which God has given us His work to do."

Her husband smiled and added:

"It is thus my Anna has kept us all to our duty; but starvation was already at work with us. I could not have remained alone to see her and our children perish, and had not your ship reached us this week, I must have gone home in the one which brought us—feeling forever a dishonoured man."

Their physical trials and torments had indeed been formidable, but Egede had never lost sight of the purpose of his visit. He tackled the language problem with tremendous zeal, and as soon as he found out that "*kina*" in Greenlandic implied "What is this?", he started systematically to ask the name for everything, and wrote it down. Paul's gift for drawing helped, too, and with a combination of pictures and signs, father and son between them began to acquire more and more knowledge of the Eskimo tongue.

One of Egede's first acts was to invite the Eskimos to

let their sorcerers try their powers against him. They did so, and the sorcerers declared with candour that Egede must be a great *"angekok"* or wizard in his own right, since they were powerless to harm him in any way. In this manner respect and confidence were gained; but, nevertheless, Egede was forced to plant a secret garden somewhere among the mountains because everything he tried to grow round his home was stolen.

Still Egede persevered and, as his mastery of their language increased, he succeeded in making converts among the Eskimos, who saw that he was devoted wholly, to their welfare. As acquaintanceship grew, Egede detected many traces of Norse influence, and it became apparent that some Eskimos had acquired many useful scraps of knowledge from the now defunct settlers. Those in the south, for instance, knew how to make morticed joints when constructing their sledges, while others had adopted the practice of decorating their gear and weapons with designs suggestive of Norse artistry.

Egede's children through continually playing with Eskimo youngsters, picked up the correct pronunciation of words, so that, in addition to enlarging his vocabulary, their father was able to coin words where necessary to convey his meaning when seeking to explain terms like "holy", "sin" or "grace", or when speaking of unfamiliar things, such as angel, manger or cross.

By 1727 some progress was being made when disaster threatened. The coast became ice-bound, and the yearly store-ship from Norway was wrecked. Egede, recognising the peril ahead, showed himself a man of action, and proposed a dash northwards in an endeavour to buy some supplies from Dutch whalers who were known to be in a region about 300 miles distant.

He and his eldest son set off across the ice and kept going day and night, using dog-sledges. They brought back all they could, but when everything was pooled, the total stores for their settlement, which now numbered thirty, consisted of three barrels of pease, three of oat-meal, eleven sacks of malt and 1,000 biscuits. Fortunately, a second supply vessel, though delayed by ice, did get through that year, or winter prospects would have been grim indeed.

The Greenland Company had by now given up trading because it saw no worth-while return for its outlay, and Egede was begged to abandon his settlement and to return. He steadfastly declined, but sent back a missionary friend from Norway.

Fortunately, King Frederik IV indicated his readiness to continue his support. No doubt he was impressed by Egede's courage and tenacity, for in the following year he sent out a special convoy of five ships, one of them a man-o'-war which carried troops and cannon, with the idea of building a fort and providing a garrison for the protection of the Greenland trade.

Jans Olaf, now a young man of twenty-one, chanced to sail with this convoy, and has recorded that many married couples now came out as prospective settlers, while masons, carpenters and other much-needed craftsmen also arrived. In this mixed company, too, were some officers who had brought horses with the express intention of exploring the interior in a new effort to trace the original Norse settlers.

Chief among the new arrivals, however, was an elderly officer named Pars, who had been nominated as the First Governor of Greenland. This tangible support, with its strengthening of links with home, must have put new heart into Egede's party.

Still more heartening from a personal point of view was the arrival of two assistants for Egede himself, named Olans Langen and Henri Milzong, because this enabled the Pastor to dispense for the time being with the services of his son, Paul, who was now sent back to Copenhagen to study for the ministry. A Greenlander named Poek and one of his companions went back with Paul at their own request; and, meanwhile, the remaining settlers entered upon a new era of progress.

III

The first consideration, now that their resources were augmented, was to move the settlement to the mainland, where Godthaab was established on its present site. But this move had scarcely been accomplished when the winter set in with a severity which appalled the new colonists. Unacclimatised, they sickened and died in numbers, taxing the stamina of the survivors, who were unable to bury their comrades in the ice-bound earth. Makeshift graves had to be scooped in the snow and covered with stones until the following summer. But before the winter ended the settlers had other trials to face. Some kind of pestilence broke out and the death-roll rose. All the horses perished, too, for want of proper fodder.

While troubles thus multiplied, the soldiers mutinied against the Governor, and even threatened to take Egede's life because they regarded him as responsible for their plight. Guards were mounted round the Pastor's house by day, and at night he crept away to sleep peacefully in the tents of his Eskimo flock.

The mutiny petered out as the men were stricken with the pestilence. Some were nursed by the Eskimos at first and then abandoned to die.

By summer the colony was plunged in gloom. All the high hopes cherished when the settlers had moved to the mainland had gone, though Egede and his dauntless wife tried by their example to rally everyone to renewed effort.

In September ships arrived with a welcome consignment of all kinds of building materials; but the death of King Frederik IV brought a new blow. A mandate arrived recalling Governor Pars, the two assistant missionaries, and all the colonists! Egede was given the

option of remaining, with permission to keep any of his
original followers who were willing to share his hardships;
but he was told frankly that if he did elect to remain he
could not expect any further assistance from home.

For Egede and his wife there was never any doubt as to
where their duty lay. The Pastor had now baptised 150
Eskimo children with the consent of their parents and was
giving his flock regular instruction. He had mastered the
language and had plans for translating the Creed and the
New Testament. Moreover, the mainland settlement, if
hard pressed, was at least established, and plantations were
beginning to thrive. How could they abandon their little
domain now, after all they had endured? It was unthinkable.

Ten staunch seamen ranged themselves beside the
Pastor and his wife and resolved to stay; a pitiful handful
for an undertaking of such magnitude, but what they
lacked in numbers was counterbalanced by their un-
quenchable spirit, and one and all drew inspiration from
Egede's favourite watchwords, "Good hope".

Poek, the Eskimo, returned from Copenhagen at about
this time, married and settled down, a loyal follower of
Egede, who baptised the happy couple and christened
them Christian and Christiana.

The next two years tested the resolution of the little
community to the uttermost, but Egede, though sorely
missing the help and companionship of his eldest son,
allowed himself no respite. He made patient experiments
in planting wheat in any sheltered nook he could find;
but though he succeeded in raising crops, they never
ripened. Today, even with all modern aids and increased
scientific knowledge, farmers in Greenland are no more
successful. Crops are raised, just as Egede raised them,
but winter sets in before they can ripen, and they serve
only as fodder for cattle.

Egede made many excursions with his second son, Carl;
sometimes seeking the abundant game—hare, reindeer or

ptarmigan; sometimes seeking the remains of the old Norse settlements; sometimes studying the flora.

At the end of two arduous but lonely years a ship came through the ice with supplies from home. There was also the welcome news that the settlement would not be left to fend for itself, after all, as the King had ordered a grant of £400 yearly to foster trade.

Messages also came from the Moravian Brethren at Hernhuth in Silesia to the effect that they were willing to place themselves under the direction of Hans Egede. A letter in the King's own hand commended the Brethren to Egede as believing that they had a call from Heaven to support him in the work he was doing.

Thus the pendulum of fortune swung alternately between good luck and bad. A few months after these heartening tidings had come to hand the settlement was smitten with an outbreak of smallpox. Terrified Eskimos stabbed themselves or flung themselves into the sea; others spread contagion by fleeing to scattered encampments.

The Moravian Brethren came in for this fierce baptism of fire, but under Egede's leadership they battled courageously. While Gertrud Egede and her daughters nursed the sick in Godthaab, the Brethren went from village to village with Egede and Carl to ensure that no one lacked any care that could be given. Many lives were thus saved and comfort was brought to the dying.

One old Eskimo who had always derided Egede in the past said on his deathbed: "You have done for us what our own people would not do: you have fed us when we had nothing to eat; you have buried our dead; you have told us of a better life."

This outbreak lasted for eight months, and traders who arrived at the end of it found scores of dwellings abandoned. By a cruel irony Gertrud Egede was among the last victims. She died blessing her husband as he knelt weeping at her bedside.

IV

News of his mother's death reached Paul Egede just after his ordination in Copenhagen, and he proceeded to Greenland immediately, having accepted the office of missionary at Disko.

It also reached Jans Olaf, now an expert ice-pilot making regular voyages aboard whalers to Disko Bay and Upernavik. He looked up his old friends, and took Egede several copies of religious works which the Pastor had translated into Greenlandic and which had just been printed in Copenhagen.

In his memoir of Egede, Olaf records that he found the Pastor sadly changed by the loss of his wife, in spite of his joy at Paul's presence. But he was still unflagging in his work and often read to the Eskimos. He had translated Luther's Catechism and several Lutheran hymns—the latter in a metre that could be chanted by the Greenlanders when paddling their kayaks or rowing their umiaks.

Anna was now housekeeping for her father, and Carl was sent back home to train as a naval officer; but first the entire family accompanied Paul to the scene of his future labours at Disko Bay. The scene can have altered little since those days. Many travellers hold the region of Disko Bay to be the loveliest part of the west coast. There the giant icebergs, many of fantastic shape, may be seen shimmering in the Arctic sunshine as, newly calved from the majestic Jakobshavn glacier, they drift towards the open sea.

Preparations had been made for Paul's reception. Building materials had been sent on in advance and existing settlers had built a trim little house for their new Pastor. But after his son was installed, and Egede returned to his own labours at Godthaab, moods of despair seemed to settle upon the father. He became subject to fits of dejection from which he seemed to find it harder and harder to rally himself with his old motto "Cast down, but not forsaken".

Only Carl remained unchanged by rigours of climate or general hardship and reverses. Olaf, faithful chronicler of the family's fortunes, observes that Carl's cheerfulness never left him. He had a great gusto for life, got on splendidly with the Eskimos, delighted in fishing with them and learnt to manipulate a kayak with a skill to match their own. It is easy to appreciate what the departure of this ebullient member of the household must have meant to the father, now left with his two daughters. Carl's company might have helped Egede to conquer his growing despondency, but he put the boy's career first, and did not count the cost to himself.

His own capacity for work was undiminished, and he even made the long trip across the coastal ice by reindeer sledge to visit Paul and to encourage him in his labours among the settlers of Christian's Hope colony. In those times it was a trading-post where fishermen and seal-hunters brought their wares; today it is the site of a flourishing shrimp cannery.

Meanwhile, the Moravian Brethren were struggling to make themselves proficient in the Danish language so that they could read Egede's notes on Greenlandic; but in practical matters they were somewhat slow. They did not take to fishing or shooting, as Egede and his sons had done, and when they went out in a boat to collect drift-wood near the shore they were nearly lost in a storm.

In the end they turned to the milder pastime of weaving, but they did not desert Egede, whose health was beginning to fail. Their trials were many, and news of their sufferings was carried back home, yet they still toiled on. Some of the more wily Eskimos seem to have taken advantage of their simplicity and good nature, even to the point of stealing their notes on the Greenlandic language.

News of Egede's failing health had also reached home, and brought a letter from the King requesting his return. This time Egede capitulated. Fifteen years of his life had been spent in Greenland, and he was a sick man. In a farewell sermon to his beloved Eskimos he said: "I have laboured in vain—I have spent my strength in vain; yet surely my judgment is with the Lord, and my work with my God!"

He sailed back to Copenhagen in 1736 in a ship commanded by his young friend Jans Olaf.

v

But Egede's work for Greenland or its people was far from ended. His return was a triumph, for he was received with great respect on all sides and sent for by the King. As a result of this latter interview he was commanded to found a seminary for students and orphans to whom he might teach Greenlandic and from whose ranks might be recruited future teams of missionaries.

He became the first Principal, with the title of Professor and a guaranteed salary. All his old zeal revived, and he organised the systematic training of missionaries to carry on the work he had begun so well.

There was also private cause for rejoicing in the Egede family. Olga, the youngest daughter, was now eighteen, and Jans Olaf, who had long admired her, ventured to offer himself as her suitor. His own account seems to suggest that he was both surprised and relieved when Egede instantly gave his consent and added that he had long regarded Olaf as a son. They were married in the spring.

The young couple made their home in Bergen, Jan having inherited a legacy from his grandfather, and it is pleasing to read that Olga scored a great social success and even won praise from her mother-in-law, who exclaimed: "Who would think that those pretty hands had ever rowed a kayak among the ice?"

Brighter news, too, came from Greenland, where the Moravian Brethren were scoring successes in the spiritual field. One of their converts brought his family and pitched his tent beside the missionaries. Three big families followed his example, and they, in turn, attracted others. Baptisms increased; and the days when mischievous Eskimos purloined the Moravians' notes were gone forever.

Egede remained as superintendent of the Mission to Greenland from 1740 to 1747. His closing years were spent in retirement on the island of Falster with his daughter Anna. He died peacefully there at the age of seventy-three—in the words of Olaf, "Long after he had received by common consent the name of the 'Apostle of Greenland'."

His son, Paul, who had succeeded him as Superintendent of the Mission to Greenland, continued to work with equal zeal. He excelled as a linguist and had produced the first Greenlandic Dictionary in 1750. Now he completed a translation of the New Testament which his father had begun, and then went on to produce a Greenlandic catechism and prayer-book and a translation of Thomas à Kempis.

Reality begins with dreams. All the fine achievements of mankind have had their seeding time. Canterbury Cathedral, the Pyramids, the Taj Mahal and the Great Wall of China were once no more than dream conceptions in the minds of men. Between them, Hans Egede and his son, Paul, brought many dreams to reality. Between them they may be said to have laid the foundation stones of Greenland's future destiny.

But now other noble figures, dreaming vastly different dreams, have their contribution to add to the growing structure as a new phase in the country's history opens and interest turns from the coastal peoples and their welfare to the hidden mysteries of the frozen hinterland.

CHAPTER V

THE ICE CAP'S LURE

OTHER men; other dreams. With the dawn of another century came a mounting interest in Polar exploration by which pioneers from many nations were drawn to Greenland's shores. Early map-makers had described most of the coastline as "inaccessible by reason of floating and fixed mountains of ice"; but voyagers like Scoresby, Inglefield, Kane, Hays, Hall, Nares, Payer, Sir A. Young, Mourier and many others were soon to give them the lie.

The first accurate chart of Greenland was produced by Captain William Scoresby, who was born near Whitby in 1789. He made his first acquaintance with Greenland when, as a young man, he served as mate aboard his father's whaler, *Resolution*; but in 1822 he returned in command of his own vessel, *Baffin*, charted 400 miles of coastline, discovered the most extensive fiord system in the world, and gained immortality by giving it his name—Scoresby Sound.

Between 1823 and 1855 many other parts of the vast coastline were explored. Captains Edward Sabine and D. Clavering visited the coast between 72° N. and 75° N., and encountered the only Eskimo seen in that region. The south-east coast between Cape Farewell and 65° N. was explored by several Danes, including W. A. Graah and Gustav Holm; Britain's E. A. Inglefield entered Smith Sound and reported on many miles of coast; America's E. K. Kane discovered Kane Basin and Kennedy Channel, and was one of the first explorers to enlist the active co-operation of native Greenlanders and to profit from their knowledge of Arctic lore, an example later to be followed by Peary with conspicuous success.

But while one navigator after another was thus adding

fresh pieces to the monster jigsaw puzzle represented by Greenland's thousands of miles of intricate coastline, other explorers felt an irresistible lure to penetrate the frozen interior. With an area of 840,000 square miles, scope for discovery was not lacking, but as the greater part of the country was ice-bound, the problem facing the would-be pioneers presented tremendous difficulties. So far as could be deduced, the interior would yield nothing in the way of food or materials, and everything required for both outward and homeward journeys would, of necessity, have to be taken under conditions comparable to a dash for the Pole.

Edward Whymper and Robert Brown tried to penetrate the Ice Cap from the west coast in 1867, but their dog-sledge broke down, and they were forced to return. Their failure was mitigated in some measure by the acquisition of geological and natural history specimens, and they did not repeat the attempt.

Three years later A. G. Nordenskiold and S. Berggren, starting from Auleitsivik Fiord, succeeded in battling 35 miles inland, reaching an altitude of 2,200 feet above sea level. This record was eclipsed in 1878 by a Dane, Jens Jensen, who climbed to 5,400 feet and reached a point 45 miles from the west coast.

A. E. Nordenskiold replied to this in 1883 by making a second thrust from Auleitsivik Fiord which took him 84 miles inland to an altitude of 5,000 feet; and two Laplanders of his party, who were equipped with snow-shoes, pressed on to 6,600 feet. An even greater achievement was scored by Peary and Maigaard in 1886, when they pushed 100 miles inland and reached an altitude of 7,500 feet.

II

All these thrusts to date had been made from the west coast, but in 1888 Fridtjof Nansen, the Norwegian explorer, departed from precedent by deciding to tackle the problem in reverse. He also planned, ambitiously, for a complete crossing from coast to coast, starting from Gyldenlove Fiord, and with Christianshaab as a possible objective.

No one had ever succeeded in getting across the Ice Cap, and Nansen thought he knew why. Previous explorers, he argued, had been beaten before they started, and had taken undue risks in launching their attacks upon the Inland Ice from the west. Were they not leaving what he termed "the fleshpots" behind them, and thus facing the prospect, if they got across, of arriving on a wild and little-known east coast in an exhausted condition, with poor chance of finding shelter or of being able to replenish their supplies?

Nansen feared no danger, but he reasoned, logically enough, that it would be better to get the worst over first, while his party was still fresh, well-nourished and adequately supplied. Every step they took would then leave the barren, inhospitable east coast farther behind them, and as they progressed they would be buoyed up by the vision of the populous west coast. Indeed, he made "Death or the west coast of Greenland!" his slogan for the trip. There was no temptation to turn back; every inducement to press on.

His companions were three Norwegians, Otto Sverdrup, Kristian Trana and Olaf Dietrichson, and two Laplanders named Ravna and Balto, who had been specially recruited in Christiania.

Their equipment included five hand-sledges on broad, steel-shod runners. All joints were lashed, the better to absorb shock and, unloaded, they weighed about 28 lb. each. Nansen based their design on a type previously used successfully for Arctic rescue work; they were light and rode high in loose snow.

A start was made on the evening of August 15 with a stage of 2 or 3 miles, which took the party to a point 500 feet above sea level, where they pitched camp for the night. When they pushed on again progress soon became impeded by crevasses that could only be crossed with caution. To rope themselves together proved impracticable, because it interfered with their hauling, so each member lashed himself to a sledge and trusted to the weight being adequate to save him from disaster. Hauling the laden sledges over snow bridges was both difficult and dangerous. Often a member of the party would fall through up to the armpits.

After two days the expedition was halted by fierce storms, and Nansen wisely reduced rations, on the theory that as they were confined to their tent and could not work, they could well afford to make do with less nourishment.

By August 21 they had reached 3,000 feet, where they had nine degrees of frost at night. The snow surface was like iron, and stages of 3 or 4 miles were as much as they could manage, though they sometimes made night marches, which Nansen felt compensated them for the heavy going by the sheer beauty and wonder of their surroundings.

"When the ever-changing northern lights filled the heavens to the south with their fairy-like display—a display, perhaps, more brilliant in these regions than elsewhere—our toils and pains were, I think, for the most part forgotten," he wrote. "Or when the moon rose and set off upon her silent journey through the fields of stars, her rays glittering on the crest of every ridge of ice, and bathing the whole of the dead frozen desert in a flood of silver light, the spirit of the place reigned supreme, and life itself became beauty. I am convinced that these night marches of ours over the 'Inland Ice' left a deep and ineffaceable impression upon the minds of all who took part in them."

On August 23 they completed a stage of 9 or 10 miles, and felt elated; but the next day they were slowed down so

Frozen giants—product of the Jakobshavn glaciers which discharge
20,000,000 tons of ice daily

Author

Drift-ice near Julianehaab. At the start of the Royal Tour of 1952 a belt 30 miles wide threatened to render many ports inaccessible, but the King's yacht got through.

A snug anchorage near Godthaab.

Author

badly by loose snow that Nansen issued a cake of meat-chocolate every mile to keep his party in good spirits.

III

So the gruelling march into the unknown wasteland goes on and on; but morale is high, and everyone learns to laugh at misfortune. To save time they decide to cook their evening meal on the march and rig up their stove on one of the sledges so that they can look forward to a hot stew on completing their stage, instead of having to sit around waiting for it to boil. But on the first occasion that this experiment is tried Nansen accidentally upsets the stew as he carries it into the tent. Fortunately, the ground-sheet has already been spread; the corners are gathered promptly, and most of the evening meal is tipped back into the pot, plus a good many foreign bodies and some spilled methylated spirit. The mess is consumed with relish, despite caustic asides from Balto.

Balto's genial grumblings recur frequently in Nansen's narrative. He is the more forceful of the two Laplanders, loyal, plodding, impervious to hardship, yet apt to speak his mind with delightful candour. He is always ready to suggest that this or that piece of equipment could be jettisoned as superfluous to requirements—so ready, indeed, that one begins to suspect that his primary concern is the lightening of his burden. He is critical of nearly every innovation; rightly sometimes, as in his condemnation of snow-shoes for such terrain; wrongly at other times, as in his first rejection of snow-glasses, which he later accepts as necessary. But, right or wrong, he never hesitates to give voice to his thoughts.

When, at 6,000 feet, some flatter expanses are encountered and Nansen suggests rigging sails on the sledges to take advantage of following winds, Balto finds this too much, and says quite bluntly that he has never encountered such a lot of absolute lunatics. Whoever heard of anyone wanting to sail on snow?

E

Nevertheless, having had his say, he assists with the rigging and helps to lash the sledges together. Two form one vessel, with the stew-stained tent-floor for sail; three form another, with two spare tarpaulin sheets as sails. The effect is crude and the practical result disappointing, for it is still necessary for two men to haul while a third steers from behind.

Nansen now begins to doubt their ability to reach Christianshaab before the last boat of the season starts for home, and the thought of being marooned there for the whole of the long winter is too gloomy to be entertained. He makes a quick decision to head for a southerly port, and suggests Godthaab. There are no dissenting voices among his party, for by this time the Ice Cap has lost a great deal of its allure for them.

But a change of route does not diminish their troubles. There are nights when they fear their tent will be ripped to pieces in the storm; mornings when, waking with rime on their faces, they have to dig out their sledges from great snowdrifts, unload everything and scrape the runners before they can get on the move.

At 6,500 feet the sun is intense at mid-day and the glare becomes unbearable. The Lapps have to suffer snow-blindness before they take to goggles and red silk veils. Trana becomes lame; the wind drops and the makeshift sails are useless; loose snow is encountered, and the ascent goes on until, by September 1, the party have reached 7,930 feet.

They are able to accomplish no more than 5 or 10 miles daily, and all round them is an ocean of snow. "No break or change in the horizon," writes Nansen. "No point to rest eye on or on which to direct course." They steer by compass or observation of the sun.

Nansen and Sverdrup unscrew the metal runners from their sledge in the hope that the wood will move more easily in soft snow; but the effect is worse—"like hauling in blue clay".

On September 11 Nansen's diary note reads: "Today Sverdrup and I found our sledge heavy to pull beyond all toleration, and it was really as much as we could do to make it move at all." Finally they abandon the sledge and take Balto's, whose kit is put on Ravna's sledge, which the two Lapps then pull together.

This change-over inspires one of Balto's typical outbursts.

"When you asked us two Lapps in Christiania how much we could pull we said we could manage a hundredweight. But now we have two hundredweight apiece, and all I can say is, that if we drag these loads across to the west coast we are stronger than horses!"

Balto also enjoys a laugh at his leader's expense when Nansen experiments with snow-shoes and keeps falling. The Lapps take to skis, and the rest of the party does likewise and find them ideal. Indeed, Nansen expresses the opinion that without them the enterprise would have been well-nigh impossible. They use skis continuously for nineteen days, in which they cover some 240 miles.

There are snow-storms in which the flakes are so fine as to suggest frozen mist, and, seen through this veil, the sun always has a halo round it. When the sun sinks so low that the halo partly disappears below the horizon, mock suns are to be seen round it.

Nansen notes that the cold intensifies as they press farther inland, but the sun is still hot at noon. During the nights ice often forms on faces and beards and hair, so that they freeze fast to head coverings and on waking it is difficult to part the lips to speak.

In one terrific storm, when Balto courageously volunteers to venture outside to reconnoitre, he is immediately blown back bodily into the tent. The storm abates next day, but leaves the explorers with the formidable task of digging themselves out of the drifts.

All these hardships are endured on a Spartan diet, a typical day's menu being as follows:

Breakfast: Chocolate or tea.
           Biscuits.
           Liver pate.
           Pemmican.
Dinner: Pemmican.
           Liver pate.
           Oatmeal biscuits.
           Lemonade poured over snow.
Tea: Biscuits.
           Liver pate.
           Pemmican.
Supper: Pemmican.
           Biscuits, tea.
           Lentil or bean soup.
           Or a stew made from pemmican, biscuits
           and soup mixed together.

Butter is issued on one day a week; and everyone chews chips of wood on the march to alleviate thirst. Slivers from their Norwegian snow-shoes, which were made from bird-cherrywood, prove best for this purpose.

By September 12 they have reached an altitude of 8,250 feet and, by their calculations, are some 75 miles distant from bare land. Balto, indeed, confidently assures his companions that he can actually see the coast. The snow certainly seems to slope away westwards now, but the surface is far from regular and the many undulations are apt to deceive the eye. Two days later they can see nothing but snow, and this time Balto remains silent, while Ravna lets off steam for a change:

"I am an old Lapp, and a silly old fool, too!" he declares. "I don't believe we shall ever get to the coast."

"That is quite true, Ravna," comments Nansen smoothly. "You *are* a silly old fool."

This makes the Laplander rock with mirth.

"So it's quite true, is it?" he demands. "Ravna is a silly old fool?"

Everyone laughs. Nansen has adroitly turned their thoughts from the pessimistic suggestion that they will never reach their goal.

On another day, after the leader has been busy with scientific calculations, Balto shakes his head dubiously and asks: "But how on earth can anyone tell how far it is from one side to the other when no one has been across?"

Nansen lets that one pass!

IV

On September 17 there is a pronounced falling away of ground. The thermometer just fails to reach zero, and Nansen records that it feels mild by comparison. A snow-bunting appears and chirrups round them, and as it is also the day for their butter issue, all are in high spirits.

The improvement in conditions continues, and they rig their sails again, and are now able to travel at speed over the sloping surface. Nansen is jolted from his sledge while trying to dislodge an ice-axe, and is left floundering in the snow. He sets off in pursuit, and finds that stores and various items of equipment have also been jolted off the sledge at intervals. Sverdrup goes sailing blithely on, unaware of what is happening until, receiving no re-sponse to some conversational effort, he glances round and discovers with amazement that Nansen is no longer there.

Sverdrup turns back, but by this time the remainder of the party have caught up, and from now onward the sledges are all lashed together.

On September 19 Balto utters a cry of "Land ahead!" And this time he is not mistaken. "We could see away to the west a long dark mountain ridge," records Nansen, "and to the south of it a smaller peak. Rejoicings were general, for the goal towards which we had so long struggled was at last in sight."

To celebrate the occasion two pieces of meat-chocolate are issued all round, with biscuits, butter and jam in addition. But shortly after, while proceeding at speed, the party has a narrow escape from hurtling into a great chasm. This sobers them. They proceed more cautiously and reconnoitre all ground ahead which appears treacherous.

Nansen's fingers are frozen during that afternoon, and in the excitement of sighting land both he and Sverdrup forget to wind their watches But they are nearly out of the wilderness of ice, and next morning they can see the whole of the country south of Godthaab Fiord—"wild and grand as the western coast of Norway".

They make a hearty breakfast, with unlimited tea and cheese and oatmeal biscuits, and start late, bearing southwards to avoid crevasses. In places it is too steep for skiing, but they stand on the sledge runners, scraping and braking with one foot to steer clear of danger. On one occasion, when slewed round sidewise on the very edge of a crevasse, the cornice begins to crumble, and they only drag their sledge clear in time to avoid disaster.

On the 29th they encounter the worst crevasses so far, and are forced to make a detour; but to compensate them for this they discover a water-hole and enjoy their first proper drink for a month. They all drink to repletion, and Balto declares that it is as good as fresh, sweet milk.

Next day Nansen slips through a snow-bridge, but happily the fissure below is narrow enough to enable him to keep hold on both sides and, after much struggling, to extricate himself safely.

He and Sverdrup now push on ahead, leaving the others to follow more slowly. For the second time that day Nansen falls into a crevasse and is left dangling perilously by his arms. Once again he succeeds in struggling out. An impassable network of crevasses then enforces more detours.

Nansen's diary for September 23 records the heaviest ice-travelling yet. They are frequently forced to carry their sledge bodily up the steep slopes of ridges, but they keep doggedly on.

On the 24th they make an early start, determined to reach the coast that day. Crossing a frozen tarn they enjoy the inexpressible thrill of feeling earth and springy heather underfoot. Now they begin their final march, taking with them only their most necessary kit. The night is spent sleeping peacefully upon the heather beside a big fire of scrub and brushwood.

Next day Nansen bags a hare, which provides a welcome change of diet, but though they keep going, their march is not yet ended. The 26th finds them following a river downward among thickets of willow and alder not much higher than a man's shoulder. Masses of mussel-shells beside the river indicate that the fiord once filled the valley. Balto, returning from a lone reconnaissance, reports having seen the fiord from a mountain top, and on the 27th work is commenced upon a small boat to be covered with the waterproof tent-floor. By evening the coracle-like craft is finished, but Nansen has his doubts.

"She was no boat for a prize competition indeed; in shape she was more like a tortoise-shell than anything else, but when we tried her in a pool close by we found she carried us both well, and altogether we were hugely pleased with her. Her dimensions I may add were: length 8 ft. 5 in.; breadth 4 ft. 8 in.; depth 2 ft."

Oars are made from forked willow branches with canvas stretched across like the webbing of a duck's foot, these ingenious "blades" being lashed to bamboo poles.

Thwarts are less easy to construct, but some parts of a theodolite stand and two thin pieces of bamboo are made to furnish "the scantiest seats it has ever been my ill-luck to sit upon . . ."

Nansen and Sverdrup embark in this frail craft on Michaelmas Day, and find that she travels far better than they had dared to hope, in spite of having to be baled out with soup-bowls every ten minutes.

It takes them four days to get clear of the fiord, and on

the fifth day they meet several kayak hunters who, being preoccupied in seeking seal, ignore the strange travellers. Rounding a point, they behold a cluster of buildings comprised of a house, some Eskimo huts and a long, slated structure with a church-like tower.

Numerous Eskimos, chiefly old women, come down to the beach to greet them, and a good-looking, fair young man in Greenlandic dress, but wearing a tam-o'-shanter, calls out: "Do you speak English? Are you English?"

"No. We are Norwegians," answers Nansen, and on giving his name he is astounded when the man immediately calls:

"Oh, allow me to congratulate you on taking your Doctor's degree."

Nansen had, in fact, taken his degree just before his departure, but he had certainly never expected to receive congratulations in Greenland. The stranger is a Dane named Baumann, Assistant Superintendent of the Godthaab Colony. From him Nansen learns that the last ship has gone except for the *Fox*, employed in the cryolite trade and now at Ivigtut, 300 miles away. Messengers are despatched to see if a return passage can be arranged, while Nansen and Sverdrup go ashore to a salute of guns, their long ordeal ended, their goal triumphantly achieved.

v

Yet that final epic voyage in their quaint home-built craft had been made in vain. Nansen and Sverdrup could, as things turned out, have completed the journey to Godthaab at a more leisurely pace with their four companions. When their request reached the Captain of the *Fox*, it had to be refused with regret. The vessel, which had once carried Sir Leopold McClintock on his celebrated search for Franklin, was at this time the property of the company operating the cryolite mines at Ivigtut; and the Captain, being unfamiliar with the coastal waters round Godthaab, was unwilling to risk being delayed in the approaching winter darkness.

So Nansen and his followers were forced to resign themselves to the prospect of wintering in Greenland, after all; though, being men of action, they took advantage of their enforced stay to sift the knowledge gained in their march across the Ice Cap and to make a serious study of Eskimo habits and customs.

Of course, they were made much of by the people of Godthaab, and a local poet, Christian Rosing, commemorated their achievement in some verses which were published in the Greenlandic paper *Atuagagdliutit*—a news-sheet which flourishes to this day.

Here is an English translation of these verses which Nansen included in his own account of the crossing.

> Six men
> Journeyed from Norway;
> Four were Norwegians,
> Two were Lapps;
> They sailed upon a Norwegian ship
> Landed on the eastern coast;
> And carried all their implements
> With them.

> They journeyed across the Inland Ice
> And suffered much by the way;
> They had no great store of food,
> And only one suit of clothes;
> Their coffee came to an early end
> And likewise their tobacco.
> And yet they crossed the Inland Ice
> And reached the western coast.

> Two of them came to Godthaab
> Out of Ameralikfiord;
> They had a boat
> Which was exceeding strange.
> Four of them had been left behind;
> We heard that there were Lapps among them.
> We longed much to see them.

At last they came,
The Lapps and the Other two;
We went as usual down
To the sea-shore to receive them.
One of the Lapps was somewhat lame;
He was very small
And had a tall, pointed cap.
The other big one of the Lapps
Had a four-cornered cap.
He had trousers upon his legs
And a great plisse.
He was very kind
And very talkative;
For this reason the little Greenlanders
Grew very fond of him.

Readers will probably have guessed that the talkative Lapp so beloved by the Greenlanders was Balto? They seem to have worshipped him for his genial good humour and high spirits and for his readiness to throw himself wholeheartedly into the life of the capital.

Balto even tried to master the kayak. The inevitable ducking on his first attempts and the unrestrained laughter of the watching Greenlanders could not quench his ebullient spirits.

"Well, I am *almost* wet," he observed with a smile as he tried and tried again. "And I will say that that kayak is a very devil of a boat!"

No wonder the Greenlanders loved him.

In the hour of his triumph Nansen could record human little stories such as this, just as he set down the fact that on the day on which he landed at Godthaab he heard "The Last Rose of Summer" played upon a musical box in his host's home—"an air which will hereafter never fade from my memory".

The magnitude of his achievement in being the first man to cross the Ice Cap will never fade either; though other great explorers must now take the stage.

CHAPTER VI

PEARY, RASMUSSEN AND OTHERS

WHILE Nansen was making his crossing just below the Arctic Circle, Peary was active in the far north, following up his initial reconnaissance of 1886. The American had fallen completely under the Ice Cap's spell, and year after year he carried out expeditions upon the Inland Ice. But always he was drawn irresistibly northwards, and there is no doubt that the experience thus gained served him in excellent stead when he finally came to launch his onslaught on the Pole itself.

Peary saw Greenland as a "pendant brooch in the glittering necklace of snow and ice which circles the Pole", and in 1891 and 1892 he made two 1,200-mile sledge journeys which were prolonged endurance tests and which provided tough foretastes of what a Polar dash would involve.

He has recorded that the traveller upon Greenland's Inland Ice—a misnomer, since it is really impacted snow—sees only three things: the infinite expanse of frozen plain; the infinite dome of cold, blue sky, and the cold, white sun. Yet he himself succumbed to the lure again and again, and the sufferings endured on one trip seemed only to accentuate his yearning to face the perils of the Ice Cap anew. He planned each successive expedition with increasing zeal.

His reconnaissance with Christian Maigaard, the Danish assistant to the Governor of Ritenbenk, provided a harsh enough baptism. In three weeks they reached an altitude of 7,525 feet, and awoke one morning to find themselves completely snowed under. For forty-eight hours they could only lie there "with wind and snow driving in one incessant, sullen roar" across the drift above them. Then, during a slight lull, they were able to scoop out a shallow pit, which they covered with a rubber blanket. Digging out their bags and sledges, they threw their belongings into the pit, crawled in after them and dragged the sledges over the edges of the blanket to weight it down.

When the weather finally cleared they had only six days' provisions left, so they lashed their sledges together, rigged a sail and devised a rudder from a snow-skate, lashed to a hatchet. The early part of their homeward journey was impeded by crevasses, some of them 50 feet wide; but they rushed their craft over snow-bridges, resisting the temptation to look down and admire the fascinating patterns of frostwork and giant icicles with which the bottomless pits were festooned.

Once past the crevasses, however, they made rapid progress, and were soon down to 2,125 feet. But here they encountered impassable slush, and were forced to wait for this to freeze before they could make their last dash for the coast and safety.

In April 1895 Peary set off with Hugh Lee, Matt. Henson, six Eskimos, six sledges and sixty dogs on a trip which, in spite of careful pre-planning, was destined to be fraught with one difficulty after another. The expedition had barely started when one of the Eskimos decamped, taking a sledge and a dog-team with him—a loss which compelled a troublesome rearrangement of loads and which upset all calculations.

Yet good progress was made in marches of 22, 28 and 30 miles a day, although a food cache prudently laid down in the previous year could not be located. This in itself was a shattering blow, for it involved the loss of 1,400 lb. of pemmican; but Peary and his companions, though all suffering from frostbite, decided to press on. The five remaining Eskimos were sent back.

Without Eskimo assistance, the three explorers found the handling of the dog-teams a problem, and on one occasion they were held up for five hours while they battled, with frozen fingers, to unravel the tangled traces. A great storm overtook them at the head of Petermannfiord Basin, and one sledge had to be abandoned.

By now they had reached 7,865 feet above sea level, but were still making from 10 to 25 miles daily. Then, when they were 400 miles inland, the runner of one sledge broke and had to be patched up. It lasted for another 12 miles and then gave out beyond repair. The original pack of sixty dogs had dwindled by this time to seventeen, and there was no more walrus meat on which to feed these.

A few days later, when 500 miles from their base, only eleven dogs remained. Three of these were at the point of collapse, and the others were quite unfit for any great exertion. Leaving Lee to snatch what rest he could and to look after the dogs, Peary and Henson (a negro) set off, with three days' pemmican rations, a spare cooker and their rifles, in search of game.

Storms plagued the would-be hunters for two consecutive days, then they had the good fortune to bag a hare and several musk-oxen. They were then so ravenous that they could not trouble to get their cooker going. "Never have I tasted more delicious food than was that tender, raw, warm meat," wrote Peary in *Northward Over the Great Ice*—"a mouthful here and a mouthful there, cut from the animal as I skinned it. I ate until I dared eat no more, although still unsatisfied."

Back in camp, the remaining dogs were permitted to gorge themselves to repletion, and the explorers cooked some ox-meat for themselves before starting upon their return journey.

When they took stock of their situation on June 1 it was found that they had fourteen days' rations for their dogs, which now numbered only nine, and seventeen days' rations for themselves. They met this situation by deciding to limit their own diet to biscuits and to reserve all the meat exclusively for the dogs, in the hope of maintaining their pulling power.

On June 3 they achieved a run of over 25 miles, but on the following day the going proved much heavier, as biting head winds were encountered and all were suffering from tender and aching legs and feet.

Two days later the wind dropped, but the going was still difficult, as the snow became looser and heavier. Lee became utterly exhausted after the first 3½ miles of the day's march and had to be kept going on quinine, brandy and hot tea. Yet it was impossible to linger while the dogs were pulling well. So they kept on until two dogs dropped, to be devoured by their companions.

They were still 400 miles from their base on June 7; Lee was now very unwell, and all the dogs showed signs of flagging. Everything was now transferred to the smaller sledge, but after pressing on for a time, the party was obliged to camp so that Peary and Henson could devote themselves to nursing their sick comrade.

During a fifteen hours' rest Lee was fed on a treble allowance of milk, brandy and other stimulants, which enabled him to stand another march which lopped 20 miles off their long journey. On the 11th only five dogs were left, and for the last few miles of the day's march the explorers pulled the sledge themselves, and the exhausted animals were barely able to follow in their tracks. Peary estimated that by putting themselves on half rations of biscuits, tea and milk, they could last out for another nineteen days.

Four dogs were left on the 12th, and the only encouragement for the hard-pressed men was that they were now on a downward gradient. They managed to maintain an average run of 20 miles daily, though often delayed by heavy snow and the necessity for stopping to bury the sledge-runners when the sun was at its zenith to prevent the ice from melting.

By June 15 all their precautions proved in vain, for the

surface of the runners began to loosen. They now had only three dogs and all the dog-food was gone. Still they pushed on, through squalls on the 17th and snow-storms on the 18th and 19th, accomplishing runs of 20 miles and 10 miles. But two days later, with only one surviving dog and their own strength ebbing, they were obliged to camp after a march of barely 2 miles.

The remaining dog was fed on old sealskin boots and some yards of raw-hide line; then the march was resumed, though Lee soon dropped behind. After three hours the coastal fringe was sighted, and in due course all reached their base to find everything as they had left it three months before. Peary soon had the stove going and prepared food and coffee; but before he touched a morsel himself he fed his surviving dog by hand, passing it tender pieces of unfrozen venison until the poor creature could eat no more.

II

With the dawn of a new century Danish explorers began to turn their serious attention to the north-east coast of Greenland. Preparations were made to launch a big-scale expedition, and in the spring of 1906 a picked team of scientists and technicians left Copenhagen under the leadership of Mylius-Erichsen.

The enterprise was known as the Denmark Expedition, after the vessel in which they sailed. The party consisted of the commander of the *Denmark*, Lieutenant A. Trolle, his second officer, Lieutenant H. Bistrup; Lieutenant (later Colonel) J. P. Koch; Lieutenant H. Hoeg-Hagen; H. Jarner, geologist; A. Lundager, botanist; F. Johansen, zoologist; A. Manniche, conservator; A. Wegener, meteorologist; Peter Freuchen, his assistant; J. Lindhard, physician; Thostrup, boatswain, and three Greenlanders, Jorgen Bronlund, Tobias Gabrielsen and Hendrik Olsen. Two artists, Achton-Friis and A. Bertelsen, also accompanied the expedition.

Their vessel reached Danmarks Havn on August 17, and for two consecutive winters the party made this their base. After numerous small scientific excursions, major thrusts were attempted in the spring of 1907 by two teams. The first of these, consisting of Koch, Bertelsen and Gabrielsen, made for Cape Bridgman, then thought to be the most northerly point in Greenland; the second, consisting of Mylius-Erichsen, Hoeg-Hagen and Bronlund, made for the north-west with the task of determining whether Pearyland was an island or joined to the mainland.

Koch and his companions reached their objective and got back to base safely; but Mylius-Erichsen and the others were ill-fated. They had planned to augment their rations by hunting, but game proved scarce; and though they, too, gained their objective and established that Pearyland was indeed part of Greenland, they perished from exposure and starvation on their return march.

Bronlund's body was found in the spring of 1908 by a search party consisting of Koch and Gabrielsen. Notes that he had left revealed that after his two companions had died he tried to press on alone; but realising that he, too, was doomed he had used his last remaining strength in writing down all details of their trip until the final moment.

The other members of the Denmark Expedition returned to Copenhagen that summer, and though the enterprise had been so marred by tragedy, it yielded very important results in the way of new cartography and discoveries in the realms of physics, natural history and ethnography.

In the following year Captain Einar Mikkelsen set out in a small ship, the *Alabama*, in the hope of finding diaries and other papers belonging to Mylius-Erichsen and Hoeg-Hagen. He reached Shannon Island at the end of August, after battling through ice-fields. Winter quarters were established, and in the same autumn Mikkelsen, with two companions, managed to reach Jorgen Bron-

Women of Thule still find the *amaut*— a capacious hood devised by early nomadic Eskimos— ideal for carrying their babies in comfort.

The young Greenlander also favours the same method when called upon to play nursemaid.

A polar-bear hunter gives his son an early lesson in handling a rifle.

This typical man of Thule looks across North Star Bay. He and fellow huntsmen make long sledge journeys across the ice in search of walrus, narwhal and bear.

lund's last resting-place. After giving him a proper burial, they returned to their base in mid-December, having searched in vain for any further papers.

In the following spring two expeditions were planned. Mikkelsen and the ship's engineer, J. Iversen, pushed north; Lieutenant Laub and two companions set off to map the country north of the great nunatak in Dronning Louise's Land.

The second party got back first to find that the *Alabama* had sprung a leak and was sinking. With commendable foresight, they immediately set to work to build a house against the return of Mikkelsen and Iversen; then, with the rest of their ship's company, they were given a passage home on a Norwegian whaler.

Meanwhile Mikkelsen and Iversen pushed on by dog-sledge up Danmarks Fiord and came upon a cairn in which Mylius-Erichsen and Hoeg-Hagen had cached their papers and reports relating to the last stages of their journey. These were found to be full of vital information, not the least interesting item being their confirmation that there was no channel cutting off Pearyland from the mainland.

On their return journey Mikkelsen and Iversen experienced some of the hardships which had brought disaster to their pioneering comrades. Lack of game meant a greater drain on such supplies as they carried with them. They were forced to abandon their sledge, tent and even their sleeping-bags and to kill their sole surviving dog. They, too, might have perished had they not had the luck to stumble upon a cache of supplies that had been left by the Denmark Expedition. Thanks to this find, they were able to keep on until they finally reached their base at the end of November, exhausted but triumphant.

The shock of finding their companions gone and their ship sunk was mitigated by the discovery of the house and stores that had been prepared for them. They wintered

there together, but early in the spring they were pushing
northwards once more to retrieve their diaries and all the
gear they had been forced to abandon on their gruelling
march in the preceding autumn.

This errand was successful, and they returned to their
base to await the arrival of help. None came, and again
they were compelled to spend a lonely winter, cut off from
the rest of the world. It was not until the summer of 1912
that a Norwegian whaler appeared and was able to bring
them home.

III

In that same summer a Swiss, Dr. A. de Quervain,
crossed the Ice Cap between Ritenbenk and Angmagssalik by dog-sledge in forty-one days; and Captain J. P.
Koch headed a new Danish expedition to Dronning
Louise's Land and across the Inland Ice, with the German
physicist, Dr. Alfred Wegener, as his chief assistant.
Danmarks Havn was reached by the end of July, but one
mishap followed another. Wegener broke a rib and Koch
a leg before they reached the margin of the Ice Cap. They
were not deterred, however, from starting their journey
across the ice in the following April.

Ill-luck still dogged them. Bad weather involved
delays, which in turn upset calculations where supplies
were concerned. A novelty of the expedition was that
Iceland horses were being employed for the first time; but
the experiment proved no more successful than it had
when the military had brought horses to Godthaab in
Hans Egede's day. They perished piecemeal, and the last
one had to be shot, as fodder was by that time exhausted.

Nevertheless, they succeeded in getting across the
Ice Cap to Laksefiorden, between Upernavik and Proven,
after a march of nearly three months' duration. They
crossed the fiord on an improvised raft, and were finally
picked up by a boat when almost at the end of their
tether.

IV

While various scientists, coming from all parts of the world in their pioneering zeal, were thus adding to the widening knowledge of Greenland, the country was nurturing an explorer of her own—a man who was to plan on a greater and more consistent scale than any before him and to inspire a series of expeditions unparalleled in the history of exploration. That man was Knud Rasmussen.

The son of a Danish pastor, Knud Rasmussen was born at Jakobshavn in 1879. He could scarcely have wished for a more appropriate birthplace. It is a majestic setting which suggests the very spirit of Greenland. There the Ice Cap spills over in great glaciers, and no one who has seen the immaculate expanse of ice in Jakobshavn Fiord can ever forget the spectacle.

In this setting, then, Rasmussen grew up, considering all Greenlanders as his brothers, learning their ways, sharing their secrets and developing a love for them that never waned. Young Knud was nine when Nansen made his epic Ice Cap crossing, and still in his teens when Peary was making his northern journeys. No doubt he fell early under the spell of the Ice Cap's lure, and no doubt his imagination was fired by stories of these and other explorers.

At twenty-one he was in Lapland, where, with future possibilities in Greenland in view, he made a special study of the conditions necessary for reindeer breeding. At twenty-three he turned explorer himself and joined the Danish Literary Expedition under Mylius-Erichsen, other members being Count Harald Moltke, the painter, and the Greenlandic catechist, Jorgen Brønlund, who, as already related, was to perish later with his leader in the subsequent Denmark Expedition.

The Literary Expedition, which extended between 1902 and 1904, involved a sledge journey across Melville Bay to Cape York, where the party wintered among the

Polar Eskimos who had not previously come under Danish influence. Today the Polar Greenlanders, who number about 275, are the most northerly tribe in the world. Their hunting grounds embrace the coast of Greenland between Humboldt Glacier on the north (lat. 79° N.) and Melville Bay on the south. All have been converted to Christianity, and school attendance is general.

First discovered by John Ross more than sixty years before Rasmussen was born, this tribe was cut off from the inhabitants of Greenland's west coast by a desolate stretch of 400 miles. Its members were accustomed to making long journeys to Ellesmere Island and to even more distant parts of the Arctic archipelago in search of musk-oxen and other game.

One result of the Cape York expedition was to bring these isolated Greenlanders into the family. On his return to Denmark in 1904 Mylius-Erichsen launched a virulent attack upon the administrative system, and in 1909 a Danish Mission was established in the forgotten district, at North Star Bay.

A year later, on this same site, Knud Rasmussen founded the trading-post of Thule. Besides providing a trading centre for the Polar Greenlanders, Thule was also to become a base for further expeditions (seven in all) which were to constitute Rasmussen's life work and which were to win him honorary degrees from the universities of Copenhagen and Edinburgh.

The First Thule Expedition was conducted in 1912 by Rasmussen and Peter Freuchen, and involved a journey across the Ice Cap from Thule to Danmarks Fiord and thence to Independence Fiord. Natural history and meteorology were studied on the way, and special attention was devoted to Eskimo culture, their tricks in constructing snow huts and their general way of life. Valuable lessons were also learned on the vital problem of arranging supplies for long marches across frozen wastes.

For his Second Thule Expedition, Rasmussen was thus

able to plan more ambitiously, and his party included Dr. Lauge Koch, geologist; Dr. Thorvild Wulff, Swedish geologist and botanist; and four Greenlanders; Hendrik Olsen, veteran of the Denmark Expedition was also included, and preparations for a closer examination of the regions between Independence Fiord and the north-west coast were begun in 1916.

A start was made from Thule in the spring of 1917, and objectives were gained without undue difficulty. The return journey across the ice, however, was dogged by disaster. At the head of Sherard Osborne Fiord one of the Greenlanders failed to return from a lone hunting trip. Time was lost and extra provisions were consumed in a fruitless search for the missing man, and most of the party were exhausted by the time they reached Humboldt Glacier. They had been obliged to kill all their sledge-dogs during the journey.

Dr. Wulff's strength was failing, so Rasmussen and another of the Greenlanders, named Ajakio, being the freshest of the party, pressed on towards the post of Etah with the intention of sending back help. They reached the post and were able to send back a sledge-party at once, but it was already too late. Dr. Wulff had collapsed and died after insisting that the others should proceed without him. The survivors reached Thule at the close of October, and it was only with the utmost difficulty that they were able to preserve the scientific fruits of the expedition intact.

Rasmussen immediately turned his thoughts to a Third Expedition and, as usual, devoted much time to careful pre-planning. Active preparations were spread over 1919, and the expedition started on March 8, 1920, Rasmussen delegating leadership to Captain Godfred Hansen, whose party consisted of a Greenlandic minister, Gustav Olsen, several Eskimos and dog-sledges.

The object of this mission was to lodge a cache of supplies at Cape Columbia as a possible aid to Roald Amundsen, the Norwegian explorer, who had set off on a

North Polar expedition two years previously. Captain Hansen reached Cape Columbia on April 20, carried out his assignment and then pressed on to the east side of Grant Land to pay a visit to Fort Conger before returning to Thule on May 25.

In the same year Rasmussen personally led the Fourth Thule Expedition—a trip to Angmagssalik* on the east coast to collect old Eskimo tales and legends. These he later published in book form, thus rescuing them from oblivion.

By far his greatest achievement, however, was the Fifth Thule Expedition, in which, between 1921 and 1924, he explored the whole region between Thule and Bering Strait, accomplishing in the process a thorough scientific investigation of all the Eskimo tribes. From his discoveries on this epic journey he formed the conviction that the Greenland Eskimos were in fact descendants of Red Indian tribes which had wandered east and west in Polar regions 1,000 years before. It was after his return from the Fifth Expedition that he received his Doctorate degrees, in recognition of his contribution to ethnographical knowledge.

Today the 16,000 relics and exhibits which Rasmussen brought back from his various trips may be viewed in the National Museum at Copenhagen, to which he presented them.

In the same museum a special section has been set aside as a permanent tribute to his genius, and is known as the Knud Rasmussen Memorial Room. Here may be seen the Caribou Eskimo coat that he wore on the Fifth Thule Expedition and the Danish flag he carried from Thule to the Bering Strait. Here, too, are the skis he wore on his first expedition, and two paintings by Count Harald Moltke depict Rasmussen alone on the inland ice, and again with Mylius-Erichsen in Melville Bay on the Danish Literary Expedition. There are other portraits and, on a plinth of Greenland marble, a bust by

* Pronounced Ammassalik.

Svend Rathsack, while close by may be seen the medals awarded to Rasmussen by geographical societies of Europe and America.

It was a fitting gesture to establish this small chamber with its intimate personal mementoes; but many a visitor must feel that Rasmussen's true memorial lies in those 16,000 exhibits he contributed to the adjacent galleries—exhibits which make the Museum's Arctic collection the most complete in the world.

v

The stories sketched in this and the preceding chapter comprise only a few highlights in the record of Greenland exploration. Many names have had to be omitted to keep this narrative within bounds, and little has been told of the numerous navigators who combined through the years to chart the coastal waters, although their part in helping to open up the country and in moulding Greenland's destiny must not be forgotten. Some record of their achievements may be found in the Chronology at the end of this book.

It is also impossible to attempt any assessment of individual efforts. These men have, in their own way, made their personal contributions to the Greenland story, paying for every offering in hardship and suffering and sometimes, as in the cases of Mylius-Erichsen, Hoeg-Hagen, Jorgen Bronlund and Dr. Thorvild Wulff, with their lives. All may be equally honoured.

The story of Greenland explorers is a long one, and it will be necessary to return to the subject in later chapters; but now it is desirable to renew acquaintanceship with the west coast settlements, and to find out how the Greenlanders themselves have been faring since we left them at the close of the missionary crusades of Hans Egede and his son Paul. For, while explorers from many lands were sacrificing everything to probe the hidden mysteries of the Ice Cap, other men, no less adventurous, were dedicating their lives to the welfare of the Greenlandic people.

CHAPTER VII

GROWING PAINS

In the century which followed the departure of Hans Egede from Greenland there was little change in the pattern of the people's everyday life. By 1733 the Moravian Brethren, under Count Zinzendorf, had established six mission stations besides the Ny Herrnhut in Godthaab, and were ministering to the spiritual welfare of the Greenlanders at Kungek, Umanak, Lichtenfels, Lichtenau, Frederiksdal and Igdlorput. These selfless men were mostly lay preachers without recognised theological qualifications, but with a great fund of sincerity and of devotion to their chosen calling. There is no doubt that they did good work in the cause to which they had dedicated their lives.

On the material side, after providing for their own needs, the Greenlanders were given scope for trading in anything surplus to their requirements through a merchant named Jacob Severn, who had been entrusted with the management of the Greenland commerce in 1734, and who received a State subsidy from Denmark.

In 1742, Severn, in association with the College of Missions in Copenhagen, appointed a resident physician in Godthaab. This was a step forward, though there had been surgeons or surgeon-barbers in Egede's time. But the appointment ended after three years, and the physician was not replaced.

Severn continued to handle the colony's commercial affairs until 1746, when, dissatisfied with the results, apparently, the State gave control to a General Trading Company, which, in turn, gave way to the Royal Greenland Trading Company in 1774.

In the meantime at least two individuals had made their

presence felt in Greenland. One was David Cranz, who came to Ny Herrnhut in 1761 and, in one active year, gathered material for a *History of Greenland*, which he published in 1765. The other was Otto Fabricius, linguist and scientist, who between 1768 and 1773 identified himself with the life of the people and published improved editions of Paul Egede's Dictionary and Grammar.

On the general administrative side there seems to have been little advancement, although the country was divided into North and South Inspectorates in 1782.

From 1774 until 1793, when the Directors of the Royal Greenland Trading Company began to appoint physicians, there was no medical attention available at any of the settlements except for a lone surgeon who practised in the whaling-stations of the north. Contact in emergency could be made only by sledge or boat, and by the time medicine or advice had been brought back by the same means the patient might well be beyond aid.

The country was, in fact, drifting along in a rather haphazard fashion. There was a need for a man with the faith and vision of Egede: someone who could feel a similar devotion to Greenland and its people; someone with an unshakeable conviction that the destiny of both was of paramount importance to the world.

In the middle of the nineteenth century such a man appeared in the person of Dr. Hendrik Rink.

II

A scientific mission, remote from his ultimate destiny, brought Dr. Rink to the northern inspectorate of Greenland in the spring of 1848. As a brilliant geologist and mineralogist, he was charged with the task of making a survey of graphite deposits in the Upernavik and Umanak districts. He arrived with the expectation of completing his duties within a matter of months—and stayed for twenty years!

Rink's career is remarkable. Having obtained his

doctor's degree at Kiel, he sailed, as a young man of twenty-six, aboard the corvette *Galathea* on a round-the-world scientific expedition. He was entrusted with technical duties connected with the construction of a temporary trading-station on the Nicobar Islands, but after six months, his health undermined by climatic fever, he was compelled to return home. It was then that he was sent to Greenland.

His scientific survey there was completed within a year, as expected, but by that time the country and her people had cast their spell upon him. He found immediate benefit from the invigorating Arctic air. Greenland gave him back his health, and thereupon he resolved to give his life to Greenland.

He soon became immersed in geological and geographical studies, but his interest in the people and his sympathy with their problems grew steadily, and he asked the Government to permit him to remain. His request granted, he plunged into numerous activities. Apart from his purely scientific work, Rink charted long stretches of coastline and marked off all trading-posts, outposts and experimental stations, as well as existing and former dwelling-places of Greenlanders, taking especial note of natural resources and the general living conditions of the people in each locality. He even prepared statistics on the sealing industry, showing that about 50,000 seals were being killed yearly in North Greenland and 42,000 in the south. In later years many of the fruits of his labours were destined to prove invaluable to the authorities.

Meanwhile, all around him he saw evidence of maladministration or no administration at all, and he felt sincerely that the cheerful, courageous, resourceful Greenlanders deserved something more in life than a perpetual, unrewarding struggle for survival. He saw to his grief that the people were declining in prosperity and enterprise, and he longed to do something tangible to help them.

In 1851 he was given a seat on a Commission for Greenland, in which capacity he travelled in South Greenland. As his knowledge thus increased, it strengthened his resolve to impart culture and civilisation to the people and to help them to attain a stage of maturity that would qualify them to take an active part in the direction of their own affairs. He recognised, though, that this aim would have to be achieved in easy stages and under effective controls, to avoid the pitfalls which might otherwise attend the too-sudden contact of a primitive people with the outer world.

The absence of adequate medical services was one of the things which struck Rink's imagination. Doubtless it had struck others also, but here was a man capable of expressing what he felt in forcible terms, and a man whose reputation lent added weight to his comments.

"A physician in Denmark," he declared, "could more easily visit patients distributed over three different continents than the physician in Greenland could get about to the patients in his district."

In 1853 his marriage to Signe Møller brought him a wife who was to prove an inspiring helpmeet to him, just as Gertrud Rask had been to Hans Egede. Born in Godthaab, Signe Møller not only knew the language but had collected a store of local folklore. She was, moreover, a woman of culture, and the authoress of novels with Greenland settings.

She was able to help her husband in his efforts to master Greenlandic, and when he later made a collection of Eskimo tales and legends, her assistance was invaluable.

At the time of his marriage Rink held the post of Manager of the Julianehaab settlement, with the authority of inspector. A year or two later he published some observations on the Inland Ice (a term which he coined), ice-fiords and icebergs which caused immense interest throughout the scientific world. He was the first person to draw attention to the fact that Greenland presented wonderful opportunities for the study of ice conditions that could help towards a better understanding of the glacial age in other countries.

He followed this with a classical work in two volumes— later published in England as *Danish Greenland, its People and Products*—and also produced a number of treatises. With boundless industry he added map-making to his many activities, and produced an improved map of the Julianehaab District; a map of other districts of Southern Greenland; a map showing the distribution of the Inland Ice, and one of Disko Island and its surroundings.

All the time there was forming in his mind a far-reaching scheme for helping the Greenland people. He held the opinion that the old social organisation should have been adapted to the new conditions arising from the Danish administration of the country. Instead, he saw that it had been shattered. Old observances which amounted to unwritten laws had gone, and he longed to create an institution in which the Greenlanders themselves could act as local administrators in collaboration with Danish officials.

His ideas on this subject were incorporated in proposals which were laid before the Ministry of the Interior in 1856. Rink was then Inspector for Southern Greenland, and his project was openly supported by Samuel Kleinschmidt, a Moravian missionary with an equal zeal for reform, and a number of Greenland officials.

The core of the proposals was the establishment of so-called Boards of Guardians which should include Greenlanders elected by their fellows. Men known to be good kayakers and sealers or who had otherwise distinguished themselves would thus be given the opportunity of running their own affairs under the guidance of the inspectors or officials of the Danish Ministry of the Interior.

While waiting for these proposals to bear fruit, the indefatigable Rink pushed on with his collection of Eskimo tales and legends. He sought out Greenlanders capable of illustrating the work, which he published in Godthaab in 1860, as one of the first volumes to emanate from a printing office he had established there.

In the following year Rink launched a paper called *Atuagagdliutit* ("Reading"), which still flourishes. It was prepared in monthly parts and then issued yearly in volume form. Rink entrusted the editorship first to a head catechist, Rasmus Berthelsen, and then to Lars Møller, who was also an excellent illustrator.

He then set about discovering Greenlanders with a talent for writing, and some notable contributions are said to have come from the pen of a seal-hunter, Ungaralak, in a series dealing with hunting adventures among the small settlements. Translations of various classics were also serialised in *Atuagagdliutit*, including *Robinson Crusoe*, *Robin Hood* and *Captains Courageous*. Eskimo legends were also given prominence, and readers were kept informed of events in other parts of the world, with notes on the latest discoveries and scientific progress.

Their interest in culture thus fostered, the Greenlanders were ripe for experimental moves that were made in 1862–3 to apply Rink's Board of Guardian proposals in Southern Greenland. Rink hailed the move as "the corner stone in the building up of the modern social order in Greenland". Regulations for the Boards of Guardians were issued in 1863, and the people were kept informed of progress in published communications known as *Nalunaerutit*, from which may be traced the beginning of an effort to develop the Greenlandic language to express ideas of a social and political nature, for previously the vocabulary had been confined more or less to necessary hunting terms or terms associated with everyday life.

In some measure the ends visualised by Rink began to be attained. He sought to abolish old abuses in all fields— especially a prevalent borrowing system which tended to make the Greenlanders wholly dependent on the traders. He longed to see a self-supporting Greenland.

III

A Board of Guardians was established for each colonial district, composed of Danes and Greenlanders, and meetings were held twice yearly. Responsibilities included the dispensation of aid for the needy, and rewards and encouragement to the deserving; in other words, poor relief and the distribution of part of the State revenue in the form of refunds to hunters and providers where merited.

Always Rink had in mind his early dictum that "The population itself is the only really productive power in the country", and he felt that the people should enjoy the full fruits of their labours.

At the same time, order had to be guaranteed, and the Boards also had powers to settle minor disputes and to try any delinquents who might be brought before them. Offenders found guilty, however, were passed to the Inspectorate for punishment.

In theory, the Boards were also to act as vigilance committees and to draw attention to any circumstances thought to be unfair or harmful to the Greenlanders.

In practice, this combination of trading and welfare did not prove very practical. Friction became frequent, and Rink, one of the first persons to recognise the deficiencies of the system, began to advocate a much sharper distinction between trade and administration.

Meanwhile, though his health was suffering as a result of the many journeys he had made into bleak, uninhabited regions, Rink continued to overwork himself, and his activities, as usual, extended into an amazingly wide variety of fields.

Mention has already been made of his studies of the Inland Ice, and these included a period of observation at Jakobshavn Fiord, from which he subsequently developed certain theories concerning the formation of icebergs. He also carried out personal investigations on the sites of old Norse ruins. Somehow, too, he found time for enlarging the scope of his studies of the Greenlandic language and for collaborating in the production of both a Grammar and a Danish–Greenlandic Dictionary.

But his reforming activities were perhaps a little too zealous for some people. His constant advocation of new ideas met with considerable opposition, and after years of battling, increasing ill health forced him to resign.

On his return to Denmark, however, he asked that he might be allowed to continue to associate himself with what he termed the "Greenland Institution". With characteristic self-effacement, he declared his readiness to serve in an advisory capacity in "any kind of work that might be entrusted to me", his one desire being to be able to devote all his time and energy to the welfare of the Greenlanders, for whom he had formed an undying affection.

His modest request went unanswered for a time, and he was consulted only once or twice on queries which arose regarding the administration. Not until 1871 did he get the chance he longed for; then an appointment as Director of the Greenland Trading Company seemed to offer excellent prospects of being able to accomplish something worth while. Certainly his directorship can be said to have marked a new era in the history of Greenland, though he encountered plenty of obstacles and a frustrating lack of understanding.

One of his first acts was to collect and arrange all the official regulations then in force for employees of the Royal Greenland Trading Company, both in Copenhagen and in Greenland. These he re-drafted and simplified and re-issued in January 1873 as new instructions, which he subsequently supplemented with additional regulations.

He also made it a rule that all Danes proceeding to Greenland to take up administrative posts should first undergo preliminary training in Copenhagen to ensure their fitness for the tasks ahead of them.

He continued to put forward suggestions for the steady

development of the Boards of Guardians, always maintaining that the principle of law being the foundation of the State must be applied even in a small Arctic community.

One of his most enlightened acts was the founding of a hostel on the outskirts of Copenhagen where students from Greenland could stay while training to take a more active part in the development of their country. Those who lacked his deep, first-hand knowledge of the people were unable to share his vision. Many of his schemes for the advancement of the Greenlanders in cultural spheres and for the stabilisation of their economic life could not be carried through. In the end, saddened, disillusioned and broken in health, he was forced to resign; but even in relinquishing his burdens he voiced the belief that "a change will set in once more and that these tasks will be taken up again".

In the immediate post-Rink period, however, there was a phase of stagnation in which many new reforms and experiments he had started were more or less neglected. A "permanent" committee he had established met spasmodically until 1889, and in 1893 passed a resolution not to meet again!

Worse still, Rink's pet scheme—the Home for Greenlanders in Copenhagen—was allowed to decline, and with the closing of the Home all plans for training Greenlanders in Denmark petered out, too.

For a long time there were no improvements of any kind; no reforms and no experiments. The guiding rule followed by Rink's successors seems to have been to keep administration costs down to a minimum. Because of this cheese-paring policy, vessels engaged in the Greenland trade were allowed to fall into disrepair; buildings, too, deteriorated sadly, and trade itself began to decline.

There was one moment, in 1889, when a change of Directors seemed to open up possibilities of improvement; but the go-slow policy was by then too firmly rooted, and only a few minor reforms were, in fact, carried out. Rink's

Once these Thule Greenlanders had the wastes to themselves; now a monster air-base has sprung up beside their former settlement.

Thule girls and their sledge dogs.

Jette Ban

Bringing in a whale is always a great event in the lives of the Greenlanders.

Women perform the work of flensing seal and also dress the skins, while their menfolk seek fresh prey.

Jette Ban

broad, far-seeing plans for progressive development were forgotten.

Embittered by the trend of events, Rink turned his back upon his native land and went to Norway, where he died in 1893. Today, like Hans Egede, Dr. Hendrik Rink is honoured with a monument in Godthaab. At its unveiling a Greenlander said: "On Rink's work for Greenland everything rests which, until now, has been undertaken in this direction, for, up to the present, his thoughts and work are both unsurpassed."

And, thirty-five years after his death, one of Rink's pioneering ideas was revived successfully by the establishment of a new hostel on the outskirts of Copenhagen for young Greenlanders sent to Denmark for training. Thus the fruits of Rink's selfless labours still endure and, in the words of one historian, "he is a man who, above all others, has inscribed his name in the history of Greenland".

IV

With the turn of the century another champion of the Greenlanders arose in the person of Mylius-Erichsen, the distinguished Danish explorer. On his return to Denmark in 1904, after leading the Literary Expedition to North Greenland, Mylius-Erichsen aired his views on the country's affairs with considerable vigour and launched a violent attack upon defects in the administrative system.

A man of his achievements and integrity could not be ignored. His disclosures aroused widespread discussion, and the controversy which followed culminated in a complete reorganisation of the Government of Greenland in a new Act dated May 27, 1908.

This had the effect of creating two new co-ordinate offices: the Chief of the Administration and the Chief of the Royal Greenland Trade. It was harking back to Rink's ideas for separating the two functions; but, unfortunately, it did not bring the benefits hoped for, so the arrangement was terminated by a further Act in 1912.

G

Responsibility for the management of the Colony was now vested in a Director, who in future was to be assisted by a subordinate Manager of Trade—an expert on whom he could rely for advice on all commercial matters.

In the meantime there had been developments in a number of fields. In 1900 the Moravian Brethren had been recalled from Greenland on the grounds that their services were now superfluous. With their departure from Greenland after a long record of devoted service to the people their mission-stations were taken over by the Church and schools.

In 1905 long-overdue improvements were effected in the country's medical services. The number of doctors was doubled, and at the same time new and more modern hospital buildings were provided in several centres, some of them being staffed with trained nurses sent out from Denmark. As a further step forward doctors were also equipped with motor-boats to replace the slower sailing-craft on which they had previously depended.

Simultaneously, too, action was being taken by the authorities to modernise the schools, and a new series of text-books was published by C. W. Schultz-Lørentzen. The College at Godthaab also produced on its own press the first Greenlandic song-book and the works of two Greenland poets, Jonathan Petersen and Hendrik Lund.

There were also new efforts to test other industrial possibilities, and sheep-breeding on rational lines was started, first at a small experimental station at Frederiks-dal, and then at a much larger establishment in the Julianehaab District.

On the scientific side a Danish Arctic Station was opened at Godhavn for intensive research on the flora and fauna of the country; and another innovation was the appointment of veterinary surgeons, whose chief work was among the sledge-dogs of the northern settlements, then afflicted by mange, distemper and rabies.

The Polar Greenlanders, hitherto left out of any

schemes for the betterment of living conditions, were, thanks to the initiative and energy of Knud Rasmussen, at last furnished with their own trading-post by the foundation of Thule at North Star Bay in 1910.

Thus, up and down the entire west coast the pattern of life in Greenland began slowly to change. The stagnation period which had followed Rink's retirement was ended; Greenland's march of progress had been resumed. There were still inevitable growing pains, but in the maze of widely varied activities in different parts of the country could be discerned a consistent thread of development.

Then, in 1914, when the rest of the world was plunging into war, occurred an event which would have delighted Rink's heart. From the Godthaab Press, which he himself had founded, there came a significant volume by one Mathias Størch, bearing the title *Singnagtuak* "A Greenlander's Dream". It was the first Greenlandic novel.

CHAPTER VIII

GREENLAND'S OTHER FACE

ALTHOUGH the east coast of Greenland lies closest to the lands of the Norsemen, it was the last part of the country to be explored. The silence and the solitude which strike the traveller in the west are accentuated tenfold in the east, where the eternal procession of pack-ice and icebergs forms an aggressive coastal defence, declared by early map-makers to be inaccessible. Even today the ice serves all voyagers with its "KEEP OFF" notice, and the advent of radar and other modern aids to navigation has not lessened the respect which even the most skilled ice-pilots feel for its menacing challenge. All must advance with caution and thread their way through the broad floating belt before they can gain the clear channel which runs between the pack-ice and the coast.

Thus it came about that East Greenland remained virtually unknown for more than a century and a half after the opening up of the west coast. It was Henry Hudson who first sighted the east coast in 1607 and who gave names to distinctive landmarks—Cape Young, Mount of God's Mercy and Cape Hold-with-Hope. Dutch whalers, venturing from Spitzbergen to the margin of the ice, also christened land they could not reach—Land van Edam and Land van Lambert. British whalers, too, attracted by the success of the Dutch, sought those waters. In 1777 twelve whalers from various countries were trapped in the dread pack-ice. One vessel after another was crushed, until a remaining ship was crowded with surviving members of different crews. Then it suffered the same fate, and only a few survivors, shivering upon an ice-floe, drifted to Cape Farewell and lived to tell the tale.

II

Through the years the whalers continued to brave the perils of the dread east coast, and at the beginning of the nineteenth century an eleven-year-old boy made his first voyage to Greenland aboard his father's ship. He was William Scoresby, junior, apt pupil of a remarkable father. Together they spent hours in the "crow's nest" (a device the father had invented), and William Scoresby, senior, an unrivalled ice-navigator at that time, imparted many items of Arctic lore to the eager boy. At the age of seventeen the son was a capable chief officer to his father, and at twenty-two he was commanding his own ship.

In yearly whaling voyages off the East Greenland coast the younger Scoresby developed a growing interest in the country itself. He was, moreover, keenly interested in scientific exploration, as was evidenced in 1820 by his publication of *An Account of the Arctic Regions*, a two-volume work which kindled fresh interest in northern discovery.

But he was not content merely to point the way. In 1822 he set off in a specially constructed vessel, the *Baffin*, accompanied by his father in the *Fame*, and a whaler, on a voyage of exploration. In the course of this voyage he followed the east coast of Greenland from the 72nd parallel to the 69th, making a detailed survey while his father explored Scoresby Sound. Altogether the son mapped about 800 miles of coastline, landing at many points to sketch details of the scenery and to make notes of flora and fauna. He discovered that the apparently deserted land had been visited before. Here and there were traces of abandoned camps, old utensils, discarded arrow-heads and similar relics of the early Eskimos. All this he told on his return in a second book, *Journal of a Voyage to the Northern Whale Fisheries*, a title which scarcely suggests the romantic scope of the narrative. He was, above all, a skilled and exact observer, whose contribution to knowledge of the Arctic is of outstanding value.

A year after the above voyage, two other British captains, E. Sabine and D. Clavering, explored the north-east coast. Sabine set up an observatory on Pendulum Island, and Clavering penetrated Gael Hamke's Bay by small boat and encountered a tribe of twelve Eskimos—the only ones ever found in that part of the east coast. How they came to be there can only be a matter for speculation. They may have been stragglers from a former migration, but whether they had come from the north or from the south must remain a mystery. Fifty years elapsed before other explorers visited the region, and by then nothing remained but a few pitiful relics of that tiny encampment. Clavering's Eskimos had perished.

III

Nomadic tribes of Eskimos from the north-east sometimes reached a few of the settlements and mission stations in the south-west tip of Greenland, coming by kayak and umiak, but finding difficulty in making themselves understood because their dialect differed considerably from that of their cousins in the west. Their habits and customs differed, too, for their fight for survival as they followed the harsh, ice-bound east coast had induced a degree of toughness which shocked their kinsmen of the west. Often, when prey failed and starvation faced them, they were forced to resort to cannibalism. They were unwelcome guests, though some trading was carried on between them, the men from the east coast bartering skins for iron.

Since they came by kayak and umiak, the same mode of travel commended itself to more than one explorer, curious to know more about their origin and the districts, from whence they came. As early as 1751 a European named Peder Walloe had used an umiak for exploring the coast round Cape Farewell; and in 1806 Ludwig Giesecke, the German mineralogist commissioned by the Danish Government to report upon ores, found the same mode of transport ideal for coastal work.

The first real expedition to south-east Greenland, however, was made by a Danish naval officer, Lieutenant W. A. Graah, in 1829. With two kayaks and two umiaks, the latter rowed by women, he reached a point north of Return Island, 65° N., before the ice made further progress impossible.

He met a few Eskimos, who confirmed that those regions were being depopulated by hunger owing to the scarcity of game. Sailing through open water inside the ice-belt, Graah mapped the southernmost stretch, and christened it Frederik VI Coast. After wintering in the Eskimo village of Imarsivik, Graah made a second attempt to push northwards in the spring, but without success. Nevertheless, he had by his enterprise added considerably to the knowledge of the mysterious east coast.

No further attempt was made to explore East Greenland for forty years, though in the meantime reports filtered through to the people of the south-west of an unknown tribe called Angmagssalimiut (those who live where there are many *angmagssat*—the latter being a small, herring-like fish, also known as the capelin).

In 1868 a German geographer, Dr. Petermann, fitted out a small ship at his own expense and gave the command to Captain Karl Koldewey. An attempt to reach the northeast Greenland coast failed; but in the following year Koldewey succeeded in establishing winter quarters on Pendulum Island. Then, with Julius Payer, he pressed northwards by sledge for 150 miles, past Cape Bismarck. Steaming homeward in the spring, they discovered Franz Josef Fiord.

But, with all these enterprising ventures, vast stretches of East Greenland remained unexplored. In 1879, two Danish naval officers, Commander Mourier and Lieutenant

Wandel, voyaged among the pack-ice in the region of Denmark Strait to determine its nature and extent.

Five years later two other officers of the Royal Danish Navy, Lieutenant Gustav Holm and Lieutenant Th. V. Garde, set out with seven kayaks and four umiaks to follow the coastal route explored by Graah, in the hope of being able to press on beyond the point of his return.

Headquarters were established at Nanortalik, and a well-stocked depot was built farther south. After three months' intensive exploration, the expedition split up. Garde and one of the scientists of the party returned to headquarters with two umiaks, while Holm pushed on with two other companions and an interpreter. Holm, who now carried sufficient provisions to keep him going for a year, reached Return Island within a month. From there onward the advance was into unknown territory.

He explored much of Sermilik Fiord, made some geological studies, and recorded movements of the ice; but by far his most momentous achievement was the discovery of the legendary Angmagssalimiut at their settlement of Angmagssalik. This primitive community, which numbered 416, had never before been visited by white men. They were a Stone Age people living completely segregated from their fellow Eskimos of the west coast, of whom they had heard only vague rumours. Holm and his companions decided to spend the winter among them.

They soon realised that the tribe was in decline. The remnants of numerous dwellings made it quite obvious that many more people must have lived there. Gradually the Danes gathered that fishing, once good, had ceased more than a generation before; and the older men at the settlement declared that seal-hunting had declined rapidly within their memory. The Eskimos told of severe periods in which their fellows had died in large numbers from starvation. In one such period, two years before the arrival of Holm and his companions, a small settlement of nineteen people had been so hard pressed that only two had survived the winter, which they had done only by consuming the flesh of their dead.

Living among these primitive people for nearly a year, Holm saw that there was small hope of their surviving for long without Danish assistance. Determined to do something about it, he set off for the west coast, rejoined Garde, and returned with him to Copenhagen.

There were still unexplored gaps in the long, straggling coastline of East Greenland, but gradually they were filled in as one expedition after another sailed into the unknown. Another officer of the Royal Danish Navy, Lieutenant C. Ryder, penetrated for hundreds of miles into Scoresby Sound and mapped many branches of the vast fiord before heading southwards for Angmagssalik and home.

An expedition financed by the Carlsberg Foundation, and led by Lieutenant G. Amdrup, who had already conducted research near Angmagssalik, completed the charting of the coast between Cape Farewell and Cape Bismarck.

All along the east coast various explorers discovered evidence of former Eskimo settlements. Although the tribes who once peopled them migrated from the west, by way of Cape Farewell, they developed certain artistic characteristics. Their clothing and hunting and fishing gear differed little in design, but they showed a tendency to embellish everything with fanciful ornamentation.

By using strips of dark and light skin alternately they contrived to give their clothing a distinctive and attractive appearance; and nearly all their utensils, throwing boards, pails, eye-shades, boxes and spoons were decorated with little bone figures of men and women and seals and narwhals, skilfully rivetted to the surface.

All these arts and crafts still survived among the people Lieutenant Holm had found at Angmagssalik, notwithstanding their grim battle for existence. Such people merited aid.

Governments move slowly, and nine years elapsed

before it was decided to establish a proper settlement at Angmagssalik, but by a happy choice, Holm, now a Captain, was charged with the task. He selected a site upon a gentle slope on the east side of a large island at the mouth of Tasuisarlik Fiord and appointed his old interpreter, Johan Petersen, as first colonial manager.

There was no question of making trading profits or of covering expenses, even. The welfare of the distressed Eskimos came first, and arrangements were made to import the kind of things calculated to help them to help themselves—steel tools to replace stone ones; modern weapons to replace Stone Age harpoons.

The rate of decline may be gauged from the fact that when the authorities thus intervened the population had dwindled to 352 from the 416 counted by Holm nine years before.

Training in the use of firearms now helped to improve the yield from hunting, which meant an improvement in the standard of nutrition. Imported food was added with discretion, and the trading manager had strict instructions to buy from the Eskimos only such goods as were superfluous to their requirements. Any vital need—like train-oil for heating huts—was safeguarded by placing an absolute ban upon its purchase.

By these and similar measures the people of Angmagssalik were saved from extinction.

IV

Today there are some 1,500 East Greenlanders—all descendants of those 352 Eskimos. Angmagssalik is a thriving little community, with a church, a general store, a wireless station, a school, a hospital, a meeting hall and its own monthly local paper. The people, like their west-coast kinsmen, have proved themselves skilful and adaptable. In the words of Einar Mikkelsen, the famous Danish explorer, who served for some years as Inspector for East Greenland:

"The Stone Age man's sons and grandsons are now efficient handymen, able to do wonders with broken-down or refractory motors. They are employed as carpenters, or as foremen on big communal jobs in the settlement or at outposts. They unload the ships which bring all the goods they can no longer do without. East Greenlanders of high intelligence are employed as store managers under the settlement administration or as clerks at the settlement office, where, with fair skill and great application, they can operate typewriters and comptometers.

"They make efficient pilots, engineers and crew of the settlement's flotilla of large and small motor boats. At the modern wireless station a number of young East Greenlanders with some knowledge of electricity hold trusted posts as engineers or general assistants."

As in the west, young Greenland women have been trained as nurses and midwives; and both men and women are eligible for election to a Settlement Council that was set up in 1947, and through which they can make their own recommendations on all matters affecting public welfare.

It seems hard to believe that less than sixty years back the ancestors of these happy people were battling for survival under the most primitive conditions imaginable, conditions which had not changed in 1,000 years. So desperate was the struggle for existence that the loss of a hunter through the hazards of the chase could mean starvation and death for his dependants. The vigorous and the able-bodied fought on to exist; the others went to the wall. New-born infants would be left to die; the aged and infirm would be turned adrift. Yet this barbarism was born from dire necessity, and with the feeling of greater security which Holm and his helpers brought to Angmagssalik, the Eskimos turned their backs upon savagery and eagerly grasped the new opportunities held out to them.

In the old days blood feuds and knife duels were common, and might was right. Now members of the Settlement Council assist the head of the settlement to administer justice. They also award loans to applicants who wish to improve their lot by building a new home or acquiring a boat of their own; it is at their discretion, too, that grants are made for the benefit of orphans or the aged and distressed.

Gradually public funds have been built up for this purpose by setting aside 20 per cent of the purchase price of all hunting products sold to the administration. All Danes and Greenlanders employed in the settlement also contribute 2 per cent of their wages.

Trading conditions vary from year to year, and at present the biggest item in the list of exports is shark's liver for salting. In a peak year this may rise as high as 17,721 kilograms. Seal-hunting, still important, has a yearly surplus of 6,500 for export in good times. Minor items are blue and white fox-skins, blubber-nosed seal and blue seal.

With the growth of population a necessity arose to spread out in an endeavour to develop new communities and avoid over-hunting in one area. In 1924 a voluntary committee addressed itself to this new problem with initiative and imagination. There was room enough for 100 settlements along the vast east coast; but everything depended on making the right choice. It was imperative to select a place where Eskimos had been known to live formerly and where there was reason to assume that good hunting was to be found. After much thought and discussion, the committee decided that the place most suited for its experiment would be Scoresby Sound.

v

Necessary funds with which to finance the migration were raised by a nation-wide collection. When the committee had completed its spade work and the site for the new settlement had been prepared, the Board of Greenland took over and organised the transfer of eighty-two volunteers from Angmagssalik who were to form the nucleus of the new settlement.

These pioneers, who began to open up their virgin territory in 1925—the year in which the first effective steps were taken towards the political reorganisation of Greenland as a whole—found that hunting conditions in the north were good. In their lonely, but beautiful setting they throve to such purpose that today their numbers have trebled and, in the opinion of experts, there is scope for still further expansion, and it is felt that the district could support a much larger community. The settlement has developed on the pattern of other Greenland centres. It has a picturesque little church, a school, a hospital and a wireless station. On a smaller scale it produces a valuable quota of shark for salting, whitefish blubber, seal, fox and bear-skins.

The success of this migration prompted the authorities to attempt a similar experiment in 1938, when about 150 people eased the congestion at Angmagssalik by moving south to a hunting district of known repute at Skjøldungen. They, too, have settled down and are thriving.

Throughout the years explorers and scientists of almost every country have been drawn to East Greenland, and in meteorology especially their work has gained world-wide importance. Norway was the first country to establish a weather-station in East Greenland, which she did in 1923; but when, ten years later, the International Court of Justice at The Hague awarded Denmark full sovereignty over the whole of the country, a complete network was developed.

The part played by the east coast weather-stations and the Sledge Patrol during the war years is dealt with in another chapter. The Americans also established a war-time air-base, Bluie West 2, near Angmagssalik. After the war the Danes constructed seven modern weather-stations between Danmarks Havn and Prins Christian Sund. Each is staffed by a dozen or more technicians to provide a twenty-four-hour meteorological service. A meteorological station at Skjoldungen, of immense importance during the war, has since been developed by the Danes. There are Greenlanders in the Meteorological Service, and their number will increase as more of their countrymen graduate from the wireless school in Godthaab.

In 1932 the Geodesic Institute embarked upon the colossal task of mapping Greenland. For the east coast survey the expedition made its headquarters at Angmagssalik. Aerial photography, in which Danish naval flyers co-operated, has helped to speed up the work, and large sections have been completed. The difficulties of terrain and climate and the vast area to be covered will keep successive surveying teams fully occupied for many years to come.

East Greenland, with its three scattered communities of Scoresby Sound, Angmagssalik and Skjoldungen, presents its own problems, which, like those of the hunters of Thule, lie outside the scope of development schemes for the west-coast settlements. The authorities, alive to this, have taken various steps to ensure that the progress already achieved shall continue. There are measures to protect rarer animals, such as the musk-ox or walrus, from being over-hunted, and the possibility of opening up new fields of endeavour has not been overlooked. The mineral resources of the east coast, which are constantly being prospected, may well be developed economically one day. Some hopes are pinned on the newly discovered lead deposits just north of Scoresby Sound. Difficulties of exploitation and shipment of such finds are, of course, immense; but they should not prove insuperable in a modern age.

CHAPTER IX

SOME AERIAL PIONEERS

A YOUNG man, on a sledging and mapping expedition in Labrador in 1929, dreamed of wider conquests. A year later, though only twenty-three, he was in Greenland as the head of the British Arctic Air Route Expedition, investigating the possibility of establishing a regular flying route from London to Winnipeg by way of Aberdeen, the Faroes, Reykjavik, Angmagssalik, Godhavn, Baffin Island, Southampton Island and Fort Churchill.

He was H. G. Watkins—"Gino" to his many friends— a born leader, whose interest had been fired in undergraduate days at Cambridge by lectures on Polar travel. He was also a practical visionary. Convinced that all the great air routes of the future would lie across the Arctic, he was quick to point out that before anything could be achieved it was essential that the territory over which the planes would have to fly should be scientifically explored.

Even as a schoolboy he had the reputation of being able to make others do anything he wished. That quality had so developed at twenty-three that he found ready backers in the Royal Geographical Society and the famous Courtauld family. He also secured the co-operation of the Air Ministry, the War Office, the Admiralty and the Danish Government. He even gained a free hand in picking the thirteen men who constituted the expedition, and said afterwards that he would not have picked otherwise had he been given the choice again. Certainly the men themselves would not have wished for another leader. At nineteen he had led a Cambridge University Expedition to Spitzbergen to map Edge Island. In Labrador during 1928–29 he explored the upper reaches of the Hamilton River and gained valuable experience with dog-teams; so, in spite of his extreme youth, he had a wealth of experience behind him when he sailed for Greenland in Shackleton's old ship *Quest*.

His companions were J. M. Scott, who had been with him in Labrador; Augustine Courtauld, who had been in Greenland with J. M. Wordie; A. Stephensen, chief surveyor, assisted by J. R. Rymill, Lieutenant Martin Lindsay and F. Spencer Chapman; Flight-Lieutenant N. H. D'Aeth of the R.A.F.; Flying Officer W. E. Hampton of the Air Force Reserve, ground engineer; Flight-Lieutenant H. I. Cozens, photographer; Captain P. Lemon, of the Royal Corps of Signals, wireless operator; L. R. Wager, geologist; Quintin Riley, who had spent some time at Kew Observatory, and Lieutenant E. W. Bingham, surgeon.

Flight-Lieutenant N. H. D'Aeth, lent by the Air Ministry, was in charge of flying operations, being the only pilot in the party with experience of seaplanes. Hampton acted as second pilot and engineer, and Watkins, Rymill and Cozens were all qualified pilots.

Two De Havilland Gipsy Moths were used, one being fitted with a special locker for rifle and emergency gear for long-distance flights, and with a special attachment to enable vertical and oblique photographs to be taken. Two undercarriages were provided, one with floats, and these were specially strengthened for landing on snow or ice.

The second machine was more or less standard, except for a ski undercarriage. Both had coupe heads and exhaust-heated cockpits, as well as extra fuel-tanks to allow for a maximum of 600 miles of flying in good weather.

Financial considerations limited the amount of spare parts that could be taken, but these included one float and one ski. Most of the equipment was carried on S.S. *Quest*, but some followed on later in the Danish Government steamer *Gustav Holm*.

Jette Bang

A seal-hunter stalks his prey upon the ice, creeping within range behind a small camouflage screen, which he pushes slowly before him as he advances.

e milder south sheep-farming is being tried, and a flock is here being shipped from Julianehaab to Narssak.

Varvara Ingram

Danish Press Photographers' Assn.

Godthaab, with the statue of Hans Egede, its founder, seen upon the skyline to the left of the church.

M.S. *Umanak*, one of the latest vessels of the Greenland Department, lying in the inner harbour, where new wharfs are now under construction.

Danish Press Photographers' Assn.

II

A base was established at Niarunak on July 27, and a
first flight was carried out on August 3. The weather was
clear and perfect for both flying and photography; but one
ever-present menace was to cause considerable anxiety.
The vast areas of moving ice were constantly changing,
and the flyers could never be sure whether an open
stretch of water from which they had taken off successfully would still be open on their return.

Nevertheless, this risk had to be taken. Daily flights
were made during the first week, including three reconnaissance trips over the edge of the Ice Cap. On August 9
Gustav Holm arrived with the second plane, and two days
later *Quest* left to survey the coast north of Kangerdlugsuak Fiord.

There a reconnaissance flight was made with a passenger, and though this was of barely forty-five minutes'
duration, ice closed in during that interval, and the pilot
had difficulty in setting his aircraft down. It was obvious
that it would never be safe to fly in such circumstances, so
Quest moved north again to an unnamed fiord near an
ice-free lake, 3 miles long, which Flight-Lieutenant
D'Aeth saw as an ideal seaplane base. At the first opportunity he flew from the fiord alone and moored his plane
on the lake. From this tranquil base he made two
flights on August 18, another on the 19th and a fourth
on August 20. *Quest* pressed on to Kangerdlugsuak
Fiord.

By the end of the month the flyers were photographing
the coast south of the fiord and the fiord itself. They also
observed another ice-free fiord and a range of mountains
which seemed to tower above the coastal fringe.

On August 31 Watkins and D'Aeth flew back to their
base, where Hampton built a hangar from packing-cases
large enough to hold both Moths when their wings were
folded. The summer flying programme was completed by

mid-September, and the second Moth was then rigged for winter flying.

But now bad weather set in, with gales which made nonsense of meteorological forecasts prepared in London, and which compelled severe curtailment of flying plans.

In the meantime a station had been established on the Ice Cap at an elevation of 8,000 feet, some 140 miles inland, where it was intended to take continuous scientific readings from September to May. The original plan was to man this station in relays, relieving the occupants every month, but as blizzards and gales intensified it became clear that regular sledge journeys would be impossible. The route from the base to the Ice Cap Station was marked with flags, but sledging parties could not leave their tents for days on end, and such delays meant inroads on precious food and oil intended for the station's stock.

Soon they had to face the fact that if two men were left on the Ice Cap stores would be exhausted by March, with no guarantee that relief would then be possible. One man, however, could expect to eke out supplies until May, by which time it was reasonable to suppose that conditions would be better for the relieving party. Augustine Courtauld volunteered for this lone vigil, and prevailed upon the others to leave him there on December 6.

The Ice Cap Station consisted of a dome-shaped tent with two thicknesses of canvas and an air-shaft in the top. The sides were closed, and entry was gained through a tunnel which, being below floor level, precluded any escape of warm air from within the tent itself. Two smaller tents on either side of the tunnel served as stores for oil and food.

Courtauld was kept very actively employed at the out-set drying his clothes and sleeping-bag, digging the space between the tunnel walls clear of snow and getting stores inside. He had twenty-six gallons of paraffin for his Aladdin Lamp and primus stove; six ration boxes, each of which held food to last for twenty-four days, two bottles of concentrated lemon-juice and one bottle of cod-liver oil.

Six times daily he put on his full Arctic kit and went outside to read his instruments and to make general weather observations. During the early weeks he had frequently to clear the tunnel of snow, and could only reach his instruments in the end by crawling through the small space he was able to keep open.

At about Christmas time he made the alarming discovery that nearly four gallons of oil had leaked away, so he immediately resolved to dispense with the primus stove for warmth and use it for cooking only from then on.

On January 4 a very severe gale closed his tunnel completely, and he was obliged to cut an emergency exit through the top of one of the store-tents. On returning he closed the aperture with a packing-case and pressed snow all round to seal any cracks.

During January the main tent was completely covered by snowdrifts. Ominous creaks and groans smote the ears of the lone scientist, and he watched the walls of his submerged home bulge under increasing strain. At other times he heard weird subterranean roars and crashes, but he retained his serenity.

By March, however, the station was so heavily snowed under that Courtauld found himself a prisoner. At first he feared that the air would be vitiated, but the ventilation sleeve in the roof continued to function satisfactorily. He was naturally disappointed at being cut off from his instruments and being thus unable to complete his mission, but he kept himself occupied drawing and reading. He drew plans of boats and meteorological instruments, composed imaginary dinner menus and read most of the books he found among the effects of earlier occupants. There was *Vanity Fair*, *Guy Mannering*, *Jane Eyre*, *The Forsyte Saga*, *Kidnapped*, *The Master of Ballantrae*, the Bible and *Whitaker's Almanack*.

This Crusoe of the Ice Cap often found inspiration in

the Bible, and in a report which he subsequently contributed to F. Spencer Chapman's official account of the British Arctic Air Route Expedition he told sincerely of his conviction that some outer Force was in action on his side.

A curious growing feeling of security as time passed dispelled any earlier doubts.

". . . as each month passed without relief I felt more and more certain of its arrival," he wrote. "By the time I was snowed in I had no doubts on the matter, which was a great comfort to my mind. I will not attempt any explanation of this, but leave it as a fact, which was very clear to me at that time, that while powerless to help myself some outer Force was in action on my side, and that I was not destined to leave my bones on the Greenland Ice Cap."

This faith sustained him even when, on May 5, his primus stove uttered its last gasp. But back in the base his companions had every reason to be anxious for his safety. It had been hoped to fly out and drop luxuries and mail for him, but this project, with others, such as photographic missions inside the coastal mountain belt, had to be abandoned.

III

On January 1 Cozens flew south to Angmagssalik to buy stores, but because of the short hours of daylight it was impossible to return the same day. The Moth was secured on the ice, and the next night a gale sprang up and continued for nearly thirty hours. When it subsided the aircraft was found to be seriously damaged, and Hampton flew down in the second machine to supervise repairs.

He and Rymill started work on the machine on January 19, and kept at it for two months, toiling for ten hours a day in below-zero weather, without proper workshop facilities and without adequate spares. They were obliged to make a new tail-plane and elevator spar from driftwood supplied by a Greenlander, checking all measurements from the second machine.

By March 18 their task was accomplished and the repaired plane found to be airworthy. But gales still persisted, and the biggest project of all—a flight across the Ice Cap via Godhavn, Cumberland Peninsula, the western shore of Hudson's Bay and Port Nelson to Winnipeg and back again—had reluctantly to be abandoned.

A few flights were carried out in an attempt to locate the Ice Cap Station, but these proved futile. Winds were found to vary considerably on the Ice Cap at different heights, and this complicated navigation. The flyers were further misled because they did not then know that the station had been completely blotted out by snow.

Weather also hampered photographic missions. On dull days clouds almost always came down to the surface of the Ice Cap before the position of the station had been reached. On sunny days wind-drifts threw confusing black shadows on the white snow surface, making it impossible to distinguish anything in the patchwork of deep black and dazzling white.

Although May 1 had been fixed for Courtauld's relief, a sledge party of four set off from their base on March 8. It was well that they made this early start, for they soon encountered violent storms, which reduced their progress seriously. They reached what they knew to be the vicinity of the Ice Cap Station, but extensive searching failed to locate it. As their food was running out, they were obliged to return to base, and a second relief party, led by Gino Watkins himself, set out without delay. By May 4 this second party had reached a point which, according to their calculations, was one mile north-west of the station.

Moving in that direction, they gained the crest of an undulating ridge, from which they sighted a distant speck. As they drew nearer they saw it to be the tattered and shrunken Union Jack, fluttering from its pole amid great snowdrifts, from which protruded the tops of meteorological instruments and the handle of a spade. Their emotions as they skied on may be imagined; but before they could speculate on the possible fate of their comrade, buried somewhere beneath the great mound of snow, they spied the ventilator pipe. The ensuing moments of tension are best described in Chapman's official account:

"A moment later Watkins knelt down and shouted down the pipe. Imagine our joy and relief when an answering shout came faintly from the depths of the snow. The voice was tremulous, but it was the voice of a normal man."

When an exit had been cleared, Courtauld emerged, a little weak, but able to walk. Five months' growth of hair and beard gave him a wild, unkempt appearance, and Chapman records that his cheeks seemed leaner. But he was none the worse for his long vigil, and quickly gathered strength, though his companions made him don the darkest glasses they had to protect his eyes from the unaccustomed snow-glare.

A Swedish Junkers monoplane, piloted by Captain Ahrenberg, had been sent out to help locate the Ice Cap Station, but the sledge party was already on the march. Repeated joint flights were made, however, in the hope of being able to drop a note to Watkins and his companions. Fog frustrated early efforts, but on May 7 contact was made, and it was found that the sledge party was on its way back with Courtauld.

Several photographic flights were subsequently attempted, but it was impossible for the Moths to climb high enough to secure pictures of any value inside the coastal mountain belt. A summary of the expedition's flying work which Flight-Lieutenant D'Aeth prepared for the *Geographical Journal* shows that even though the full ambitious programme was not realised, truly commendable results were achieved. In forty-four possible flying days during the summer twenty-three flights were made, total duration being thirty-two hours fifteen minutes. Nine of these, which totalled eighteen hours twenty minutes, were for purposes of photography, and 450 plates were exposed, covering all the coast from Bjorne Bugt up to and including Kangererdlugsuak Fiord, as well as parts of Sermilik Fiord and Angmagssalik Island.

Forty-nine winter flights, totalling forty-six hours fifty minutes, were carried out, and at intervals the flyers found time to give a few Greenlanders free "flips". Throughout the expedition's stay Greenlanders proved themselves most co-operative, and when the crashed plane was being repaired their help was found especially valuable.

As the Winnipeg flight could not be made, Watkins conceived the project of flying back to England with Hampton in one of the Moths. The machine was actually overhauled for this purpose, and arrangements were made to obtain special meteorological data; but the London Committee wisely vetoed the flight, feeling no doubt that sufficient risks had been taken already and that, in any case, it was outside the scope of the original expedition.

In spite of his youthfulness, Watkins greatly impressed members of the Royal Geographical Society when he made his report to them in London. Already he was dreaming of a big Antarctic expedition, but in 1932 he received an offer of £500 through V. Stefansson, Arctic adviser to Pan American Airways, as an inducement to continue a general investigation into flying conditions in East Greenland. The Royal Geographical Society supplemented this with another £200, and The Times added a further £100 for Press rights. Finally, the Meteorological Office agreed to help by lending whatever instruments were required.

This total backing of £800 seemed meagre enough— the British Arctic Air Route Expedition had cost £13,000 —yet Watkins was too keenly interested in the work itself to let the opportunity pass. He was forced, however, to limit his companions in this new enterprise to three—Chapman, Riley and Rymill.

IV

The new expedition sailed from Copenhagen on July 14 aboard the *Gertrud Rask*, bound for Angmagssalik. Watkins had selected Lake Fiord, 100 miles distant, as the base for his operations, but the work had barely got under way when sudden tragedy overwhelmed it. On the morning of August 20 Watkins set off early in his kayak on a lone seal-hunt. As he failed to return, a search was started, and though some of the leader's discarded garments were found upon an ice-floe, there was no sign of their owner. The widest possible search was made without success, and to this day the mystery of Gino Watkins's end remains unsolved.

Any ordinary kayak accident may be ruled out because Watkins, who had had his craft specially built to his own measurements, had achieved complete mastery, even to the point of being able to turn turtle and right himself again in expert Greenlandic fashion. Indeed, his skill and the speed at which he had learned all the tricks had won the admiration of the Greenlanders. Various theories have been advanced to account for the disaster, the most-favoured being that Watkins had landed upon an ice-floe, dragging his kayak after him. Then, possibly, the kayak slipped back and, swimming after it, he was perhaps seized with cramp, and drowned. But speculation is idle. The numbing fact remains that the expedition lost its beloved leader within a few weeks of landing in Greenland, and British exploration lost one of its most promising stars. Nevertheless, nothing could detract from the work that he had already achieved.

In August 1952, twenty years after his untimely death, a number of his former companions and supporters participated in a special radio programme to his memory.

They included his old nurse, Nanny Dennis, his sister Pamela, and her husband, J. M. Scott, F. Spencer Chapman, Quintin Riley, Augustine Courtauld, Wilfrid Hampton, Sir Raymond Priestley, Professor Frank Debenham and Richard Murdoch, who was at school with him. The title of the programme was illuminating—"Watkins, Explorer, England", for this forceful young man, whose name is forever enshrined in Greenland's story, became so well known in his brief lifetime that a telegram so addressed would reach him without delay.

v

The work of the pioneers went on. By the close of 1932, through the combined efforts of Lauge Koch, Einar Mikkelsen and Knud Rasmussen, the entire east coast had been photographed from the air. Lauge Koch and Mikkelsen conducted a large expedition north of Scoresby Sound, while Rasmussen, with two ships, numerous motor-boats, a seaplane and sixty followers, combined his scientific activities with the production of a film based on the life of the Angmagssalik Eskimos.

Then, in 1933, a Lockheed Sirius seaplane swooped unheralded out of the skies over the west coast. It was piloted by Colonel Charles Lindbergh, who, accompanied by his wife, was scouting for Pan American Airways, looking for possible bases and studying conditions along the various alternative air-routes between America and Europe.

That these new arrivals meant business was evidenced by the equipment they carried. They had a specially built folding rubber boat with waterproof cover and a small sail as an insurance against being forced down at sea; they had a waterproof radio set; eight gallons of drinking water; food for several weeks; a sextant, and an assortment of other equipment. They calculated that they could have survived at least a month at sea if forced to abandon their seaplane; but, happily, their theories were never put to the test.

"Our most difficult problem for an emergency landing was the possibility of being forced down on the Greenland Ice Cap," wrote Lindbergh in retrospect. "On our flights in Greenland we were prepared to walk half-way across the Ice Cap if it became necessary. This equipment consisted of a sled in three sections, snowshoes, six weeks' food, heavy clothing, and many other articles. We also carried full hunting and camping equipment, so that we could have lived comfortably for an indefinite period wherever game was available.

"In all, there were several hundred articles of emergency equipment. We planned first to avoid as far as we could the possibility of forced landings; second, to equip to meet them under any combination of circumstances."

But here again the American flyers were fortunate enough not to be put to the test, although they flew over the Ice Cap on two occasions—once from west to east, from Christianshaab to Clavering Island, and again from east to west, from Angmagssalik to Godthaab.

Writing of their first crossing of the Ice Cap, Mrs. Lindbergh describes the experience thus:

"We were approaching the Ice Cap now, climbing slowly upward. That smooth white dome seen beyond the rim of mountains was so unreal that I had nothing in my mind to compare to it. When we were actually over the Ice Cap, it did look like snow, but dirty and streaked as though raked by snow ploughs. The long crooked lines were melted streams running down into fiords, the longitudinal wrinkles were crevasses."

She goes on to say that this crevassed area was soon passed and that they found themselves flying over clean white snow, dotted with occasional ice-blue pools. Ahead, everything was a dazzling white.

"We were flying by dead reckoning now. There were no landmarks. Everything looked the same below us, and even above us, for the sky was overcast. With no horizon distinguishable, the whole world looked like a gigantic white bowl. My husband pushed back his hatch and put on a pair of amber glasses with which he could see through the haze and glare to wind ridges in the snow below."

When they were about half-way across, Lindbergh passed his wife a reassuring note. It was brief, but very much to the point: "EVERY FIVE MINUTES WE SAVE A DAY'S WALK!"

A little later came reassurance from another quarter. Wireless communication was established with Dr. Lauge Koch's base ship, still engaged in aerial survey work on the north-east coast, and they were told that they would find good weather and an ice-free anchorage off Ella Island. Course was changed accordingly, and a safe touch-down was made after a flight of seven hours.

In addition to meeting Lauge Koch, the Lindberghs also encountered Knud Rasmussen when they later flew down to Angmagssalik prior to making their shorter Ice Cap crossing to Godthaab.

Before they flew on to Iceland and Copenhagen, the Lindberghs covered the entire coastline of Greenland, from Clavering Island to Cape Farewell round to Ritenbenk on the west coast. Though the Greenland visit was just one phase in a world-wide itinerary which took the flyers to Norway, Sweden, Finland, Russia, Great Britain, Holland, France, Spain, the Azores, Africa, South America, Puerto Rico and Haiti, it could not have been more thorough. Both on the west coast and the east coast of Greenland they had the support of the Pan America Airways Expedition ship *Jelling*, and it is interesting to note that, with the exception of Thule, all the points where America was subsequently to establish her air-bases were flown over in turn.

The Danish Government representative, Commander Dam, followed their progress aboard the *Jelling*, and wherever they touched down they received a true Greenland welcome. Kayak fishermen turned out in force to escort them when their seaplane was towed into the harbour at Godthaab, and the local populace entertained them with song and dance. It was not long before a Greenlandic nickname had been given to Colonel Lindbergh's plane—*Tingmissartoq*, "the one who flies like a big bird". While they were at Angmagssalik a local boy lettered this name upon the fuselage, and though he painted it parallel with the water instead of following the lines of the machine, the flyers would not have had it changed for anything.

At Angmagssalik, too, Colonel Lindbergh met some members of the Second Watkins Expedition, whose base was at Lake Fiord, some 100 miles distant. Spencer Chapman, in his book, *Watkins' Last Expedition*, records that the American Ace thought Greenland "a wonderful country to fly in". But later, in a foreword he contributed to an article by his wife in the *National Geographic Magazine*, Lindbergh qualified this in some measure by saying:

". . . where distances between land are the shortest, the climatic conditions are most severe. Consequently, the great advantage of the Greenland route from the standpoint of frequent bases and refuelling facilities must be weighed against the extreme climate, while the attractions of a more southerly route must be discounted due to the much greater distances between land."

That, however, was in 1934, and as subsequent developments have shown, rigours of climate have not deterred the nations from working persistently to establish Polar air-routes. Progress has been rapid, and the results already achieved probably eclipse even the most ambitious dreams of those early pioneers, though everything is based upon their efforts and would have been impossible had they not blazed the trail.

CHAPTER X

THE WAR YEARS

On the outbreak of the Second World War in 1939, Greenland's future became fraught with uncertainty. Those responsible for the country's administration had had the foresight to stock-pile supplies against emergency, but it was quite impossible to determine how the situation would develop. Then, with the occupation of the mother country on April 9, 1940, Greenland's fate seemed black indeed. In some respects history had repeated itself, and the vast Arctic colony was once more isolated, as she had been at the time of the early settlers. Her struggles, already hard enough, would now be all the harder, and overnight she was thrown back upon her own resources.

"At one blow all connection between the colony and the motherland was severed," wrote Knud Oldendow, Director of the Board of Governors of Greenland. "The Board in Copenhagen became like a general staff without an army."

But the Board did not sit down and accept the situation as irretrievable. Attempts were made to maintain contact with the work in Greenland, and on the day the German Army invaded Holland, Mr. Oldendow left Copenhagen by air with two experts, intending to fly to America by way of Italy in the hope of being able to organise some means of keeping Greenland supplied.

Unfortunately, a serious setback was encountered at Genoa, where their visas were cancelled by the United States Consul-General on special instructions from his Government. German pressmen had got wind of the mission, and had cabled messages to America to the effect that Hitler was sending a delegation to Greenland.

For the next three weeks Mr. Oldendow argued and

pleaded with the authorities in Rome, but the mischief was done, and it was impossible to obtain permission to proceed.

"From then onwards," to quote Mr. Oldendow, "throughout the entire separation from Greenland, the role of the Board was cautious and expectant, outwardly passive, but inwardly active. Under the radically changed conditions, work of various kinds was undertaken that might benefit Greenland in the future.

"We were careful not to try to interfere with the administrative work in Greenland by telegrams and other means, for we quickly realised that absolute independence of the mother country was an unalterable condition for the Americans and Canadians, Greenland's neighbours if the autonomous Danish Government of Greenland was to continue through our local officials. We understood, and resigned ourselves to the situation."

Meanwhile, in Greenland, the people were more concerned for the plight of the mother country in enemy occupation than for their own immediate future. Gradually, however, they became alive to the fact that their supplies could not last if the war dragged on. The emergency stock-piles had been augmented on the very eve of war, when a specially chartered ship had got through with 1,000 tons of essential goods which had been off-loaded at Julianehaab and Godthaab; but in time there would be inevitable needs—especially vitamin foods like butter, vegetables, potatoes and milk.

Fortunately, the Danish Minister in Washington, Henrik de Kaufman, was a man of great initiative and, in consultation with the Greenland administration, he laid the colony's problems before the United States and Canadian Governments. Action followed swiftly, and an efficient organisation was devised under which a staff of Greenland officials took up residence in New York.

Functioning in place of the Copenhagen Board, these

officials were successful in establishing a two-way traffic, and arranged for the marketing of Greenland products in America on one hand and for the shipment of necessities to Greenland on the other. This prompt action restarted a regular flow of supplies well before the emergency stocks were depleted, and also enabled Greenland to maintain a measure of independence in an admittedly difficult world situation.

Mr. Oldendow has paid tribute to both Canada and the United States for the readiness with which they came forward to help. "It is not easy to imagine how Greenland would have managed had these two countries not given evidence of the fullest and friendliest understanding of the colony's special difficulties," he declared in 1947. "This will never be forgotten by Greenland and Denmark, and we feel deeply grateful."

II

Early in 1940 the Greenland Provincial Councils held a joint assembly at Godhavn, on Disko Island, and the general situation was thoroughly discussed. Loyalty to His Majesty the King of Denmark was pledged anew, and the United States Government was cordially thanked for the consideration shown to the people of Greenland in a situation where Greenland law and the Danish flag were exposed to serious dangers.

The Provincial Governors were virtually responsible for exercising the powers of the Danish Government where the Board of Governors in Copenhagen was precluded from so doing, and to simplify the local administration during the emergency it was decided that a central co-ordinating office should be set up in Godthaab.

One of the Provincial Governors was put in charge of this office, and under his leadership the administration was carried on from the capital. To advise him in all economic matters, and to act as inspector of trade, he had a sub-administrator, who was also an expert on shipping.

The second Provincial Governor was to reside in New York, and it was planned originally that they should change office alternately. The powers of whoever was in New York were to be delegated to his colleague in Godthaab.

Later, however, this plan was amended. Mr. Eske Brun remained permanently in charge in Greenland, and Mr. Aksel Svane stayed in New York. In the United States a special office was established by the Greenland delegation in conjunction with a Danish–American Greenland Commission appointed by the Minister, Mr. de Kaufman. A Danish–American business-man, Mr. H. C. Sonne, was its chairman.

Serving on the Commission were several prominent Americans and Canadians associated with, and friendly disposed towards Greenland and Denmark. Until the autumn of 1941, when it was dissolved, the Commission performed much useful work in mapping out Greenland's future. Through its efforts shipping, trade and other problems were successfully smoothed out.

Not the least of the difficulties was the problem of accountancy and auditing, for available skilled personnel in Greenland was inadequate for the task. This was solved by calling upon the services of an American firm.

Throughout the separation from the motherland ecclesiastical and educational affairs were delegated to the Dean of Greenland, Pastor Aage Bugge. Medical services for the two districts were combined under Dr. S. M. Saxtorph, of the North Greenland Province, who acted as adviser to the Provincial Governor of Godthaab in all health and medical matters.

The United States and Canada opened Consulates at Godthaab in May 1940, and the Colony settled down to its war-time routine. But, though the country was cut off from the motherland and seemingly remote from the struggle that was rending Europe and Asia, the war was to come much closer to Greenland. Greenland weather,

Royal Yacht, *Dannebrog*, at Faeringerhavn, international fishing port chosen for rendezvous before the start of the tour.

Harbour at Umanak, most northerly point visited by Their Majesties.

People of Godthaab, celebrating the first Royal visit for thirty-one years, follow
Their Majesties on a pilgrimage to the church.

The children mass on a garlanded landing-stage under the genial supervision of
a lone policeman.

for all its caprices, is of fundamental importance for pre-
dicting conditions in the North Atlantic and in western
Europe. Germany was already thinking of Greenland in
terms of weather outposts which might gather data that
would give her the whip hand in the Battle of the Atlantic.
The defence of Greenland was now a new matter for grave
concern.

III

Once again the necessary foresight was forthcoming,
and on April 9, 1941, the enterprising Danish Minister,
Mr. de Kaufman, signed a defence agreement with the
United States Government, which the two Provincial
Governors of Greenland endorsed soon afterwards. This
document gave the Americans the right to establish bases
in Greenland, and arrangements were made to construct
three airfields—two on the west coast at Narsarssuaq and
Sondrestromfiord and the third on the east coast at
Angmagssalik.

Twelve months of close co-operation in commercial
and administrative spheres had paved the way for this
momentous move. The first United States Consul to
Greenland, Mr. James K. Penfield, was already installed
at Godthaab, having arrived in the 165-foot Coastguard
cutter, *Comanche*, soon after the signing of the first agreement. There had been no consulate, but the local medical
officer, a bachelor, gave up his residence in the interests of
international relations and moved into a room in the
hospital.

Once the second agreement was signed, Americans
began to arrive in force. "Soldiers and hardy workmen
from our mid-northern States," according to the Consul,
"poured in to build commodious air-bases complete with
runways, hangars and snug cabins."

Within a year, war-planes, including speedy pursuit
craft, were able to take advantage of these bases for short
hops to the Western Front.

I

Let Knud Oldendow testify to what this stupendous achievement amounted.

"The technical and military achievements of the Americans in Greenland," he declared in 1947, "considering the extremely difficult conditions, are a source of wonder and admiration. The bases were set up at the cost of tremendous effort; hospitals, sports grounds, hotels, canteens, cinemas, roads, and harbours were constructed. The Greenland authorities assisted in the construction and in the realisation of the American plans. Relations between the American troops and the local authorities were good, loyal and cordial. The Americans fully respected and appreciated the special conditions operating in Greenland. They understood the reasons for our traditional policy; there were therefore no relations between the American troops and the population beyond what in the nature of things was necessary and advisable. In general the troops kept to their special districts, from which they had little contact with the rest of Greenland. Greenland labour was not employed on the military bases or other constructional work."

Nevertheless, the Consul had a busy time helping to solve the problems of American soldiers and sailors as they kept arriving throughout the spring and summer. Of course, he visited the bases in turn and marvelled at the highways which had sprung into being and along which trucks and jeeps (some of which had been flown in by commercial transport planes) were already speeding.

"Our Arctic soldiers live in model camps in a womanless world," he reported. "Nearly all barracks, comfortably insulated against the cold, have running water and toilet facilities."

He found a barber's shop, an excellent library and a cinema, at which he was able to view the latest news-reels, just arrived by plane.

Notwithstanding the provision of these home comforts and amenities, the Greenland assignment was a tough one, involving immense labour under severe climatic conditions. Plagues of mosquitoes harassed vanguard troops (men of the Marines had landed on the day the defence pact was signed!) until nets and veils could be shipped in sufficient quantities. It is said that some homesick men christened the country "Groanland", but in the main they were all kept far too busy to dwell upon their hardships.

While weather permitted, heavily laden transports, escorted by swift naval craft, kept arriving at Simiutak at the mouth of the fiord leading to Narsarssuaq, and at other selected points on the west coast. Much material had to be transhipped to smaller coastal craft, or just rolled ashore to be stacked in dumps in the absence of suitable wharfs or warehouses.

In addition to the air-bases, various weather and radio stations were established at isolated posts from Walrus Bay on the north-east coast to Egedesminde on the west.

East Greenland attracted the attention of the Germans immediately after the occupation of Denmark. Reconnaissance ships and long-range aircraft were despatched on a mission which resulted in a Nazi weather-station being set up at Torgilsbu in south-east Greenland. That same autumn a landing party from a Norwegian gunboat under British control raided this station and captured its personnel.

The first commandant at Sondrestromfiord was Bernt Balchen, who had been chief pilot for Admiral Byrd in the Antarctic. From here he organised a bombing raid on another German weather-station on Sabine Island.

Enemy attempts to get a footing in Greenland for meteorological purposes were also harassed by land and sea. A Greenland Sledge Patrol was established, under the command of Captain Niels Jensen, and manned by picked Danish hunters. This patrol ranged far and wide across the coastal ice, and acted as scout for the American

Forces. Wherever Nazi activity was seen prompt counter-measures would be applied.

The U.S. Coastguard service also took a hand, for the enemy was persistent. Greenland weather reports were doubly vital to the Nazis, first in helping them to forecast possible Allied bombing raids on the Continent, and again in enabling them to plan their own submarine attacks during periods of good weather in the Allied shipping lanes.

At least four German weather-stations in Greenland were accounted for by the combined forces, and German armed trawlers and sealers were also put out of action. A patrol from the U.S. Coastguard cutter *Eastwind* surrounded a weather-station on Little Koldewey Island and captured the entire staff with their stores and equipment.

Stores were particularly acceptable when they included such delicacies as Hungarian plums in syrup and various nourishing tinned foods sent to sustain the lone weather-spies. On one memorable occasion American Army units came upon a miniature food dump piled beside an abandoned Nazi trawler caught in the ice off Shannon Island. The vessel had served as a weather and supply ship, so the stores were of the best. Some cases were broached there and then, a blazing fire was kindled on the ice, and the men enjoyed the feast of their lives before returning to base with the balance of their treasure trove.

Of course, the fortunes of war in Greenland did not always run like this. The cutter *Northland* sustained a damaged rudder, and also bent her screw following an engagement with the enemy. Fortunately, her sister ship, *Eastwind*, was able to come to her assistance and, by masterly seamanship, succeeded in taking the crippled vessel in tow. It was necessary for the cutters to manœuvre within 5 feet of each other in heavy swells before the rescue could be effected.

Action apart, there was always the Greenland weather to contend with. Battling against one fearsome northeaster, often at full speed and never under one-third speed, a cutter is said to have taken two and a half days to cover 7 miles.

Grim ordeals were likewise plentiful for the flying services. A plane flying from Iceland crashed on the Ice Cap, and a second plane, a Flying Fortress, sent out with other searchers, crashed near Comanche Bay. The crew were all injured, one seriously, and for nine days they were imprisoned in the cabin of their helpless plane. Then the operator got the radio working and managed to tap out an SOS. His message was picked up and the plane's position re-broadcast, and help was soon on the way.

A plane from Sondrestromfiord located the wreckage and dropped supplies; and at about the same time a party of scientists who were studying Arctic conditions in the area dispatched Lieutenant Max H. Demorest and Sergeant Don T. Tetley by motor-sledge. Demorest actually reached the plane on foot, but when he attempted to bring up his sledge he crashed through a snow-bridge to his death at the bottom of a deep crevasse.

Among those who had also picked up the radio messages was the cutter *Northland*, and it sent out its small amphibian plane under Lieutenant John A. Pritchard, junior, who made a successful landing on the Ice Cap. He was able to take only two of the injured men off, but on the following day, though weather was by now worsening, he attempted a second trip. He picked up another injured man, but crashed in swirling fog and snow. The wreckage of his plane was subsequently found, but he and his passenger were never seen again. Apparently they had wandered away to perish in the snow.

Meanwhile a fifth fatality attended the rescue attempts. While striving to reach the coast by motor-sledge with one of the injured, Pte. C. Wedel, shared Lieutenant Demorest's fate and plunged into a crevasse.

Colonel Bernt Balchen now suggested the daring experiment of attempting the rescue with a big Catalina flying-boat. The Navy offered full co-operation and placed two machines at the Colonel's disposal. The perilous mission was entrusted to Lieutenant B. W. Dunlop, who, in three trips, succeeded in rescuing all the remaining men.

Deeds like this were frequent on the forgotten front, and while most eyes were turned to the war in Europe, or the desert, or in the Far East, Greenland had many sharp reminders of the reality of the world conflict. Two blows which perhaps brought this reality home to the Greenlanders more than anything else involved the loss of their most famous vessels.

The *Hans Egede* steamed from Ivigtut one day in 1942 with a cargo of cryolite for America. She never made port, and no one knows what fate befell her or her picked Danish and Greenlandic crew. As German U-boats were reported to be operating up the St. Lawrence, it can only be assumed that the ship was torpedoed and sunk without trace.

At about the same time the East Greenland ship, *Gertrud Rask* was sunk off the coast of Nova Scotia on a voyage from America. In this case, happily, all the crew were saved; but the loss of these two ships, with their sentimental attachment for Greenlanders, stirred the people deeply.

IV

Despite setbacks and the inevitable restrictions of war-time, various technical development schemes, visualised long before by the Board of Governors, went steadily forward. Electric light was introduced in several settlements, chiefly in the public buildings, offices, schools and hospitals, but to some extent also in the homes of officials. As it became necessary during the long dark months to keep all commercial enterprises moving at an increasing tempo, this innovation was a tremendous boon.

It became evident as the war dragged on that the

Greenlanders' ties of affection and loyalty with the mother-land were strengthened rather than weakened. The people held fast to an unshakeable faith in their future, and found repeated means of reaffirming their loyalty to the Danish Crown in resolutions and messages of good-will.

"During all the years of separation," declares Knud Oldendow, "there was not even the shadow of a tendency to dissolve or limit the very close relationship. . . . The people of Greenland were distressed and angry at the treatment meted out to Denmark and they tried to show it where they could."

They showed it in a practical way by public collections which raised nearly 200,000 kroner—"a large sum for a poor country with only 20,000 inhabitants, engaged in a constant and hard struggle for their daily existence".

This money was devoted firstly to the British war effort in 1942; then to bring succour to Danish refugees in Sweden. A further collection, initiated solely by Green-landers themselves, was devoted exclusively towards re-construction work in Denmark.

With the regular arrival of supply ships from Canada and America, some parts of Greenland began to experience better times. Often as many as five ships would be anchored off Godthaab, and the handling and distribution of so much material meant plenty of work for everyone.

A considerable amount of building went forward. New houses were needed for the growing band of Danish administrative officials, and adequate American and Canadian Consulates had to be provided. The United States Consul has recorded that his own Consulate was a prefabricated building ordered from a mail-order cata-logue, while the Canadians contrived to adapt an Arctic reindeer-inspection station for themselves.

Sealing and whaling went on, and fishing developed steadily. The war-time demand kept the cryolite mines busy, but one industry, the quarrying of marble at Marmorilik, had to be abandoned completely once the Danish market was cut off. This raised quite a problem, as 400 Greenlanders had been employed in the quarries. A full-scale migration took place in which buildings, plant and machinery and the 400 workers were transferred to the coal-mining industry on Disko Island.

Problems of a different kind were posed by the existence of isolated outposts which had to be kept serviced and supplied with some degree of regularity. Such outposts were manned by about ten volunteers, including five radio operators, four weather men, and a cook. Sometimes there would be a medical orderly among them.

Men get on their own and on each other's nerves when thrown together for months on end in snowy solitudes. Like lighthouse-keepers, men for the Greenland outposts were always carefully studied for physical and psychological stability. Most volunteers were put through an Arctic Training School, and it was claimed that if they survived it could be taken that they were balanced, steady and dependable.

The staff of remote stations could be relieved only once a year, between July and October, but letters and emergency supplies were dropped by plane every month or six weeks.

To help relieve the tedium of their year's turn of duty the radio and weather men were equipped with baby cine-projectors and films, books, games and hunting kit. They were also able to send stock "radio letters" to their people at home by a system that was in effect a modern variant of the famous field postcards used by Tommies in the trenches in the First World War. All that was necessary was to transmit certain code numbers to the base at Narsssuaq, where they were converted into written messages which conveyed a variety of stock expressions to friends and family at home.

For the most part, duty for the outpost men was comparatively uneventful, but on at least two occasions the monotony was broken by dramatic interludes. Men of the Prins Christians Sund weather-station looked out one day to see two strangers approaching their post. They grabbed their rifles quickly and called upon the strangers to give an account of themselves. In the absence of adequate identification, the strangers were kept under restraint while a message was flashed to Narsarssuaq. It was ultimately established that the two prisoners were scientists engaged upon an authorised survey, but through an oversight the outpost had not been warned of their presence in that area.

The central figure of the second incident was an Army weather observer named John E. Schneider, in charge of hydrogen balloons near Kulusuk, East Greenland. Each station had to manufacture its own hydrogen for the weather balloons, and Schneider had just left his generator shack when it blew up. He was hurled 30 feet into the air by blast, but was fortunate to survive, slightly singed and bruised, but otherwise sound.

v

One picturesque figure who played an active part in helping to keep the remote settlements supplied throughout the war years was Commander Donald B. Macmillan. A veteran of Peary's Polar expeditions, "Captain Mac", as he was familiarly known, was thoroughly at home in Greenland waters. Moreover, he loved the Greenlanders, and welcomed this opportunity of rendering them a practical service. He also worked on Navy air surveys and visited most parts of the east and west coasts, thus renewing acquaintanceship with more than one Greenlander who, like him, had served with Peary.

On the whole, adequate supplies were always available, and though a modified form of rationing was introduced in Greenland, this was only in the latter stages of the war, by which time the supplying countries were themselves feeling the effects of world shortages.

Four transit ports were organised—Egedesminde, Sukkertoppen, Godthaab and Julianehaab—and all supplies were brought to these centres, either in the Greenland Board's own vessels or in specially chartered ships, and distributed to all smaller settlements by coastal craft.

While the economic life of the country was stabilised, the work of the churches and schools was carried on without undue interruption. In the early years of the war some of the older Danish children who would normally have been sent home to Denmark were sent to Canada and the United States. But the opening of special schools at Egedesminde, Godthaab, Sukkertoppen and Julianehaab later made this unnecessary.

Medical services functioned smoothly, and all posts were kept up to strength. The influx of defence troops and technicians and the stream of shipping from across the Atlantic brought no new diseases and there were no serious epidemics. A threatened outbreak of typhus in one area was speedily brought under control by action in surrounding medical districts.

One significant development which undoubtedly did much to help Greenlanders through the years of separation from the motherland was the opening of Godthaab Broadcasting Station in 1942. From then on they were kept supplied with news in both Danish and Greenlandic, besides being entertained with talks, plays and music. From 1942, too, a Danish newspaper, *Gronlandsposten*, appeared fortnightly, which helped further to cement the ties between Greenlanders and Danes.

When, at last, news of Denmark's liberation was received in Greenland there was joy and jubilation throughout the entire country. Telegrams of congratulation and fervent messages of goodwill showered upon the authorities in Copenhagen; and many were addressed to King Frederik IX in person. The return of peace and freedom to Denmark was the return of peace and freedom to Greenland. The two countries had never been closer.

PART TWO

NEW DEALS

CHAPTER XI

A ROYAL COMMISSION

WITH the return of peace and the re-establishment of close contact with the motherland, the loyal Greenlanders eagerly sought for help in tackling the numerous problems which had, of necessity, to be shelved during the long period of separation. The Danish Prime Minister therefore requested the Provincial Councils to elect a delegation of six representatives to discuss all such problems with the permanent Danish parliamentary committee on Greenland.

The delegates from Greenland arrived in Copenhagen at the close of 1945. Discussions opened in January 1946 and continued until mid-June, representatives of the Greenland Board of Governors also participating.

Although a great deal of ground was covered to the satisfaction of all parties, it was felt that the agreements reached did not go far enough, and that social life in Greenland had undergone such marked changes in recent years that every aspect of the country's affairs ought to be thoroughly reviewed.

Various reforms were initiated, but in the summer of 1948 the then Prime Minister, Mr. Hans Hedtoft, decided to see things for himself. He accordingly went to Greenland and conferred with the North Greenland and South Greenland area councils in Godthaab. This joint session ended with the adoption of a unanimous resolution calling upon the Prime Minister to take the earliest opportunity of appointing a representative committee of Greenlanders and Danes to investigate all current social, cultural, economic and political problems in Greenland and to make whatever recommendations they considered appropriate to further the interests of the Greenland people. It was especially suggested that consideration should be given to proposals for terminating the Government trading monopoly, so that initiative and private enterprise could play their part in helping the people to make more effective use of their economic resources.

Action followed swiftly. The Royal Commission asked for was set up in November 1948 and plunged into its work in January 1949. By February 1950 it was in a position to issue an 1,100-page report, thereby setting an example to Royal Commissions of other countries, which too often are characterised by protracted deliberations.

Moreover, the report did not share the fate of so many official documents and gather dust in a pigeon-hole. Its recommendations were acted upon with commendable swiftness. Legislative proposals, chiefly of an administrative and organisational character, were drawn up and submitted to the Danish Parliament in April, adopted with a few minor amendments, and accorded the royal signature on May 27.

The Commission paid much attention to the question of developing local administration. It proposed that in future there should be only one head of the administration in Greenland, the *Landshovding*, or Governor, who should have expert technical assistance at his disposal.

In addition, the whole structure of local government was to be changed. The existing sixty-six local councils and thirteen district councils were to be replaced by a number of local councils. There was also to be a National Council for all Greenland, elected by the population as a whole.

Local Councils were to be charged with administering general social welfare and general local government responsibilities like drainage, road maintenance, fire services, etc. The National Council was to be responsible for drafting general legal regulations (within the framework of Danish legislation) for the local governments and the Greenland people. It was also to be the mouthpiece of the people of Greenland in voicing the country's opinion on any proposals affecting Greenland. It was recommended that a future amendment to the Danish Constitution should make provision for Greenland to be represented in Parliament when the time became opportune; but that meanwhile the National Council would nominate two representatives of the Parliamentary Greenland Committee.

One of the principal functions of the National Council was to be the allocation of funds. Under existing conditions the bulk of public expenditure in Greenland had inevitably been a charge on the Danish nation, and it was agreed that the people of Greenland should now assume financial responsibility for certain local government affairs, especially for social welfare.

The possibilities available for raising the necessary funds came under careful review, and it was suggested that a system of indirect taxation on goods sold to the Greenlanders might be applied. The proceeds of these commodity taxes were to be placed to a national account, and grants would be made as authorised by the National Council towards local government administration after local budget proposals had been considered.

This strengthening of the self-government of the Greenland people would, the Commission argued, give them a more positive interest in and a greater sense of responsibility for the solution of their problems.

Further, it was suggested that the time had come to separate administrative and judicial authorities. It was a leading principle in every modern society which it was now felt should be introduced in Greenland, where hitherto both functions had been vested in the sheriffs.

II

Judicial reforms recommended by the Commission included the establishment in Greenland of a Court of Appeal, with a legally qualified judge as its president and two lay magistrates to be appointed by the National Council. Lower courts were to be set up within the territory of each local council, and each would in turn have a president appointed by the president of the Court of Appeal and two lay magistrates nominated by the local council concerned, their term of office to coincide with the period for which the local council was elected.

The main aim was to assure the proper hearing of all cases—especially those of a penal character. Happily there is very little crime in Greenland, and it was not felt necessary in present circumstances to appoint legally trained defending counsels. Instead it was suggested that a small force of Danish police officers could be sent to Greenland to supervise detection and prosecution in penal cases, always with the assistance of local authorities and under the direction of the head of the administration. To ensure the protection of any accused party it was provided that the court should appoint either assessors or counsels for his defence.

Lower courts were henceforth to try all cases in the first instance, and the accused would have the right of going to the Court of Appeal. On the other hand, lower courts would have the option also of referring any particularly complicated or difficult cases direct to the Court of Appeal for trial, while the accused would be further safeguarded by having the right of appeal to Danish Courts.

III

Except that it advocated the separation of education from the Church, the Commission did not recommend any ecclesiastical changes. It had, however, a great deal to say about educational problems. As children under the age of twelve form 36 per cent of the country's population, these problems are certainly pressing.

"A small population like that of Greenland, scattered

Glacier Fiord at Jakobshavn, where the ice is pushed out at the rate of 60 feet a day.

Seal-hunters' summer encampment on Peat Island, Egedesminde.

Royal Yacht *Dannebrog* and M.S. *Umanak* at Godhavn, Disko Island.

Her Majesty Queen Ingrid, escorted by Mr. Eske Brun, Chief of the Greenland Department, at the Arctic Station. Dr. Poul Gelting, its Director, exhibits a radish grown under glass; his daughter seems more interested in the cameras trained on the scene.

and speaking a language of its own will," according to Hans Henrik Koch, Chairman of the Greenland Commission, "always have difficulty in making contact with other peoples and other cultures. It is impossible technically and economically, to translate ordinary fiction and technical literature into the Greenland language. But the Greenlanders' desire for a share in general culture is so persistent that their children and young people must be given effective instruction in Danish together with a general cultural outlook which places them on a level with other Danish subjects."

Koch hinted that some might query whether the Commission had been sufficiently radical in this respect and might favour making Danish the only language in the Greenland schools, but he explained that the answer to that is that "the people feel the Greenland language to be their mother tongue—with all the association of ideas and emotion which that implies".

Anyway, the Commission was unanimous in advocating the retention of the Greenlandic tongue; but it also recognised that the people themselves had a strong desire to master Danish as well.

With the separation of education from the Church, a Board of Education was to be established, with a new official, the Director of Education, in charge. More Danish-trained teachers were advocated, with the suggestion that it should be a rule that there should be such teachers at all schools having more than forty pupils.

One proposed innovation was for the provisional establishment of dual-language schools at three colonies, with boarding facilities for pupils from outlying districts. Instruction during the first two years at such schools would be in Greenlandic, but in the third year those who wished would have the option of transferring to the Danish side, provided the educational authorities deemed them sufficiently advanced. Thereafter all instruction

K

would be given in Danish, except for religion and the actual study of the Greenlandic language. The Commission looked forward to the time when this form of school would be general in all the larger settlements.

Until then special continuation schools must be maintained from which those who wished could go on to high school, where the instruction should be on the lines of a Danish secondary school, leading by a four-year course to a final examination.

Those who then desired further education in Greenland could, subject to passing this final examination, embark upon a two-year course at the training college, either on the theological side in preparation for entering the Church, or on the teaching side for those bent upon a scholastic career.

In addition, it was recognised that opportunities for advanced training in Denmark were desirable, in order to ensure a flow of qualified persons for administrative posts and skilled technicians and artisans of the standard that would be increasingly required in the Greenland of tomorrow.

A comprehensive programme was also worked out covering a system of evening classes, to include the subjects of arithmetic, Danish, Greenlandic, first-aid and domestic science.

IV

On the health side, the Commission paid considerable attention to problems of housing and medical services. Its recommendations called for more doctors, more nurses, better housing and sanitation, and the establishment of a central sanatorium for tuberculosis patients.

On the economic side it proposed the conversion of the Royal Greenland Board of Trade into an independent body, organised to include all undertakings in Greenland and Denmark as one unit. It was agreed that the Danish Government's present obligation to provide the Greenlanders with consumer goods, implements and equipment could not be abolished, as there was no guarantee that private enterprise could or would assume such a responsibility.

Nevertheless, the abolition of Government trading was regarded as a desirable aim.

According to Hans Koch, problems of supply and import were comparatively easy for the Commission to deal with, but the proposed expansion of Greenland production and the marketing of the products raised a number of problems of a far-reaching economic and theoretical character.

The aim was to expand the economic life of Greenland, while at the same time making it more efficient.

"We were aware that this aim could scarcely be achieved without some assistance from Denmark," Koch declared. " But the objective throughout was the development of the Greenlanders' independence and ability to exploit their economic resources, thereby securing better economic conditions for the population. It was not, under its terms of reference, one of the Commission's basic objectives to provide better economic opportunities for individuals from Denmark. Interests will, to a large extent, coincide; but where they are opposed the people of Greenland must come first.

"What is new in the Commission's recommendations is that Danish private enterprise is given the opportunity, and offered assistance, to share in Greenland production."

The Commission recommended that all exports from Greenland should pass through one central sales organisation, by which means it was hoped to standardise Greenland production and render it more effective and marketable. Such an organisation would also have the effect of regulating prices by setting aside suitable reserves in good years to offset the bad.

V

Naturally, these far-reaching recommendations represented a formidable undertaking, and the total estimated cost was put at 95,000,000 kroner. It was also calculated that at least fifteen years would be required in which to carry through the complete programme, and that the cost would have to be spread over that term.

But the Commission considered such expenditure absolutely essential to ensure the transition from a primitive hunting community to a modern society with a specialised economic structure and a monetary economy to replace barter.

"It only remains to hope," declared its Chairman, "that not only the Danish Parliament but the people of Denmark as a whole will feel it their natural duty to render our Greenland fellow-subjects this assistance. The raising of the economic, social, and cultural standards of the people of Greenland which was the Commission's purpose will therefore be achieved in fruitful co-operation between Greenlanders and Danes, and there will be a further strengthening of the bonds which bind Greenland to the Danish motherland."

This hope has, in fact, been fully realised. As intimated earlier in the present chapter, a series of Acts were rushed through the Danish Parliament within a few months of publication of the Commission's report. These in turn were supplemented in the following year by a further series of Acts initiating legislation to meet all the Commission's recommendations.

"Through this legislation and through practical measures simultaneously set in motion to expand and develop the economy and cultural life of Greenland," declares Eske Brun, "Denmark hopes to promote what has always been her policy in Greenland—namely, the spiritual and material welfare of the population—in con-

tinued close association between Greenlanders and Danes
and with the final end * in view of complete partnership,
formally and actually, between the Greenland people and
their fellow-subjects of the Danish Crown."

VI

A Report on Greenland published by the Prime
Minister's Second Department, the Greenland Department, in 1951—a year after the Royal Commission's
recommendations—gives a graphic idea of the progress
being made towards the fulfilment of the fifteen-year plan.

A modern, well-equipped new hospital at Upernavik; a
large wing added to the existing hospital at Frederikshaab, with X-ray room and dark-room, waiting-room,
dressing-room, consultation-room, laboratory and dis-
pensary; a new house for the medical officer. Godthaab's
hospital was provided with new sanitation and a new
electrical installation; Sukkertoppen's hospital got electricity and X-ray equipment; Egedesminde got a temporary hutment with beds for eleven patients and a new
well-found doctor's boat and a dental clinic. More nurses
were appointed.

A drive to improve the standard of dwelling-houses was
started with plans for the manufacture of eight different
types of prefabricated houses eventually, but confined at
the outset to three special designs. Two of these are
bungalow style and the third has two storeys. The sitting-
rooms of houses of one type of bungalow are arranged
with four bunks separated by curtains from the sitting-
room proper. Bunks of all types are arranged so that the
old traditional Eskimo custom of an entire family sharing
a communal bedstead may be abandoned.

All these prefabricated houses are fitted with electrical
installations, with stoves in all rooms and with coal-
burning kitchen ranges. Danish skilled workers have
been sent to Greenland to supervise the erection of the

* Achieved in 1953 under Denmark's new Constitution.

houses, as at present there are not enough skilled Green-landers for the task.

Furniture especially adapted to meet conditions in Greenland is being produced in Denmark in series for shipment to Greenland, where the people will be able to obtain it, with suitable fittings, at relatively low prices.

The shipment of prefabricated houses actually began in 1948, when twenty were sent to Narssak as dwellings for some of the workers in the new canning factory there. In 1950 forty-eight bungalows of both types were shipped to different points on the west coast, six to Juliane-haab, twenty to Narssak, six to Godthaab, six to Sukker-toppen and ten to Egedesminde, and every year since then the building programme has developed.

In addition to the provision of prefabricated houses, Greenlanders have been encouraged to build for them-selves, and generous long-term loans have been granted. At least fifty new houses of varying size and quality were built in 1950 in this way.

It has also been necessary to provide accommodation for the growing army of Danish officials, experts and Civil Servants who have been sent to Greenland to further the development drive. About 110 dwellings were built in 1950 and 1951, and all forms of building and construction work are being stepped up as the fifteen-year plan gathers momentum.

Loans are being made, too, to enable Greenlanders to acquire their own motor-boats and fishing gear, or for the purchase of farming stock and equipment.

Meanwhile, to enable the Greenlanders to keep pace with the rapid developments in every sphere of their national life, and to take advantage of the growing oppor-tunities which are presenting themselves, adequate train-ing schemes have to be considered. More and more young Greenlanders of both sexes are being given the chance of going to Denmark for technical and industrial training. A steady flow of skilled labour in all the new trades and callings of modern Greenland is thus being assured. Male trainees have their fees paid for them out of public funds. Women trainees are helped by a private society receiving Government subsidies.

The training given is equivalent to that received by Danish youths in corresponding trades, and throughout their residence in Denmark everything possible is done to help the young Greenlanders to adapt themselves to strange conditions. They are given board and lodging in a hostel in the vicinity of Copenhagen run by the State on the lines of the institution run by Dr. Rink in his lifetime. It is a rallying point for all young Greenlanders in Denmark. There can be met prospective teachers, clergymen, bakers, bookbinders, printers, housebuilders, coopers, electricians, tanners, painters, machinists, machine joiners, metal workers, ship's carpenters, shoemakers, carpenters, netmakers, seamen, agriculturalists and clerical workers of all kinds.

Greenland girls are training as occupational therapeutists, as midwives, teachers, nurses, milliners, sempstresses, weavers, clerks and typists. Others are studying baking, bookbinding, hair-dressing and domestic science. A number are taking a specially prepared course to qualify them for clerical duties in the district cashiers' offices in Greenland.

A cultural board, composed of the Governor, the Director of Schools and an elected Greenland member and a permanent secretary, sits in Godthaab and makes recommendations for future developments and generally supervises cultural work throughout Greenland. Its funds have been doubled since 1950.

The nine-year-old Danish paper *Gronlandsposten*, started in the war, has been merged with Rink's famous eighty-four-year-old *Atuagagdliutit*, which is now published weekly with both Danish and Greenlandic text. It includes two juvenile pages and two pages devoted to sport.

Godthaab also has a daily with Danish and Greenlandic text which has been started as an experiment to stimulate the Greenlander's growing interest in social problems. Other settlements may follow suit. The daily Press bulletin service provided by the Greenland Radio has been greatly extended, one innovation being a daily topical transmission in which some feature of the news is commented upon by members of the broadcasting staff at Godthaab and other Greenland stations.

Music and talks are transmitted regularly from Godthaab, often supplemented by re-transmissions from Denmark or stations in southern, eastern and northern Greenland. Between 6 and 7 per cent of the population now own receiving sets. The main transmitting station at Godthaab broadcasts seven days a week, half an hour in the morning, one hour at noon and four hours in the evening.

Ten settlements now have wire recorders for covering local events for subsequent broadcasting from the Godthaab station.

New plant in the printing-shop at Godthaab has increased its capacity four-fold. Controlled by the Danish equivalent of our own Stationery Office, it is extending its programme for the publication of educational handbooks and pamphlets. The Greenland Society for the Promotion of Education, which has sponsored a score of books in the Greenlandic language, is likewise expanding its activities. Danish societies are also interested in disseminating knowledge on social questions and have published two pamphlets in Greenlandic, *Citizen of Greenland* and *What is Democracy?*

There are well-stocked libraries at Julianehaab, Godthaab and Egedesminde which serve numerous surrounding settlements and districts, and plans have been drawn up for establishing smaller libraries in forty-six scattered settlements and ten school libraries. Schoolrooms chiefly function as reading-rooms at the moment, but it is intended to provide suitable buildings as soon as possible. A very useful reference library has been built up in conjunction with the technical school at Holsteinsborg. Denmark also plans to send an expert librarian to Greenland to supervise the extension of library services there.

So far Greenland has no cinemas, except those built by the Americans for troop entertainment at their bases, but eleven 16-mm. projectors are available, and about 70 per cent of the population see regular film-shows. Two ships of the Greenland Department are equipped with projectors, and film shows are occasionally given in ports of call.

Arrangements have been made to allocate more funds to the provision of films for both education and entertainment. Distribution will be made through a Film Centre in Godthaab, and proceeds from public film-shows will go to further the work. In time it is hoped that all larger schools and most youth societies will have projectors and an increasing supply of short cultural films.

Some settlements already have assembly halls—that at Julianehaab being particularly fine—and plans are being considered for the erection of twenty more.

UNESCO has sent a collection of prints and paintings, arranged by Sir Philip Hendy of the National Gallery, and these have been exhibited in all the principal settlements—even as far north as Umanak, where Greenlanders have shown great interest and appreciation. A pamphlet on the art of painting, printed in Greenlandic, has likewise proved popular.

The range and scope offered to the landscape-painter in Greenland are limitless, and it is not surprising that the country has inspired local artists. The first appeared at the beginning of the century, and lack of proper training has not curbed ambition, and some notable work has been produced. Gerth Lyberth, of Sukkertoppen, produced cubist landscapes of true originality; Stephen Moller, who died young, left behind him some artistically mature oil-paintings and drawings. Pavia Petersen showed talent both as a writer and artist, specialising in water-colours. Another talented water-colour artist was Jacob Danielsen, whose paintings depicting scenes in and around Disko Bay have a delicate, individual charm. An East Greenlander, Karl Andreassen, did some pleasing illustrations for Knud Rasmussen's collection of Eskimo myths and legends; but perhaps Greenland's greatest painter is Peter Rosing, who was born at Godthaab in 1892.

Greenlanders are naturally musical, and love to sing. A Greenland choir was formed in the winter of 1950–51, and now assists regularly in radio broadcasts and in making strip-recordings of old and new folk-songs. When a film of the Royal Tour of 1952 was privately shown in London under the auspices of the Anglo-Danish Society, it was preceded by some songs from this choir, broadcast for the occasion, and reception was excellent.

There is now a Greenland Athletic Federation comprising some twenty clubs and affiliated to the Federation of Danish Athletes, which supports it in a variety of practical ways, besides helping it financially. Large stocks of athletic equipment have been distributed, together with instructional films and a handbook specially printed in Greenlandic. Facilities also exist for instructors to pay periodical visits to Denmark to receive training.

Finally, in this comprehensive post-war drive, it may be noted that Greenlanders are showing an increasing interest in study circles and discussion groups. In Godthaab, with little more than 1,000 inhabitants, study circles included 110 young Greenlanders who concentrated upon a survey of the Report of the Royal Commission and followed this with lively debates upon their country's future.

The faith in that future voiced so confidently by Hans Egede and Hendrik Rink is thus receiving striking vindication.

CHAPTER XII

HEALTH PROBLEMS

"In Greenland you had better be ill when the doctor is there!" is an old proverb which, unhappily, could be cited with justification for a great many years during the early colonisation of the country. Five surgeons or surgeon-barbers functioned in Godthaab in Egede's time, and there was a resident surgeon there from 1742 to 1744; but thereafter the capital was without a physician until 1839, and the nearest medical assistance was in the whaling-stations hundreds of miles away in the frozen north.

Towards the close of the eighteenth century a surgeon was appointed in the North Greenland Inspectorate at Jakobshavn, and in 1802 his "practice" was extended to take in Disko Island. Twenty-seven years later a course of training for midwives was inaugurated, but it was not until 1938 that two statutory posts for medical officers were created—one for North Greenland, with head-quarters at Jakobshavn; the other for South Greenland, at Godthaab, the posts being filled in the following year. Twelve years later a third appointment was made and a medical station was opened in Julianehaab.

From these tardy endeavours a medical service began to emerge. Greenland's first hospital was opened at Jakobshavn in 1853, but another three years elapsed before one was established in the capital. The Cryolite Mining Company at Ivigtut appointed a doctor of its own in 1866; and a year later a third hospital was opened, this time at Julianehaab. Things then remained more or less static until 1905, when various improvements were introduced and the number of doctors was doubled.

II

Much has been achieved during the past fifty years in building up the health services in Greenland. The country is divided into a number of medical districts, each with its hospital, staffed by a Danish doctor, a Danish nursing sister and a number of Greenland nurses. Some variation is rendered necessary in view of differences in population; some centres may have two doctors and three Danish nursing sisters, according to estimated requirements. The scattered out-stations still present a big problem, and many medical officers have to make considerable journeys, either by boat or dog-sledge, to treat emergency cases. The doctor at Godhavn, for instance, sometimes has to travel for a day and a half by sledge to visit scattered patients.

About 100 Greenland women to date have been thoroughly trained in first-aid, nursing and midwifery, some being sent back to Denmark to gain experience in modern hospitals. These nurses, when qualified, are stationed at various settlements, where they attend normal cases of illness and preside at births. They are also responsible for arranging transport for patients and for summoning a doctor when necessary.

The entire cost of the medical service is defrayed by the Danish State, but the service is supplemented by three privately built and administered sanatoria for children. Several Danish philanthropic institutions have also made financial grants in recent years towards the provision of homes for children, infant welfare and school meals.

Expenditure on the health service has risen from 177,514 kroner in 1923 to 474,105 kroner in 1938, to 2,171,035 in 1940, and to 3,368,100 in 1950. Today it is in the region of 6,000,000 kroner a year.

The big upward leap between 1938 and 1949 is explained by the fact that many plans for development had to be shelved during the war years. The task of reorganisation was tackled at the first opportunity, and at the initiative of the Health Service two experienced County Medical Officers from Denmark made a tour of inspection in Greenland during 1947 and 1948 and studied all the problems which had accumulated during the war. The subsequent Royal Commission had the benefit of the joint report issued by these two inspecting officers as well as the opinions of several other experts.

The result, as indicated in the chapter devoted to the Royal Commission, was a series of recommendations, including the establishment of a special post of Principal Medical Officer for Greenland; an increase in the number of medical officers, dentists and nurses; the rebuilding or enlargement of most of the existing hospitals, and an intensified drive to combat disease in Greenland—particularly tuberculosis.

A Principal Medical Officer for Greenland was, in fact, appointed in the spring of 1951. Freed from daily routine duties, this officer devotes all his energies to planning and organising. Under him there are now twenty medical officers—approximately one to every thousand inhabitants. The number of Danish nurses has been increased to thirty, and more Greenland girls are being trained in Denmark. In addition, a new system is being tried out in three hospitals of employing women stewards to undertake certain duties, and so ease the strain on the nurses themselves and enable them to devote themselves wholly to their patients.

The number of hospital beds has been increased in the last year or two. At the present time there are about 380 beds exclusive of seventy beds in three children's sanatoria. Thus, there are twenty beds or so per thousand inhabitants—a ratio that is almost double that of Denmark. Nevertheless, in the autumn of 1951 it was found necessary to transfer 130 tuberculosis patients from Greenland to sanatoria in Denmark. Although this effected some measure of relief, 70 per cent of the hospital beds in Greenland are today monopolised by tuberculosis patients. All the steps taken to improve the machinery of the health service, admirable though they are, are still not enough. Much remains to be done.

III

Despite all improvements in the facilities now available to the health authorities in Greenland, and notwithstanding a marked improvement in general living conditions among the people, the scourge of tuberculosis has yet to be mastered. New cases are reported regularly, and the mortality rate from this disease is still high.

As far back as 1930 an attempt was made to introduce Calmette vaccination. Indeed, it is claimed that Greenland was one of the first countries in the world where it was tried as a systematic measure of protection against tuberculosis. Unhappily, the campaign had to be abandoned because it was found that the vaccine could not be kept in store in Greenland. It was only after the war that technical improvements made it possible to resume vaccination.

In 1949, after negotiations between the Greenland Department and the National Health Service, almost the entire population of Greenland was tuberculin-tested. Special personnel, sent out by the Danish Red Cross, co-operated with the local medical officers in Greenland for this drive. About 85 per cent of the population was tested, and all T.B.-negative persons were Calmette-vaccinated.

Since then the practice has been to Calmette-vaccinate every new-born child as a matter of routine.

Today all the hospitals throughout Greenland are equipped with X-ray apparatus. In two large districts— those of Julianehaab and Holsteinsborg, whose inhabitants total about 6,200—98 per cent have now been X-rayed. An intensified drive is proceeding in all the other settlements, and an X-ray boat is being fitted out so that the same facilities can be made available to small hunting communities scattered in the remotest out-posts.

Work is proceeding, too, on the building of new hospitals at Egedesminde, Holsteinsborg and Angmags-salik, and a sanatorium at Godthaab with accommodation for 200 patients.

At the moment, however, it is admitted that much of this good work is likely to be nullified unless an improvement in general living conditions can be speeded up. Though the standard is much higher than it was, especially in some centres, it is still far too low. Sanitary conditions generally, as well as personal hygiene, leave much to be desired. A report published by the Greenland Department in 1951 has this to say:

"Almost all medical officers report this low standard, and only at a few settlements some few Greenland families evince a real understanding of the importance of hygiene and sanitation. The country has still too many poor dwellings, in which interior hygienic amenities are very primitive, the houses are over-populated and generally too small and only sparsely equipped with the most necessary furniture. And it is quite true when a medical officer reports that in many cases a new house will not suffice if 'the bad habits' from the old dwellings are transferred to the new one, which unfortunately they often are. There is, however, reason to believe that in time these conditions will be remedied."

This same report goes on to explain that, thanks to improved economic conditions and greater earning possibilities, it is no longer so difficult for a Greenlander to live on a hygienic and cultural level approaching conditions in Europe. In addition, educational facilities open possibilities for better enlightenment and knowledge. Education in matters of hygiene is carried on by pamphlet and poster. This, with the big drive to provide new housing in all parts of the country, forms an important part of the crusade against tuberculosis.

It is said that no reliable figure is available for the number of tuberculosis patients in the whole of Greenland. It is intended, however, to make registration of all observed cases compulsory in future, so in due course a true picture may be obtained. The very fact that 70 per cent of the patients now under treatment in the hospitals are suffering from some form of tuberculosis indicates the gravity of the problem.

As different groups of the population are subjected to X-ray examination, card-index systems are established. Regular re-checks will then render it possible to diagnose the disease at an early stage, with better possibilities of effecting a cure.

Nutrition experts have also been sent to Greenland and are making detailed studies at the moment, checking the vitamin-content and nutritive values of average Greenlandic diets. The result of these studies is eagerly awaited by the health authorities, to whom the data gained may prove invaluable.

No speedy solution of the T.B. problem can be expected, though the authorities believe that they will be able to achieve satisfactory results more quickly than was the case in Denmark itself, where an organised campaign against tuberculosis was started more than fifty years ago.

Both the Greenland Department and the National Health Service admit quite frankly that all the present measures can only be regarded as a beginning of the re-organisation of the Health Service in Greenland. But they add that each year should now see an improvement in the general state of health, until the ultimate goal of a standard comparable to that of the mother country is obtained.

IV

Greenland has been visited by several very serious epidemics, the worst, perhaps, being a particularly

Danish Press Photographers' Assn.

The hospital at Umanak nestles at the base of the heart-shaped mountain which gives the settlement its name.

Ithaab's hospital also stands beside the shore and commands extensive view across the bay.

Author

Erik Peters

The Danish Royal Family, King Frederik IX, Queen Ingrid, and Princesse
Margrethe, Benedikte and Anne-Marie. Under the new constitution, signed i
June 1953, the King's daughters may succeed to the throne; and Greenlan
becomes a part of the Danish Kingdom, with 2 Members of Parliament.

virulent form of whooping-cough which attacked nearly all the settlements in 1949. While the sufferers, particularly the infants, were still in a debilitated state, a second epidemic, described as "a very violent, influenza-like, catarrhal affliction with numerous complications", smote all the settlements in turn. The complications referred to included pneumonia (especially prevalent), a form of meningitis and diseases of the ear.

Some details of this epidemic are worth recording here for the light they throw upon the difficulties which face the health services in a country like Greenland. An interesting feature, too, is that in certain districts persons of more than twenty-five years of age seemed to escape. The explanation of this curious phenomenon is that just twenty-five years had elapsed since a similar epidemic hit Greenland. In that instance it spread right along the west coast, and *no one* escaped! From this it follows that the adult population acquired a certain immunity as a result of the first epidemic, and thus escaped in the second one.

The number of cases reported during the 1949 epidemic is 3,140, and at least 1,800 of these occurred in the northern area between Egedesminde and Thule.

The disease was traced as being brought by a passenger from Denmark, whose ship reached Godthaab in May. Within two months every child in that locality was infected. Rigorous attempts to enforce isolation could not keep the affliction from spreading. Vaccination had been started throughout the country immediately the disease was detected in Godthaab, for, as luck had it, fresh supplies of vaccine had just been received in several centres. Additional supplies from the Serum Institute in Copenhagen followed by air and by sea, so that every medical officer was equipped for the emergency in good time.

Infants received priority vaccination, with T.B. patients in the inactive stage and others deemed to be less resistant. Red Cross nurses then in Greenland for the purpose of completing the Calmette vaccinations at all stations

L

were able to assist the busy medical officers, and but for these measures the epidemic would undoubtedly have been far more serious. But the toll was terrible enough. Even in Sukkertoppen, which, by comparison with other centres, was regarded as escaping lightly, there were eleven deaths.

At Holsteinsborg vaccination was performed immediately news of the Godthaab outbreak was received. But when the epidemic hit Holsteinsborg two months later, almost everyone under the age of twenty-five was infected.

Qutdligssat, the coal-mining centre on Disko Island, did not escape. Brought by a young man from Godthaab, the disease spread with great violence and in malignant form, so that thirty infants died. In some places the toll was so sweeping that no child born in 1949 survived.

In one settlement after another the secondary epidemics smote patients before they had fully recovered from the first, and very many succumbed. In many cases it was almost impossible for harassed physicians to determine how many deaths were due to whooping-cough or how many to following complications. At several places, indeed, the two epidemics seemed to be almost simultaneous.

It was difficult to foresee where the ravaging course would be halted. There was every reason to hope that Upernavik would mark its limit, for special provisions existed to ensure that everyone travelling northwards from there must first report for examination. This measure, designed expressly to protect the Polar Eskimos at Thule, proved abortive in this instance, for a family with an infected child carried the epidemic literally to the end of the world. Whether they were unaware of the regulation, or whether they ignored it, hardly matters now. Thule suffered as the larger settlements had suffered. There were three deaths in the little community of 130, and many children, whose vitality was already lowered by malnutrition due to a poor hunting season, suffered severely from debilitating after-effects. Vaccination had been carried out in Thule proper, but lack of transport facilities had made it impossible to include outlying districts.

A schooner carried the disease to the remote east coast, where it spread with inevitable rapidity. In Angmagssalik it took the same course as in other districts, and thirty-five people died. Complete figures for the whole country were never obtained, but it is thought that there were at least 5,000 cases and 250 deaths from whooping-cough alone. The low power of resistance in the native population is emphasised by the fact that all Danish children in Greenland, though afflicted, got through the disease without much trouble, with none of the subsequent complications and without a single death.

The secondary, influenza-like epidemic which in most cases followed immediately after the whooping-cough spread in precisely the same manner, and affected both children and adults. Sometimes the following epidemic was even more widespread. For example, in the Umanak medical district there were 850 cases of whooping-cough, followed by 1,300 cases of the catarrhal affliction.

It is a grim reflection that even in a country of vast open spaces, with scattered settlements and limited communications, epidemics such as these can spread at tremendous speed and reach the most isolated outposts. Apart from suffering and loss of life, the cost to a small population can be incalculable. When such epidemics occur in the middle of the best trading months, depriving the community of many thousand working hours, their whole economy may be temporarily disrupted. Measures for keeping possible future epidemics within bounds provide yet a further problem for those now charged with the task of reorganising Greenland's health services.

V

As an illustration of the thoroughness of medical research, an interesting story may be told of methods used to combat a troublesome affliction which was reported from various quarters, including Disko Island, Egedesminde and Holsteinsborg on the west coast and Angmagssalik on the east coast. Some ninety cases were observed, but none in a district where eight deaths had occurred in the preceding year.

Known as *trichinosis*, the infection is nearly always attributable to the consumption of the meat of the walrus or bearded seal that has been insufficiently cooked, or meat which is in a slightly dried condition. It was assumed that the people in the district that had escaped had learned their lesson and, after repeated official warnings, were now cooking their own supplies of fresh walrus meat sufficiently well to kill the parasites which cause the disease.

Many samples of meat were sent back to the Hygienic-bacteriological Institute of the Royal Veterinary and Agricultural College in Copenhagen for analysis; but medical men and scientists were in some doubt as to whether *trichinosis* could be considered a new disease in Greenland or not.

An original solution to the problem was provided by Dr. Hans Roth of the Institute, who subjected all the old skulls of polar bears in the zoological collections of the college to special scrutiny. Carefully he scraped minute particles of dried flesh which still adhered to the skulls of bears known to have been killed more than fifty years before. The microscope revealed *trichines*, from which it was deduced that the disease could certainly not be new to Greenland, as Eskimos who fed upon raw meat in the past could scarcely have avoided infection.

Although some bad cases were reported in 1949, there were no deaths; but the incidence of the disease is being closely studied, because it sometimes brings serious heart complications.

VI

The average Greenlander has a very sweet tooth, and the consumption of imported chocolates and sweets is said to be disproportionately high. This, coupled with the introduction of European food into the general diet, is blamed for an increasing deterioration of the once-sound teeth of the population. It is said that the average Greenlander tends to suffer more and more from ordinary dental troubles. A rational dental system has been inaugurated, but, as with the medical services, the vast distances and the scattered nature of the settlements and outposts present overwhelming problems. There are permanent dentists in the larger centres, like Julianehaab, Godthaab and Umanak, who, besides conducting actual clinical work in the settlements, provide mobile services for visiting surrounding districts. The medical officer at Frederikshaab has established his own dental clinic, where twice a week he undertakes treatment. A number of other medical officers also perform elementary dentistry, and a new clinic was recently opened at Egedesminde. All this, however, is not enough. It is recognised that many more dentists are required, and the problem is now being considered in conjunction with other medical matters. The solution may lie in the provision of sufficient mobile units to make dental service available to everyone. Meanwhile, the hope is expressed that import duties on sugar, chocolates and sweets will bring about a material reduction in consumption, with an ultimate beneficial effect on the teeth of the nation.

Financial considerations must naturally govern the speed at which a comprehensive health service can be brought to perfection. Yearly expenses, as already stated, have risen from 697,612 kroner in 1945 to nearly 6,000,000 kroner. There is also a special fund in connection with the campaign to combat tuberculosis, which is being very widely supported. Proceeds of an exhibition of the many fine gifts presented to Their Majesties the King and Queen of Denmark on the occasion of their tour in 1952 and of the photographs depicting that tour helped to swell this fund.

But all problems associated with Greenland's development are inevitably interlocked. The successful expansion of all trading activities presupposes a healthy nation, which, in turn, must depend on an efficient health service to protect the working capacity of the individual citizen.

In the same way, there are many problems in which the co-operation of the community is essential, and which depend on education and cultural development generally. Equally inseparable, too, is the problem of re-housing the people in healthy homes.

The all-embracing aim is summed up by the Greenland Department thus: "To achieve an harmonious development of the conditions obtaining in Greenland both in regard to the state of health, trade, and within the cultural field". And this, in effect, is the fifteen-year plan in a nutshell.

CHAPTER XIII

SOME POST-WAR EXPLORERS

WITH the quickening tempo of administrative and cultural developments which followed the Second World War, it was natural that there should also be a resumption of interest in scientific exploration in Greenland. A man who foresaw this trend was Ebbe Munck, now Counsellor for Press Affairs at the Royal Danish Embassy in London, who throughout the war played an active part in the Danish Resistance Movement. Largely through his enterprise, a Danish Expeditions Fund was established to foster the activities of Danish explorers. Its backing made possible the three Danish Central Asia Expeditions of 1947, 1948 and 1949; the two Alaska Expeditions led by Dr. Helge Larsen in 1948 and 1949–50. It also inspired the Danish Pearyland Expedition of 1947–50 and the round-the-world voyage in 1950–51 of the deep-sea exploration ship *Galathea*.

This expedition, led by Count Eigil Knuth, set out to probe the mysteries of the vast Arctic oasis, as large as Denmark, which represents the largest ice-free territory in all Greenland. Lauge Koch, in his Bicentenary Jubilee Expedition of 1921, had made a 200-day tour of the Pearyland peninsula and had produced a rough map, but knowledge of geological conditions and animal and plant life in those regions remained scanty.

The central part of Pearyland had not been explored scientifically, though Lauge Koch had flown over it in 1938 and had observed various lakes and valleys and mountains. Many blanks remained to be filled in, and this could be achieved only by a planned reconnaissance, followed by a prolonged sojourn in the territory.

In addition to financial backing from the Expeditions

Fund, Knuth and his party had the free use of ships of the Greenland Department and three Catalina flying-boats provided by the Danish Admiralty. Reconnaissance flights were therefore carried out during the summer of 1947, under chief pilot Commander Erik Overbye, and Jorgen Bronlunds Fiord was found to be ice-free. The opportunity was too good to be missed, and it was decided to commence active operations. Scientists of the expedition were flown there at once, but attempts to keep them supplied were hampered in the initial stages because of a mishap to the one flying-boat then in service. They had to be brought back in mid-August, but not before they had gathered a great deal of botanical, zoological and archæological data and had also added to their meteorological and glaciological knowledge.

In 1948, however, it was possible to launch a full-scale expedition, for the three Catalinas were now in service. Regular flights, twenty-two in all, transported eight scientists and a vast amount of miscellaneous equipment to the heart of Pearyland, barely 540 miles from the North Pole. A base was quickly established with tents and huts and windmills to provide power for lighting and radio transmission. There were sledges and dogs and supplies to last the eight pioneers throughout the ensuing winter.

The following summer programme was hampered by drift-ice round the southern base at Zackenberg and by a breakdown in radio communication; but fifteen supporting flights were made, the original winter party was relieved, and fresh sledge-dogs, new windmill plants and a lot of miscellaneous material were brought up. In the three summers some seventy tons of material were carried in 962 flying hours, and this without any proper weather forecasts and with no facilities for emergency landings.

All this material was transformed into a miniature settlement on the shores of Jorgen Bronlunds Fiord. Long before the final cargoes were delivered, a house had been built, radio aerials had been erected and windmills had been assembled. It was the most northerly station in the world.

II

Pearyland presents a striking contrast to other parts of Greenland. It consists of a plateau of yellowish-brown limestone and sandstone, intersected by broad valleys and strange escarpments and winding canyons. At lower levels the action of merciless winds has, according to Count Eigil Knuth, an accomplished sculptor, produced "real works of art", in the form of "abstract sculpture".

From April 11 until September 2 the sun is above the horizon day and night, but at the Jorgen Bronlunds Fiord headquarters there were 158 days on which no sun was seen, because for twelve days preceding its actual disappearance and twelve days following its actual reappearance it was so low on the horizon as to be obscured by surrounding mountains.

"This alternation between nearly five months of darkness and a period of constant summer nearly as long," says Knuth, "made the year seem like one long day and night. And this rhythm decisively influences the rhythm of nature in this high-arctic region."

It was found that the barographs registered more hours of sunshine during the long daylight period than the yearly average in Denmark, thus compensating the local flora and fauna for the long dark winter.

The headquarters hut—the "northernmost house in the world"—consisted of one large central common-room girdled by two-berth cabins. In the first year it was not possible to transport enough timber for building kennels for the sledge-dogs, so caves were dug in a snow-drift to provide shelter for them. It was a far from ideal arrangement, for in bad weather it became necessary to carry out inspections every few hours, both day and night, with constant digging to prevent the caves from becoming blocked.

There was plenty to keep the members of the expedition busy throughout the dark period. Sledges were repaired in readiness for spring journeys, harness was overhauled, sketch-maps were revised and copied, ration scales and sledge-loads were carefully calculated, stores were overhauled, weighed and packed, plans were worked out for establishing depots at strategic points for the benefit of the various sledging parties when needed.

In two seasons twenty-three sledge journeys, with a total of 4,700 miles, were accomplished, and in all fields— glaciology, archæology, meteorology, geology, topography, botany and zoology—rewarding results were achieved.

A sub-station was established on the Christian Erichsen Glacier south of Jorgen Bronlunds Fiord, 10 miles distant from the headquarters hut and nearly 3,000 feet above sea level. Regular visits were made to this sub-station throughout each winter, and Knuth considers that the experts who took on this assignment, which often involved long lone climbs through storms in the dark, had the toughest job in the whole expedition. In all twenty-five ascents were made and 125 days were spent upon the glacier. Shafts were sunk for the examination of stratification; temperatures were taken in holes to a depth of 30 feet, and meticulous record was kept of the accumulation of snow throughout the winter and the rate at which it melted or evaporated in summer. By such means it was established that the glacier was steadily shrinking and that between the summers of 1947 and 1949 it receded in places as much as 200 feet. Other glaciers in the area reveal similar shrinkage, indicating that Pearyland shares the change towards a warmer climate known to be taking place in other parts of the northern hemisphere.

The station at Jorgen Bronlunds Fiord also made its contribution to the Greenland weather-service. Observations were made at three-hourly intervals day and night, and reports were telegraphed to Copenhagen every six hours. The violent winds which howled and whistled round the scientists' isolated headquarters were harnessed effectively, and in the first year all weather reports were transmitted on power derived from a 6-volt windmill. In the second year two 6-volt windmills were in service for radio work and a third mill of 32 volts provided electric current for lighting. With one accumulator being re-charged, it was possible to keep ten 15-watt bulbs burning continuously. A small motor unit was kept in reserve for emergency.

By night the radio operators were able to make contact with amateurs all over the world, from Alaska to South Africa; from New Zealand to Turkey; from Siberia to Honolulu. They even picked up a message of greeting from members of the Norwegian–Swedish–British expedition at the South Pole. The most southerly expedition in the world thus linked radio hands with the most northerly.

III

By mid-September, when the waters of Jorgen Bron-lunds Fiord were frozen over, sledge journeys began. These consisted of "depot trips" for the purpose of laying down caches of supplies in preparation for the spring programme. Scientific work never ceased. Snow-hut observatories were built close to the station; astronomical positions were noted; the earth's magnetism was measured. Geologists conducted a series of experiments to test wind erosion by putting out sets of stones of various shapes and varying degrees of toughness. The ice on the fiord was pierced regularly to register its growth or shrinkage. Measurements of ground temperatures and snow-cover in a specific valley were noted as part of the botanical research.

The sum total of work achieved between 1947 and 1950 is impressive. Apart from the meteorological and weather service, interesting discoveries were made in every field explored. The geologists found strata whose existence in those realms had never been suspected—limestone 200,000,000 years old containing corals and other marine fossils; Triassic strata with fossils of fish previously known only from Spitzbergen; and the most northerly tree-fossils yet found, some with poplar-like leaves which indicated that the climate of 100,000,000 years ago must have been considerably milder.

In the vicinity of the station the botanist found ninety species of vascular plants, 150 mosses and many lichens and algæ. Sledging parties also brought back specimens of numerous plants from north Pearyland. These included the blueberry, the Arctic harebell, purple-flowered saxifrage and the yellow poppy.

About twenty-one bird species were identified, including snowy owl, ptarmigan, eider-duck, snow-bunting and various geese, waders, terns and gulls. Small herds of musk-oxen were encountered, and there were hares, foxes, ermine and lemmings. A polar bear which visited the encampment during the early stages of the expedition was rounded up and shot, and a post-mortem revealed a partly digested bar of milk chocolate as the sole contents of its stomach.

Numerous insects came in for study, including bumble-bees, wasps, flies, beetles and ten kinds of butterfly. The fiord yielded mussels, snails, sea-urchins, starfish, cuttle-fish, worms, polar cod, bullhead, halibut, trout and the Greenland shark.

Into its busy programme the expedition crowded a great deal of highly successful archæological research. Sites of thirty-one ruins were located, with remains of 146 dwellings, some on the southern shore of Independence Fiord, but the majority in Pearyland itself. All were farther north than the remains of any habitation found anywhere else in the world, and a few were barely 470 miles from the Pole.

Most of the remains consisted of tent-rings, but many were found to have been of more solid foundation and structure, from which the explorers deduced that they were probably permanent dwellings and examples of a middle phase in Arctic "town planning", half tent, half house. This type of dwelling was especially prevalent along the shores of Jorgen Bronlunds Fiord, where ruins were closer together than anywhere else, and Count Eigil Knuth's whimsical comment on this fact is: "The country's new, airborne capital had been placed by us on the very spot where the old capital of Pearyland seems to have stood."

A search of sites on Jorgen Bronlunds Fiord revealed small fragments of tools and flint weapons identified as belonging to the Palæo-Eskimo Cape Dorset Culture, though in some respects they seemed even more primitive. Yet the men who used them probably migrated from Arctic-Canada round about A.D. 1000, and lived by hunting musk-oxen, reindeer, hares, geese and ptarmigan and fishing for salmon in rivers and lakes.

But perhaps the most interesting archæological discovery was made at Herlufsholms Strand, 150 miles N.E. of the Jorgen Bronlunds Fiord station. There, upon an almost snow-free terrace, the explorers came upon the complete wooden skeleton of a 35-feet-long umiak or whaling-boat. It was well preserved, and a few hundred yards away was an assortment of tent-remains, comprising a number of utensils characteristic of the Thule Culture. These consisted of an adze-handle, a snow-shovel, a blubber-pounder, a meat tray and a baleen cup.

All these objects were in a perfect state of preservation, and this, plus the presence of a few iron rivets in the framework of the boat, suggested that their users had been active on the eastern coast of Pearyland some 200 years ago. Repeated sledge journeys were made to this site, and the boat was brought back piecemeal and flown home to Denmark in the summer of 1950, when the Jorgen Bronlunds Fiord station was dismantled. Reconstructed, it may be seen in the National Museum in Copenhagen.

IV

Count Eigil Knuth's expedition was not particularly concerned with cartography because Pearyland has been included in the aerial-mapping programme for Greenland now being carried out by the Danish Ordnance Survey Department. Nevertheless, it was able to make certain contributions because many of the sledge journeys took its members through regions where no white man had previously penetrated. The geologists of the party travelled through the "Peary Channel"—the valley which runs from Jorgen Bronlunds Fiord to a point on the north coast where the famous American explorer, on first sighting it, erroneously mistook Pearyland for an island. A visit was also paid to G. B. Schley Fiord, on the east coast—another locality not previously explored.

On all these sledge journeys compass bearings were taken and sketch-maps were made from the vantage points of peaks and headlands. As a result it was possible to suggest alterations to previous maps, but first these were checked and verified by means of aerial photographs taken in the summer of 1950. In this way a map of Pearyland drawn by Lauge Koch in 1938 was brought up to date and published with additional data to give the best possible picture of Pearyland so far.

In all respects the expedition seems to have proved an unqualified success, and it also has the special distinction of being the very first venture of its kind to be launched and sustained from the air.

V

While the Danish explorers were busy in Pearyland during 1948, a French expedition, under Paul Émile Victor, a Polar expert who had served with the American Army in Alaska, was active in the centre of the Ice Cap. Its main purpose was to conduct long-term experiments at the station originally established by the celebrated

German scientist, Dr. Alfred Wegener, before the war; but the party, which numbered twenty-six, was also equipped with "weasels" for exploring the Ice Cap and studying glacial formations generally.

This expedition, which was financed by the French Ministry of Education, reached Disko Bay in the summer. It there split into two groups, one of which pushed northwards, while the other moved inland to occupy the Ice Cap station. The latter, by arrangement with the Danish authorities, was to be manned in relays for three consecutive years.

Those detailed for the task kept up daily scientific and meteorological research, the supplies they had brought with them being supplemented whenever possible by aerial drops. They were able to maintain radio contact with the outside world, but their long vigil, though there were eight of them to share it, had little to relieve it.

Like Wegener, Victor carried out echo-sounding experiments, setting off explosive charges at different points upon the Ice Cap and measuring the time taken for the responding echo to be flashed back from the rocks below. His mobile party was able to take such soundings over a very wide area. It was confirmed that the depth of the Ice Cap was at least 10,000 feet in places, and the fact that at some points the surface altitude was less than the depth of the ice, indicated that the underlying rock must be below sea level.

One of Victor's close associates, Captain Gaston Rouillon, declared: "We found two deep sounds running under the Ice Cap from coast to coast. The sounds were more than four hundred and thirty-seven and three hundred and twenty-eight yards below water surface respectively. They separate Greenland into three parts, bridged by the huge Ice Cap."

The maximum thickness of ice, according to echo-soundings, was said to be 3,554 yards; and one sound was said to have a maximum depth of 656 yards. Large quantities of basalt, usually found in coastal areas, were detected along the sounds.

Further echo-sounding investigations now being conducted by the British North Greenland Expedition may well be found to support the French theory that Greenland is, in reality, three islands, clamped together by ice. Someone has already pointed out that old Eskimo legends tell of a deep fiord or canal cutting right across Greenland, and the triple-island theory is certainly not beyond the bounds of possibility.

Erik Petersen

Greenland girls packing shrimps in the big new cannery at Narssak.

of one of the new fishing companies now operating at Faeringerhavn.

Author

Danish Press Photographers' Assⁿ

Most of the west-coast settlements are linked by air as well as by sea. A Catalina amphibian is seen here dipping low over the harbour at Sukkertoppen in salute to the Royal Yacht.

A large iceberg dwarfs the *Dannebrog*, moored in the inner harbour at Umanak.

Author

CHAPTER XIV

"AS TO THE SEAS..."

ALTHOUGH six-sevenths of Greenland's 840,000 square miles is locked in the implacable embrace of the Inland Ice, Nature seems to have compensated the Greenlanders for that vast lifeless tract by stocking the waters round their thousands of miles of coastline with a phenomenally bounteous hand. The seas simply teem with fish, especially round the west coast. Passengers and crews of coastwise vessels often amuse themselves by dropping unbaited hooks over the rail. A few jerks and a fish is caught. The amusement soon palls. It is too easy. One party of five amateur fishermen who put out in an open boat from Godthaab Fiord for an afternoon's sport returned within an hour with a joint bag of more than sixty cod-fish—all caught without bait! It is hardly surprising, therefore, that fishing ranks as Greenland's principal industry, in which more than 10 per cent of the total population are profitably engaged.

During the past thirty years the temperature of the northern Polar regions has been rising, and the rise has been more marked in Greenland than anywhere else. This change, which drove the seal farther north, attracted multitudes of cod, which are particularly numerous off the south-west coast.

At first the Greenlanders fished from small, home-made, flat-bottomed craft; then came the open motor-boat to give them wider range; then, in a few of the larger centres, fishing-cutters were brought into play. Thus the fishing industry expanded rapidly, until scores of centres were engaged in handling the catches.

The authorities supported the fishermen by conducting systematic biological investigations, by making available larger and better boats on easy terms and by granting interest-free loans. Stations set up by the Greenland Department are now to be found in Julianehaab, Frederikshaab, Godthaab, Sukkertoppen, Holsteinsborg, Egedesminde, Christianshaab, Jakobshavn, Qutdligssat, Godhavn and Umanak. There are also fishery stations set up by private Danish owners; but ever-increasing production makes it necessary to plan far ahead, and existing stations are constantly being extended.

A great deal of up-to-date plant has been imported. The Greenland Department operates a filleting plant at Sukkertoppen, and a Danish commercial company has a similar plant at Tovkussaq. The same company operates a floating freezing plant which also serves as a depot ship for its fleet of fishing-cutters. There are plants for cutting halibut at Claushavn and Jakobshavn and, in different centres, some twenty plants for refining cod-liver oil.

Following an investigation on behalf of the Danish Government in 1948, it was decided to carry out a trawling test. So many cod, cat-fish and small shark were caught on the first day that operations had to stop until a depot ship arrived to ease the congestion.

II

In the season 1948–49 the eleven principal fishery stations handled 11,849,129 kilograms of cleaned and beheaded cod-fish and produced 6,066,176 kilograms of salt-fish. In the 1950–51 season corresponding figures had risen to 13,059,324 kilograms and 6,540,500 kilograms, respectively.

Total production of whole cod-fish for the country during the 1950–51 season amounted to 22,300,000 kilograms, an increase of 23 per cent on the previous year's total. Biggest catches were made in the Julianehaab, Holsteinsborg and Egedesminde districts. Favourable weather conditions helped, no doubt, but other factors were an increasing interest among the Greenlanders in the use of more modern fishing methods and the growing use of motor-boats.

Although cod-fishing takes first place, other catches—including halibut, salmon, wolf-fish and shark—are quite substantial. Experiments in fishing for shark with long lines in the Julianehaab and Umanak districts resulted in a total catch of 250. Experimental fishing is being conducted all the time because it is felt that the neglect of subsidiary fisheries would hardly be prudent. Changes of climate brought the abundant cod, and a reversion to lower air and sea temperatures might well cause the cod to withdraw from Greenland waters as suddenly as they appeared. Indeed, experienced biologists say that the cod has been a periodic visitor to those waters for at least two centuries, appearing and reappearing at varying intervals.

The latest marine-biological investigations suggest that there are reasonable grounds for assuming that cod-fishing prospects for some years ahead will remain favourable; but there are also experts who take the view that variations in temperature are certain to occur sooner or later.

As a matter of policy, then, the authorities now encourage other fisheries. In any case, the fishing season is very short in the north, ranging from forty to fifty days. Southern districts can count upon about 200 days; but nearly all the fishermen follow some secondary calling, such as hunting or horticulture.

All the time the marine-biological investigations are being extended, and any commencing change in temperature in Greenland waters would be noted promptly, so that the industry would not be caught unawares. All the time, too, the supply of motor-boats and larger fishing-cutters is being increased, and the Greenlanders are being provided with modern technical aids and tackle and given instruction in up-to-date fishing methods.

III

Until 1925 fishing in Greenland waters was reserved for fishermen permanently resident in Greenland; then a special Act was introduced which gave rights of access to an area in the outer part of Greenland territorial waters to fishermen from Denmark and the Faroe Islands. Two years later there was established, some 32 miles south of Godthaab, the international fishing port of Faeringerhavn (literally the harbour of the Faroese). The site was well chosen, for the anchorage is protected by tall islets, and there is a good depth of water, free from pack-ice.

Today it is a thriving centre, with a radio station, a hospital, repair shops, a seamen's mission and a seamen's home. Besides the Danes and the Faroese, American, French, British and Portuguese fishermen all make use of the facilities. There is also a Norwegian Seaman's Club, and a concern, financed principally by Norwegian capital, known as the Greenland Industrial and Trading Company, which sells supplies of all kinds to visiting fishing-fleets.

The international character of the port is best exemplified by the bookshelves in the Seamen's Home, where works in nearly every tongue may be found. Those in English range from an Edinburgh guide-book to *Oliver Cromwell's Letters and Speeches*, or from *Famous and Infamous Cases*, by Sir Patrick Hastings, to Sir Winston Churchill's memoirs.

Harbour lights, mooring rings and similar amenities have been provided by the Greenland administration. Two Danish companies have established plants at Faeringerhavn to support the fisheries. Catches are handled by contract and converted into salt-fish for export to Catholic countries, particularly to Italy.

Danish and Faroese fishermen also enjoy special facilities at two other harbours—Ravns Store and Tovkussaq. At the latter station the Greenland Fishery

Company, Ltd., has established freezing and filleting plants, with living quarters for 100 men. There is also a pier and a crane to expedite unloading and loading operations. The same company owns a depot ship, *Greenland*, which is equipped with modern freezing plant.

Near Faeringerhavn a Portuguese schooner crew, fishing with hand-lines, are reputed to have caught 48,000 cod in six days. It is said that nowhere else in the North Atlantic are such big shoals to be found. A Hull trawler skipper netted fish worth £8,600 in his first trawl in Greenland waters. His catch included 1,000 stone of prime halibut.

When he got back the news spread, and many other Hull trawlers set off. Only those equipped with radar succeeded in penetrating the fog and ice; the remainder had to turn back. But one of the successful ones, Skipper Parkinson, of the *Loch Inver*, made a £10,000 catch.

The voyage from Hull normally takes twenty-six days, but one skipper is credited with having made two trips in thirty-five days and to have earned £18,000 therefrom. Hazards are such, however, that the wives of Hull fishermen banded together in an attempt to stop winter sailings, following the loss off Greenland of the trawler *Norman* with twenty of her crew.

The latest available figures, taken from the Sea Fisheries Statistical Tables, published by H.M. Stationery Office, show that British steam trawlers operating off the west coast of Greenland in 1951 caught 211,312 cwt. of cod and 4,732 cwt. of halibut. A further 952 cwt. of cod and 2,871 cwt. of halibut were caught by line.

Today the Hull Nautical School has established special courses of training for the benefit of trawler officers, to enable them to acquire up-to-date navigational knowledge of the west Greenland coast. The classes are well attended.

IV

The systematic scientific investigations which are carried on continuously in Greenland waters led, in 1949, to the discovery of three exceptionally rich shrimp-beds in Disko Bay. Two of them, off Christianshaab and Jakobshavn, are said to be the biggest in the world, each being 10 miles long and 5 miles wide. Ice difficulties and the prevalence of sharks in the Jakobshavn area tend to reduce the yield there, but round Christianshaab, where the shrimps are of excellent quality and a more uniform size, the fisheries are thriving. Weather and ice conditions are, on the whole, favourable. Small cutters may occasionally have to take shelter in harbour, but larger craft are able to fish more or less continuously. The shrimp-beds in the Christianshaab area alone are rich enough to support a very considerable expansion of the industry. The local harbour, too, is ideally suited as a base for the shrimp-boats.

Greenlanders have shown themselves enterprising and skilful in accustoming themselves to shrimp-fishing. One cutter has been known to deliver catches worth 21,000 kroner within two and a half months. Shrimp-fishing in the Disko Bay area is carried on jointly by the Greenland Department, the Greenland Fishery Company and one privately owned cutter. The combined yield for a season has reached as much as 162,352 kilograms. In the Julianehaab area two of the Greenland Department's cutters caught 12,768 kilograms of shrimps in about forty fishing days; but at Holsteinsborg the yield was nil, and the cannery there had to be fed with supplies from Disko Bay. This cannery dealt with 73,600 kilograms of shrimps, and could have handled more, but a proportion of the supplies had deteriorated in the voyage from the fishing grounds, and had to be condemned.

The cannery at Christianshaab, which was built in 1950 and equipped with the latest modern machinery, consists of three departments: a picking plant and packing plant; a freezing plant and cold store; and a sorting, washing and storage plant for fresh shrimps. The factory is designed for the production of quick-frozen fishery products, particularly deep-sea shrimps, with a capacity of about 3,000 kilograms of shrimps a day. Here again the ready adaptability of the Greenlanders has been demonstrated effectively. In the two months following the opening of the factory 82,500 kilograms of shrimps were processed by workers who were quite new to the job. The cannery could, it is claimed, handle 350 tons of shrimps in a three-months season should the expansion of the fisheries warrant it.

Another cannery at Narssak, near Julianehaab, has a useful capacity. Local fisheries are not to be compared with those of Disko Bay, and are liable to be impeded by ice difficulties. Nevertheless, given a regular flow of supplies, this factory could process 100,000 tins between May and September. It also produces a certain amount of smoked salmon and smoked halibut.

The potential development of the shrimp-fishing is incalculable. In 1946 the total production stood at 25,667 tins. By 1951 this had risen to 143,000. Greenland shrimps may one day find their way to tables throughout the world.

v

The growth of the cod and shrimp fisheries has not diminished the hunting of sea mammals, whale, walrus or seal. In northern and eastern districts it is still a principal calling, but as a material part of the catches is utilised by the Greenlanders themselves, it is not easy to gauge the precise results. Hunting is still regarded as important in many centres—even in places where more profitable pursuits now exist. It survives because Greenlanders in those districts still consider hunting the most honourable calling a man can follow.

These hunters are very conservative, and still prefer to resort to barter, though the designers of the Greenland currency have incorporated polar bears and whales and other Greenland fauna as decorative devices on paper money and coins. These pictorial reminders of the basis of the country's economy must appeal to the imaginative Greenlander, but old habits die hard, and it is likely that barter will endure in some of the more remote settlements for many years to come.

Few sealskins are now exported, because they are still of value to many Greenlanders for everyday use—for clothing, footwear or for repairing kayaks. To ensure even distribution, the Royal Greenland Trading Company buys in quantities of skins and resells them in those parts of the country where seals are now scarce. Greenlanders also carry on a lively trade in sealskins among themselves.

With the introduction of electricity in many centres and the importation of mineral oil, the use of seal blubber as train-oil for illumination has declined. Most of the blubber is now exported to Denmark by the Greenland Trading Company, which maintains its own oil refinery in Copenhagen. The largest supply centres for seal blubber today are Upernavik, Jakobshavn, Egedesminde and Umanak, in that order.

The Government maintains a whaling steamer, and the whaling season usually lasts from about the middle of June until the early part of October. In one recent season a total catch of forty-six whales was handled, made up of thirty-five rorquals, five spermaceti whales, four hump-back whales and two bottlenose whales. Since then a new and more modern vessel has been provided, so it is reasonable to suppose that these figures will be improved upon in future.

There is always rejoicing when a whale is brought in. The Greenlanders have their own whaling song—"The Boat is Coming in with the Whale". Everyone crowds down to the shore as the monster is towed into shallow water, where no time is lost in its dismemberment. There is meat for everyone, and the smallest children may be seen struggling along with buckets containing huge square slabs. Nearly everyone grabs a strip of *matak* (skin and blubber) to suck and chew while working; and packs of sledge-dogs clamour round for any stray morsels they can snatch. The men engaged upon the actual dismemberment wade about on the towering carcass, often sinking knee-deep in blubber, wielding their long flensing knives with consummate skill and working at great speed. Dogs and populace scramble round, some wading in the bloodstained water, others negotiating the slippery rocks. The task is long and arduous, but when it is finally completed the Greenlanders still have energy to spare for singing and dancing and general rejoicing.

Most of the blubber is shipped to Denmark for processing. The combined yield from seal and whale blubbers for one season may amount to about 600,000 kilograms of oil, apart from various other by-products.

Egedesminde is the largest whaling centre. Upernavik leads in sealing, with a total of more than 12,000 in a single season. Thule is the chief centre for the rarer walrus and narwhal. Godthaab, Godhavn and Egedesminde lead in porpoise fishing.

Shark, useful for their livers and skins, besides providing meat for sledge-dogs, are caught at many points along the west coast, the chief centres being Egedesminde, Upernavik, Jakobshavn and Christianshaab. But recent years have shown a decline in this branch of the fisheries industry because there is more inducement to concentrate upon the profitable cod.

VI

In all there are about 100 species of fish in Greenland waters. The capelin, or *angmagssat*, a small fish, somewhat like a herring, is fished by the Greenlanders both for food and bait. During the summer months it penetrates the various fiords in colossal shoals and may be netted by the ton. Large quantities are dried and stored away for the winter months, when they also serve as food for the huskies.

Flounders were once plentiful enough for some to be canned for export, but latterly they have not been found in their customary grounds. Halibut has been mentioned, but there is also a Greenland variety, the blue halibut. Other fish caught in numbers are fiord cod, lump-sucker, sea-scorpion, Norway haddock, wolf-fish and eels. The char, or "Greenland salmon", abounds in rivers and mountain lakes in July and August, when it migrates from the sea; but the true salmon is more scarce and seems to be confined to the Godthaab, Sukkertoppen and Holsteinsborg areas, where a certain amount of trade is carried on in salted salmon.

But the cod holds the key to the future of the Greenland fishing industry. Though less than forty-five years have elapsed since the first fishing-station was established, there are now something like eighty depots along the west coast where cod is landed, washed and prepared for export, either in the form of frozen fillets or as salt-fish. As mentioned, most of the supplies go to southern Europe, where they find a ready and profitable market. Experiments, however, are being carried out with the latest flash-freezing plants, and it is hoped also to find markets in America for both cod fillets and shrimps.

The development of the freezing technique opens up new possibilities of bringing Greenland's fish products to far-flung markets in a form which commands a higher price. A rational expansion of the fisheries is foreseen, and the policy of granting loans on favourable terms is designed to encourage more and more Greenlanders to acquire their own boats. Better and larger boats are promised, with the very latest gear, so that inshore fishermen of today will, if necessary, be equipped for venturing farther out.

So far they have no trawlers, but it is logical to conclude that, in order to compete with the fishermen of other nations who are being tempted towards the Greenland coast in increasing numbers, a proportion, at any rate, will develop into regular deep-sea fishermen.

Certainly the fisheries constitute the most important industry, and now that the country is being opened up so rapidly and private enterprise is being vouchsafed an opportunity of showing what it can do, big developments may be expected. Capital for expansion is not lacking. The Greenland Fishery Co., Ltd., which built the freezing and filleting plant at Tovkussaq, has a share capital of 2,000,000 kroner. Two other Danish companies at Faeringerhavn have 100,000 kroner and 200,000 kroner respectively; and the Greenland Industrial and Trading Company has 1,000,000 kroner.

Thus, both the Danish Government and private investors alike are pinning their faith on the potential wealth of the seas of Greenland, as did the wise prophet who, more than 200 years ago, penned the words which head this chapter.

"As to the seas," he wrote with inspired vision, "they yield more plenty and wealth of all sorts of animals and fishes than in most other parts of the world, which may turn to very great profit; witness the exceeding great riches many nations have gathered and are still gathering, from the whale fishing and the capture of seals and morses, or sea horses. Thus it is confessed that Greenland is a country not unworthy of keeping and improving."

That prophet was Hans Egede.

CHAPTER XV

TWO ROYAL VISITS

TWICE in their history under the Danish flag the people of Greenland have celebrated Royal visits. The first occasion was in the summer of 1921, when King Christian X, accompanied by Queen Alexandrine, the Crown Prince Frederik and Prince Knud, sailed up the west coast on S.S. *Island*, which they had boarded in Iceland. The Royal party had sailed from Copenhagen on June 17 in the cruiser *Valkyrien*, and had first visited the Faroe Islands. A change of vessel was dictated by ice conditions, as the S.S. *Island* was better suited for negotiating the difficult coastal waters of Greenland.

Contemporary reports describe the arrival at Godthaab on "a splendid, light polar night", with all the people in festival dress, and with scores of kayaks and umiaks thronging the harbour. The flotilla of umiaks presented a spectacle which belongs to the past, for very few of these "women's boats" are to be encountered today.

When the Royal Family went ashore next day the King wore Guards' uniform with a plumed cocked hat, with the broad blue ribbon of the Order of the Elephant across his breast. The Queen wore a simple coat with fur collar and cuffs, and the Princes were in naval uniform. But the simple manner in which they mingled with the people, gathered round the old dwelling of Hans Egede, touched all hearts. The impending Royal visit had been looked forward to by many with a feeling akin to awe, yet now they found their monarch greeting them as intimate friends. One elderly Greenland woman was overheard to declare: "Fancy! He is more plain and pleasant than our Danish assistant superintendent!"

There were formal receptions, of course, with presentations of gifts to the King, which included a kayak with all accessories; but there were also less formal dancing displays and much singing and rejoicing. The kayak hunters put on a "regatta" of their own, and the ablest performers were presented with rifles by the King. Some of those rifles are treasured to this day.

After leaving the capital, the Royal party visited Jakobshavn and Godhavn, and while sailing through Disko Bay their ship's wireless picked up an S.O.S. from a Swedish vessel, the *Bele*, which, carrying equipment for the Fifth Thule Expedition, had been held up by engine trouble, with the result that she was now firmly caught in the ice between Umanak and Upernavik.

King Christian gave immediate orders for the *Island* to steam northwards, notwithstanding the Captain's opinion that it might be courting trouble. They made for the Davis Strait at full speed, but on July 15 they ran into dense fog, and were thus obliged to feel their way more cautiously. Captain Aasberg, of S.S. *Island*, remained on the bridge with his ice-pilot day and night, the siren sounding continuously, with ominous answering echoes from icebergs ahead. One evening, while the Royal Family were at dinner, the vessel shuddered from stem to stern as she hove to, about half a ship's length from the towering mass of a monster iceberg which lay in her path.

But they kept on, and on July 17 they reached Darhead, to the north of Disko Island, where *Bele* lay locked in the relentless grip of the ice. Realising that it was impossible to free their ship, Captain and crew, with Swedish scientists who chanced to be aboard, had established a camp on the little island of Kinatok, where all the Royal party now found them.

The Swedish Captain, overwrought, broke down and wept when King Christian seized his hand and commended him as a brave sailor. It was a man-to-man gesture between fellow sailors, and it touched the Captain deeply. He grasped the King's two hands, muttering his gratitude and collapsed. With his fellow survivors he was taken back to Godthaab, from whence the Royal party resumed their homeward voyage.

Bad weather continued, but no further incident marked the remainder of the trip. The Royal party rejoined the cruiser *Valkyrien* in Iceland, and reached Copenhagen by the end of July.

That autumn King Gustav of Sweden paid a visit to Denmark, and bestowed upon King Christian the gold medal for outstanding deeds, and expressed the fervent gratitude of the Swedish people for the rescue of the *Bele's* Captain and crew. Subsequently the French Government also gave King Christian the nation's gold medal for ship salvage, to which it added a special plaque at the International Life-saving Congress in 1934. It is probably the only record in history of a reigning monarch earning such awards.

II

The young Crown Prince Frederik, who participated with his father, King Christian X, in the rescue of those trapped Swedish seamen, would doubtless have smiled had some seer then forecast that he would return to Greenland thirty years hence as King, and that his own yacht, *Dannebrog*, would narrowly escape a similar fate among the ice. Yet such a prophecy, had it been made, would have been justified by events, for the Royal tour of 1952 was menaced in its initial stages by factors which looked like reducing months of careful pre-planning to so much waste paper.

July 12 had been fixed for the official landing at Godthaab, but a few weeks before, Greenland experienced the worst ice conditions within memory. Ships were being delayed up to two or three weeks in consequence, and those responsible for organising the tour found themselves faced with tremendous problems.

Her Majesty Queen Ingrid was then in England on an

unofficial visit with her three daughters; King Frederik was already at sea, and Press delegates and officials from half a dozen countries were assembling in Copenhagen.

One week before the official landing date, weather conditions round the south-west coast of Greenland suddenly worsened, and a 30-mile-wide belt of pack-ice threatened to close a number of ports which were listed in the proposed Royal itinerary.

The Royal yacht, *Dannebrog*, with her graceful, slender hull, was not built for Arctic voyages, and her twin screws would be particularly vulnerable if caught among drift-ice. It was unthinkable that she should be subjected to unnecessary risk, yet the King had set his heart upon making the tour in his own ship, and by this time the *Dannebrog* was nearing the coast of Iceland. While time remained she could make detours to avoid ice, but she could not stay out at sea indefinitely.

Meanwhile, the departure of the delegates from Copenhagen could not be delayed. Indeed, they took off on July 5, some hours ahead of schedule, having been warned that if a landing in Greenland proved impossible it might be necessary to fly on to New York.

The original plan was for a two-hop flight via Iceland to Narsarssuaq, Bluie West 1; but in the event Greenland weather dictated an eleventh-hour change, and the party flew via Prestwick and thence direct to Sondrestromfiord, Bluie West 8, crossing the Ice Cap from east to west, as Nansen had done, but in hours instead of weeks. En route, a goodwill message was flashed to the King's yacht, then off the N.W. coast of Iceland.

While the delegates went aboard M.S. *Umanak* waiting for them in the fiord, *Dannebrog* steamed steadily on. Her radar had broken down in the Kattegat, but her escorting frigate, *Holger Danske* (formerly the British *Monnow*), was able to scout ahead for ice. High winds and rough weather were encountered off Greenland's coast, and they were forced to go far off course to avoid drifting ice.

A rendezvous was now fixed at the international fishing-port of Faeringerhavn, which *Umanak* reached on July 7, nosing past the small icebergs drifting around the harbour mouth.

The *Dannebrog*, following next day, was less fortunate. Rain and fog and high wind and more drifting ice forced her to abandon her first attempt to make harbour. Though obliged to haul off, she gamely made a second bid, this time with success. She dropped anchor beside *Umanak* at 1.29 a.m. on July 9. *Holger Danske* anchored a little astern.

Three units of the Royal party had thus made rendezvous, but they still had to be joined by the Queen. Her brief holiday in London over, Her Majesty was now back in Copenhagen, waiting to take off for Greenland by air. She finally left Kastrup Airport at 9.30 p.m. on the 9th in a D.C.6 of Scandinavian Airline System, which, flying via Iceland, was able to touch down safely at Bluie West 1. There, after snatching a very brief rest, Her Majesty transhipped to a Catalina amphibian and pressed on to Faeringerhavn.

Precisely at 8 a.m. on July 10 her brown-and-grey machine circled above the waiting ships, skimmed across the water and taxied to rest between the King's yacht and *Umanak* to a salute from the frigate's guns. Full rendezvous was thus achieved with barely forty-eight hours in hand before the official landing at Godthaab, 50 miles higher up the coast. The menace of the ice had been defeated.

Yet even up to the last the elements proved capricious. Godthaab on July 11 was mist-enshrouded. Chill Arctic winds whistled among its frowning crags, and rain lashed its myriad flags and banners and decorations and turned its newly-sanded highways into slush.

Even the weather-wise Greenlanders would not commit themselves when asked about the prospects of fair weather for their King and Queen. "*Imaka*", they said

Danish Press Photographers' Assn.

merican airmen parade on the tarmac at Narsarssuaq for inspection by His Majesty King Frederik IX of Denmark.

can linesman secures a "grandstand seat" for the Royal parade.

Danish Press Photographers' Assn.

Danish Press Photographers' Assn.

An address of welcome being delivered to the Royal couple in the Square at Julianehaab, founded in 1755.

Godthaab youngsters test a dancing-floor in anticipation of the Royal visit.

Danish Press Photographers' Assn.

with a shrug—"Perhaps". Nevertheless, every fisherman
and seal-hunter had a neatly furled Danish flag stowed in
his kayak in the place usually reserved for fishing-tackle,
rifle or harpoon.

The children had been flag-waving for weeks in anticipation of the great day. Parents and teachers feared the
flags would be spoilt long before the occasion; but they
were too much treasured to be treated harshly. A few
replacements were necessary, perhaps, but that was all.

Then came the day itself—and with it one of those
sudden changes which seem a feature of Greenlandic
weather. Bright sunshine and a cloudless sky; summer
warmth, akin to a May morning in Britain, to replace the
Arctic chill. King's weather.

III

July 12, 1952, is a day that will live long in Godthaab's
memory. At last the children were able to wave their flags
in earnest. Boy Scouts in green shirts and maroon
scarves joined with Girl Guides in blue dresses and green
scarves to line the route from a heather-garlanded landing
stage. Other lads in snow-white *anoraks*, blue serge
trousers and knee-boots helped the solitary police con-
stable, while local dignitaries appeared in full-dress
uniforms or ceremonial attire. Greenland women and
girls, in their beaded collars and exquisitely embroidered
sealskin boots, lent added colour to the scene which
greeted the Royal couple as they stepped ashore to a salute
from the small silvered cannon commanding the Colony
Harbour.

After the initial speeches of welcome Their Majesties
moved among the people, who very soon broke their
ranks and surged round them as they made their way
slowly up the hill towards the church. There were hand-
shakes and smiles for everyone in an atmosphere of
friendly informality.

His Majesty wore Admiral's full dress with the broad

N

blue ribbon of the Order of the Elephant across his breast. The Queen wore a brick-coloured tailor-made and a close-fitting hat trimmed with petals, and carried a small bouquet of yellow Arctic poppies that was presented to her on landing by a small girl in full Greenlandic costume.

After visiting the church the Royal couple made their way to a specially prepared enclosure outside the school, where the King spoke feelingly to the people, telling them how pleased he was to visit the Greenland fiords in his own ship, just as if he were sailing in the waters round Denmark. Thus when he stepped ashore he felt instantly that he was among a Danish people, as close to him as the people of the home country. His Majesty added that the work for Greenland had entered a new phase. "To all in Denmark," he said, "it is a question of vital importance that this task is shouldered in a way that will attach Greenland closer to the motherland, not as a colony but as an equal partner in the Danish society."*

Then came the presentation of gifts from the people of Godthaab—mounted walrus tusks for the King; a table-cover, hand-worked with Greenlandic motifs, and a sealskin handbag, and a full Greenlandic costume for the Queen. The three Princesses back home in Denmark had not been forgotten. Exquisitely worked Greenlandic costumes, similar to the Queen's, were presented for Princess Margrethe, Princess Benedikte and Princess Anne-Marie by Greenlandic girls of corresponding ages.

At a luncheon at the Governor's Residency Their Majesties were favoured with an all-Greenlandic menu, which included ptarmigan, three different salmon dishes, walrus flippers, smoked halibut, cod, shrimps, a pasty of seal's liver and a variety of sea-birds garnished with local grown radishes and greens. There was *matak*, made from the boiled skin of a narwhal, whale-steak and home-reared lamb.

* Denmark's new Constitution, implementing this, was signed by His Majesty within a year.

In the afternoon Their Majesties visited the hospital and made informal calls at a number of private houses. They met the local football team, "Nuk", and an opposing eleven from their escorting frigate *Holger Danske*, watched a little of the game, and then inspected the new reservoir under construction. A surprise item was a salute of twenty-one charges of dynamite among the mountains overlooking the site.

Later the Royal couple inspected the Ny Herrnhut, where the Moravian Brethren of old laboured so selflessly in the interest of the primitive Greenlanders. They also saw the ruins of early Eskimo settlements, which plainly thrilled Queen Ingrid, who has inherited some of her father's interest in archæology.

In the early evening Their Majesties received local guests aboard the Royal yacht, while the people of Godthaab gave themselves over to feasting and dancing. The open-air dancing-floor beside the school, where the morning's ceremonies had been held, became the focal point, and in the unfading light of the serene Arctic night the rejoicing went on ceaselessly.

It must have seemed to most of Godthaab's citizens that a day so crowded with incident could yield no further surprise, yet shortly after eleven the atmosphere became suddenly electrical as word spread that the King and Queen had come ashore again and were making for the dancing enclosure. And when the mixed cavalcade of jeeps and station wagons drew up, and Their Majesties alighted, the spontaneous cheering eclipsed all previous demonstrations, for Queen Ingrid was seen to be wearing the Greenlandic costume that had been presented to her on that very spot a few hours before. As, helped by the King, she mounted the platform with some difficulty in the unaccustomed sealskin thigh-boots, the cheering reached crescendo. Her Majesty's gracious gesture in showing herself to her people as one of themselves moved them as nothing else could have done.

ALERT

DANISH
PEARLAND
EXPEDITION
BASE

NORD

BRITISH
NORTH GREENLAND
EXPEDITION (Commander Simpson)

THULE

Clavering Isla

UPERNAVIK

Scoresby S

QUTDLIGSSAT
Disko Island
GODHAVN
EGEDESMINDE

UMANAK

JAKOBSHAVN
CHRISTIANSHAAB

HOLSTEINSBORG ● Bluie West Eight

Sondre Stromfiord

SUKKERTOPPEN

GODTHAAB (Capital)
FAERINGEHAVN

ANGMAGSSALIK

SKJOLDUNGEN

FREDERIKSHAAB
GRONNEDAL
IVIGTUT

NARSARSSUAQ - Bluie West One

IGALIKO

NARSSAQ
JULIANEHAAB

Cape Farewell

Though most of the settlements of modern Greenland are clustered along the west coast, there is activity today in many other zones. Angmagssalik has always been an important east-coast centre, and now there are settlements at Scoresby Sound and Skjoldungen, founded in 1925 and 1938 respectively. In the far north are weather-stations whose importance is increased by the establishment of the big new air-base at Thule; and the Ice Cap itself is being newly explored by the British North Greenland Expedition under Commander Simpson.

IV

In the weeks that followed, Their Majesties voyaged up and down the west coast, visiting various settlements and outposts, mingling informally with the people and seeing for themselves every facet of life in Greenland as it is lived today. Off the coast there were occasional fogs and storms, but, as if by some special dispensation, the sky always seemed to clear, and the sun to shine serenely, whenever the Royal couple stepped ashore.

It was an intensive tour, with little respite for the King and Queen. The formidable itinerary included Sukkertoppen, Egedesminde, Christianshaab, Jakobshavn, Umanak, Godhavn, Holsteinsborg, Gronnedal and Ivigtut, Julianehaab, Narssak, Igaliko and Narsarssuaq.

Apart from the inevitable repetitive ceremonial and speeches and inspections associated with any Royal tour, the trip was more than usually strenuous. In remote stations tricky landings had often to be made from small boats, with an ensuing scramble over slippery rocks or treacherous swamps. Her Majesty the Queen might well have been excused from many duties, yet, characteristically, she shirked nothing, and often donned slacks and gum-boots for long tramps across rough country.

Someone afterwards ventured to ask the King and Queen if they could place their finger upon any outstanding feature of their tour that might have impressed them particularly. Their unhesitating reply was: "Everything! We have enjoyed everything!" It was an answer that carried conviction.

That all-embracing "everything" enshrines a veritable treasure-house of memories. The enthusiasm of the Greenlanders everywhere, and especially the frank, spontaneous greetings from the children, must have delighted Their Majesties. At Sukkertoppen one small girl was observed an hour before the Royal landing gravely coaching her still smaller brother in what she deemed the correct angle at which his flag should be held. Her gaze was drawn with that of others towards the gleaming Royal yacht riding at anchor close to the shore; but half an eye was always on her younger brother, and whenever his hand began to sag she grabbed his wrist and corrected the flag's cant!

The children of Sukkertoppen, who number a third of the population, were everywhere—on the landing-stage with its gay arch extending a greeting of "Welcome!" in Greenlandic and Danish; lining the Royal route; clambering high among the overhanging rocks to gain the best vantage points from which to view the spectacle of a life-time.

A contrasting welcome awaited Their Majesties when they neared Egedesminde. The *Dannebrog* was behind schedule, having been delayed by winds approaching gale force; but as the weather began to clear, the people of Egedesminde could bear the suspense of waiting no longer. First one small boat nosed tentatively towards the harbour mouth; then another, and another. In an astonishingly short time a mixed flotilla of kayaks and motor-boats of all sizes had assembled, and, with each craft making the best speed she could command, the entire flotilla rounded the headland of Cairn Island and put to sea. It was an unrehearsed gesture, prompted solely by eager exuberance, and in the throb-throb of the countless motors could be sensed the vibrant excitement in every heart. Estimates of the size of the flotilla vary. Someone counted forty kayaks, and motor-boats can have been no less numerous. Together they made an impressive picture, silhouetted against a serene evening sky; and certainly no monarch ever received so fine a tribute from his people.

The tribute in this instance was all the more significant because that one flotilla epitomised the changing face of Greenland as nothing else could have done. The men in the kayaks were seal-hunters of the old school who represented the primitive Greenland Hans Egede knew; those in the motor-boats were new-style fishermen who represented modern Greenland. One in their loyalty to the Danish Crown, they bridged the gap of centuries.

Their Majesties had opportunities for closer acquaintanceship with both groups during their stay in Egedesminde. They visited the seal-hunters in their own encampment on Peat Island, inspected their summer tents and witnessed the dexterous flensing of two small whales among the rocks. The King even sampled a morsel of raw blubber, waving the official photographers aside with a good-natured smile.

In striking contrast to this glimpse of the Stone Age, Their Majesties saw on the mainland, barely five minutes away by launch, the very latest fish-filleting and packing plants operated by other Greenlanders in trim white overalls. Once again the centuries were spanned in a flash by visual glimpses of the old Greenland and the new.

v

At Jakobshavn, the King and Queen tramped across the mountains to the great fiord where the glaciers sweep down from the Ice Cap to discharge some 20,000,000 tons of ice daily into the waters of the North Atlantic. No one who has ever looked upon this immaculate expanse shimmering in the Arctic sunshine can fail to be moved by the splendour of the scene.

At Umanak, which takes its name from the heart-shaped mountain towering above the settlement, Their Majesties reached the most northerly point of their tour, and gained a glimpse of Polar Greenland. There they saw sturdier houses built of stone and turfs; there they saw kayaks and sledges and packs of sledge-dogs, scavenging through the settlement like hungry wolves, for in summer these animals are left to fend for themselves. They visited the hospital and sanatorium and the school and library, and attended a service in the picturesque stone-built church. They took coffee and cakes with the people in the open air and inspected a small museum where old harpoons and whaling implements were on view. And, to the delight of the 500-odd inhabitants, *Dannebrog* lay moored in the inner harbour among the icebergs, so close that those on shore could see the Royal couple walking upon her decks.

At Godhavn, on Disko Island, on the homeward trip, Their Majesties saw the Magnetic Observatory and the Arctic Station. The latter, established in 1906, boasts the largest library in Greenland, which is devoted exclusively to literature on Arctic subjects. There is also a laboratory with facilities for technical research. Its function is to advise the Greenland Department upon scientific matters concerning the flora and fauna of the country.

The Arctic Station had prepared surprise gifts for the Royal couple—a stuffed and mounted King eider-duck for His Majesty, a truly magnificent specimen in full plumage; and two fox-skins, white and silver, for Queen Ingrid. Her Majesty spent some time at the Arctic Station, being particularly interested in Greenland's flowers and plants. Throughout the tour, indeed, the Queen collected specimens and seeds to take back with her to Copenhagen. The Arctic Station at Godhavn has classified some 400 vascular plants, about 500 mosses and between 700 and 800 lichens.

While in Godhavn, the Queen walked out to the local beauty spot, Red River Falls. It was an afternoon of brilliant sunshine, though, lodged among the rocks beside the falls, large deposits of unmelted snow remained as lingering legacies from the preceding winter. The Queen spent some time watching the two strangely contrasting waterfalls—one crystal clear as it issued straight from surface springs; the other russet red from volcanic deposits washed down from the mountains above.

An even more arresting spectacle greeted Her Majesty on the return walk. The sea, within 50 feet or so of the

moss-green shore, was reddish-brown from the outflow of
Red River; yet just beyond, as if marked off meticulously
by a draughtsman with a ruler, lay a broad band of deep
blue water, bounded in turn by an irregular white line
formed by ranks of glistening icebergs.

From the dazzling sunshine of Godhavn, the Royal
convoy sailed into a belt of fog which persisted until
Holsteinsborg was reached, when it lifted miraculously a
few hours before the official landing. The people of
Holsteinsborg had prepared a reception in the vast boat-
building hall. Trestle tables in double ranks were taste-
fully laid, and decorated with segments of turf bearing
wild flowers and moss. There were home-made cakes
and biscuits in variety, while the accompanying drinks
included sherry and home-brewed beer. Festoons of
green leaves and branches and flags in profusion were
draped between the pillars, and in this festive setting
Their Majesties were entertained by some of the finest
singing of Greenlandic songs and anthems heard on their
tour.

Three picturesque figures at this gathering were representatives from Thule, who had been flown down for the
occasion in an American plane. Two were polar-bear
hunters named Sorkak and Jess, and the third was a priest
named Karl Poulsen, who acted as their interpreter. All
wore the traditional Thule dress of bearskin trousers, with
white sealskin boots and white *anoraks*—warm wear for
the comparatively mild climate of Holsteinsborg.

The hunters had been away on a long trip by dog-sledge
across the ice to Canadian territory, on which they had
bagged five bears and numerous foxes. They had been
unaware that the Thule Hunting Council had elected
them to represent the settlement for the occasion of the
Royal visit until met by Poulsen on their return at an
outpost north of Thule. Their dogs were then so
exhausted that they only kept to the trail when led by the
priest. Sorkak and Jess, incredulous at first, accepted the

high honour bestowed upon them by their fellows, and capped their gruelling three-months' sledge journey with their first flight. They were enthralled by the spectacle of the Ice Cap viewed from above and spellbound by the witchery of cloudscapes, which revealed to them a beauty far beyond their wildest imaginings.

They were received aboard the *Dannebrog*, and talked with their King and Queen through interpreters. Their Majesties particularly admired the wonderful feathery texture of their bearskin trousers, made from the skins of polars they had bagged on earlier trips.

Sorkak and Jess inspected the engineering and boat-building yards while in Holsteinsborg, and were interested in all they saw. Although they are hunters of the traditional school, they make one small concession to modernity, and use motor-boats for fishing during the short Thule season. After seeing the workshops at Holsteinsborg, they expressed the opinion that it would be useful to have a blacksmith in Thule to repair their boats!

While the King and Queen were in Holsteinsborg a sizeable whale was brought in, lashed to the side of a vessel which circled the Royal yacht to enable Their Majesties to view the catch before it was towed into shallow water to be flensed.

The people of Holsteinsborg had prepared a surprise send-off for the Royal convoy, and as it steamed away, beacons were kindled on surrounding headlands and islands. One after another they leapt into flame, their cheerful blaze, visible long after Holsteinsborg had been left behind, serving as a reminder of a momentous visit.

Once more the weather turned a somersault, and storms and fog greeted the convoy as it ploughed southwards to the cryolite mining centre of Ivigtut. When the fog finally cleared, the skies became leaden and rain teemed down; yet on the morning earmarked for the Royal inspection of the mine the skies cleared just as suddenly as they had clouded, and the weather became bright and sunny and warm.

Their Majesties also inspected the adjoining naval station of Gronnedal, headquarters of the Greenland Command.

VI

Now, as the Royal convoy pushed southwards on the final stages of the trip, it ran into the belt of drift-ice which a few weeks before had placed the tour in jeopardy. It had thinned a little in the interval, but was still dense enough to keep the ice-pilots on their toes. For mile after mile it was necessary to proceed at half speed, nosing cautiously between the floes. At intervals, too, large icebergs reared their formidable bulk, often in freak formations. But the flourishing settlement of Julianehaab was reached in safety, and here, in contrast to the ice-fields, the Royal party saw vast stretches of pasture-land where sheep and cattle grazed in the shadow of green hillsides. Here, too, the setting seemed for once to vindicate Eric the Red's choice of name for the land of his adoption.

From Julianehaab the Royal couple proceeded to Narssak to inspect the huge refrigerating plant designed for handling the rapidly expanding trade in home-killed mutton. They also saw the largest shrimp-cannery in the country and the plant where the unique Greenlandic delicacy, "smoked halibut", is prepared.

On the following day Their Majesties made a 2-mile pilgrimage across swampy country to the pleasant, pastoral outpost of Igaliko—the Garder of the early settlers—where the ruins of Greenland's first "cathedral", the Church of St. Nicholas, may still be seen. Igaliko has long been a dairy-farming centre, and the handful of present-day settlers entertained their Royal visitors with glasses of fresh milk, and with creamy butter spread generously upon slabs of delicious home-made cheese.

With this quiet, homely scene, the Royal tour came to

its official end. The smallest community in Greenland had not been forgotten. The King and Queen had come among them as equals, had shared their simple fare, and, with a friendly wave of the hand, had departed as they had come, over the hills and across the swamps, leaving behind a memory that the people of Igaliko will treasure for ever.

VII

On the next day, after Queen Ingrid had taken off by plane from Narsarssuaq bound for Copenhagen, King Frederik, who was to follow in his yacht, reviewed the American airmen who man the base. Brilliant sunshine flooded the runways, though icebergs floated in the adjoining fiord, and the legend "Welcome to Sunny Southern Greenland—the Miami of the North" was more than justified.

Nearly 2,000 Americans paraded before the King, and after he had ridden down the lines, standing in a jeep, they marched past his saluting base eight abreast with the precision of guardsmen. On the fringe of the airfield the Stars and Stripes and the Danish flag flew side by side, symbolising the unity between two nations, one large, one small, but both equally great in their determination to do everything possible to preserve world peace.

CHAPTER XVI

MANY ENDEAVOURS

WHEN a visitor to modern Greenland notes the deftness with which both men and women handle intricate machinery, he cannot fail to marvel that a primitive people should have proved themselves so adaptable in mastering devices so alien to anything they can ever have encountered before. The truth is that their dexterity is inherent. For generation after generation Greenlanders have been accustomed to using their hands in constructing, often with the crudest implements, all the elaborate paraphernalia necessary for their survival. Because their choice of materials was limited, they learned to adapt them to a variety of uses; and what they lacked in materials or tools they had perforce to make up by intelligence and skill.

Consider the kayak. Just bones and driftwood and skin: but bones and driftwood and skin assembled with superlative intelligence, artistry and skill, so that the resultant craft is perfect for its purpose. It is exquisitely streamlined, though those who devised it had never heard of industrial design. The same may be said of every item of hunting equipment—clothing, harpoons, bird-spears, "bladder darts" and the rest. Everything is perfectly designed and beautifully fashioned; down through the ages the Greenlanders have always taken a pride in good craftsmanship.

It has been said that they are born mechanics, and a story is told of a Greenlander taking the only watch he had ever seen to pieces and putting it together again. Whether this is true or not, it might well be; for when a shrimp cannery was first opened at Christianshaab, local girls mastered the imported machines in a week.

At the Magnetic Observatory in Godhavn, two Green-landers are employed to take readings of various scientific instruments. Professor Knud Lassen, the scientist in charge, has paid tribute to their great skill. Their zeal is also remarkable. One, whose duties included the regula-tion of a master clock, became very thoughtful and worried as to who would take on that duty during an approaching period of leave. He was to be absent from Saturday to Wednesday, and it had always been impressed upon him that the clock must be wound without fail every Monday. "Don't worry," said his manager. "I'll see to that."

But the Greenlander did worry. When Saturday came round and he was saying good-bye to his colleagues, his parting words to his manager were: "Don't forget to wind the clock on Monday."

"I won't," said the manager, with a reassuring smile, and a little later, on turning over the papers on his desk, the smile broadened to a grin, for the Greenlander had also left a written injunction: "Don't forget to wind the clock on *Monday*."

After that he could hardly fail to remember. Monday came, and the clock was duly wound; the work of the Magnetic Observatory continued smoothly. But as soon as the manager returned to his home that evening, his wife thrust an envelope into his hand. It contained a further note from the Greenlander, which ran: "Did you remember to wind the clock?"

II

There is no field of endeavour in modern Greenland in which the adaptable Greenlander cannot find employ-ment. The readiness with which he took to the motor-boat is matched by his achievements in the boat-repairing and boat-building yards. In a single year at Holsteinsborg repairs and conversion work were performed on hundreds of vessels. These included five steam and motor-ships, nine schooners, 134 miscellaneous craft of all sizes and five lighters. In the same year a number of new craft were built, including a medical officer's boat, a hopper barge, two working floats and two dories. For good measure the yards carried out repairs on electrical installations, machinery and motor engines that had nothing to do with shipping.

The smaller boat-yard at Egedesminde has been equally active, building eight 22-foot motor-boats and two of 20 feet in a single year, besides carrying out a considerable amount of repair work. Another year's work included the construction of eight 22-foot motor-boats; the installation of engines in five other boats and 174 miscellaneous small and large repair jobs.

And all the time the yards are being expanded and developed. New building-sheds; new engine-testing sheds; new slipways; new repair-shops; new carpenters, blacksmiths' and machine-shops are going up everywhere to cope with the growing demand as more and more Greenlanders acquire boats of their own. Julianehaab, Frederikshaab, Godthaab, Jakobshavn and Upernavik are some of the centres where such facilities have now been provided.

Greenland's oldest industry is the mining of cryolite, a quartz-like mineral of many uses. It is also the most profitable, for the open-cast mine at Ivigtut, which has been worked for more than a century, is said to be the biggest in the world. Indeed, there are only two other known deposits, one in Colorado and the other in the Urals. Both are considerably smaller than that at Ivigtut, which has yielded nearly 1,000,000 tons since mining first began, and almost a like quantity of granite.

The yearly output at Ivigtut at the moment is 110,000 tons of ore, against 10,000 tons produced in Colorado. The mine is operated by a private company in which the Danish State owns a half interest. There is an ever-increasing demand for cryolite, and though its principal use today is in the manufacture of aluminium, it can also be employed in the production of soda, opal glass, alum and various other items. Production is kept ahead of demand. For instance, in 1952 32,000 tons of ore were shipped direct to America, 34,000 tons to Denmark and 44,000 tons were added to the stock-pile.

Opinions vary as to how long it will be before the mine is worked out. Excavations have now reached such a depth that lifts have been installed to take the miners up and down, and the workings resemble a large quarry. They can also be reached by a gradual gradient, running through a long tunnel, ore being removed by light railway which runs alongside the loading wharfs. The most pessimistic experts estimate that ten years will see the vein worked out; the most optimistic say fifteen. Meanwhile, extensive experiments and tests by diamond-drilling are being carried out all the time in the hope of locating fresh deposits.

There are about eighteen Greenlanders employed at Ivigtut, against 100 skilled Danish operatives. All work eleven hours a day, but wages are good and tax-free, and there is also free board and accommodation. Most Danes sign on for a term of five or six years, but at least one man claims to have completed twenty-five years' service.

Ten or twelve men share living quarters, and Danish girls are employed as housekeepers, meals being prepared in a central kitchen. It is the custom for everyone to come together on Sunday, when meals are served in a central mess-hall.

Danish workers may be joined by their wives and children during the summer, a round sum of 10 kroner per day being charged for their board. Applications from Danes anxious to come and work at Ivigtut pour in so briskly that today the management has a waiting list of 4,000 names!

Nearby is the Danish naval station of Gronnedal, which formerly served the Americans as an oil-base during

Danish Press Photographers' Assn.

Seal-hunters mass in their kayaks at Egedesminde. Frigate *Holger Danske* (a former British vessel, *Monnow*) acted as Royal escort throughout the tour.

Slipway at the boat-building yards of Holsteinsborg.

Danish Press Photographers' Assn.

Danish Press Photographers' Assn.

All modern aids are used in the mining of cryolite at Ivigtut.

Cryolite, used in the manufacture of aluminium, is a profitable export which helps to pay for many reforms and development schemes.

Danish Press Photographers' Assn.

the war. A reminder of the American occupation may be found in the centre of Ivigtut, where a signpost bears the legend: "Philadelphia 2,993 Miles; Copenhagen 3,452 Miles; North Pole 3,199 Miles."

As the Danish State's share of the profits from the cryolite mines is allocated to the Greenland accounts and applied exclusively to the country's development, it is hoped that the mines will continue to flourish for many years to come. Experts have been wrong before, say some, and refuse to entertain the thought that their oldest and most profitable industry may one day come to an end.

III

Open-cast coal-mining has been carried on in Greenland for the past twenty years in several places, chiefly on Disko Island, at Qutdligssat. The deposits in the latter mine are said to be very considerable, but the quality is poor and the calorific value too low to justify export. However, some 7,000 or 8,000 tons are mined yearly, and it is hoped to expand this production because it is very useful for home consumption. Compared with British household coal, though, it is very low grade, our own having nearly twice the calorific value. Indeed, the supplies are unequal to the demand, and some 8,000 tons of foreign coal are imported every year, almost wholly from Britain.

Because of this, coal-mining in Greenland is conducted at a loss. At present the cost of procuring local coal exceeds the cost of purchasing coal from the United Kingdom plus freight charges. A loss of 1,000,000 kroner was sustained in 1951–52, and at one time the authorities even entertained the idea of abandoning the industry altogether. A plan was actually worked out for transferring the miners to other districts and training them for alternative trades, but subsequent changes in the world situation have caused this plan to be shelved.

Instead, a policy of modernisation of mining methods has been initiated, with the object of cutting production

o

costs and increasing output. Meanwhile, new deposits at Atanikerdluk, to the east of the Qutdligssat, are being re-investigated. One seam has already been examined, and the quality of the coal is said to be high. Samples mined at three levels produced good-sized lumps, and the fact that no dust occurred is considered encouraging. So much so, that an agreement has been entered into with a leading firm of British mining engineers, whose expert has made a trip to Greenland to study conditions both at Qutdligssat and Atanikerdluk. It is hoped that his report may provide some basis for a long-term solution of Greenland's coal-mining problems.

Other mining activities have not been attended by much success. During the past 100 years attempts have been made to exploit finds of copper, iron ore and graphite. All have been abandoned as uneconomic because of the high costs of procuring supplies and the long distances involved in their transportation.

Yet at a meeting in Copenhagen in the summer of 1952, presided over by Mr. Erik Eriksen, Prime Minister of Denmark, Danish Government representatives, Danish industrial, commercial and banking interests, and Canadian and Swedish mining experts, decided to set up a company to extract rich mineral deposits of lead, zinc and wolfram discovered in the King Oscar Fiord region of East Greenland.

Dr. Lauge Koch, the famous explorer and scientist, was the discoverer, and the Danish Government has undertaken to make available immediately a sum of 7,500,000 kroner * (refundable when the new company is formed) to finance preparatory work and exploration.

Known as the Nordic Mining Company, Ltd., the new enterprise will have a capital of 15,000,000 kroner, divided in the following proportions: the Danish Government, 27·5 per cent; Danish Industrial, Commercial and Banking interests, 27·5 per cent; Frobishers Ltd., of

* 19·34 kroner = £1.

Canada, and the Swedish Boliden Mining Company, jointly, 45 per cent.

Investigations already carried out have revealed lead deposits of at least 400,000 tons under the ice. Further drilling is expected to confirm still larger deposits of lead, zinc and wolfram over an extensive area. In the event of further investigation establishing the possibility of large-scale exploitation of such deposits, the Company will require to increase its total capital to 100,000,000 or 150,000,000 kroner. But it is thought unlikely that regular mining operations could be commenced before about 1956. A group of 140 scientists, technicians and workers are tackling the present investigation under the chairmanship of Mr. Per Kampmann, an engineer with experience of big-scale projects in many parts of the world, who organised the preliminary probes.

IV

What of the land? No worth-while agriculture exists because it is only in the south that small patches of pasture are to be found. This is the region where early settlers sought to establish their farms; the region which, as noted in an earlier chapter, American airmen have dubbed "the Miami of the north". There is sunshine and shelter and warmth at times, certainly, but not enough to ripen crops, and the soil is poor. There are two main types of soil: one, the product of erosion and disintegration, is a mixture of sand and gravel and humus, with innumerable stones; the other boggy, with a thin peat layer much intermixed with gravel, sand and clay.

Drought is not uncommon, because the soil does not hold the moisture, and the upper layer may be dried by prevalent Föhn winds which sweep the districts. These winds blow down from the Ice Cap, and derive their warmth from the compression of the air as it drops suddenly from 10,000 feet to sea level. Round about Narsarssuaq they occasionally attain a velocity of 125 miles an hour. Observers at the base there have seen 6 inches of ice and a foot of snow vanish within three hours when the Föhn winds blow. Buildings have had to be snugly sited, and some are anchored by stout cables as an added precaution.

So far there have been no attempts at introducing an irrigation system for farmers, but something of the sort may be tried eventually. Cultivated bog areas are drained by means of open ditches, closed drains being impracticable because of the great depth to which the soil freezes.

In the main, only grass is cultivated as winter fodder for livestock—sheep, cattle, goats and Iceland ponies. Little agricultural machinery is used, except for some ploughs, harrows and sundry hand implements. Some farmers use horse-drawn mowers; but a scheme is afoot for forming a pool of tractors and other machinery on which all can draw.

Any Greenlander who wishes to take up farming may, on request, be granted permission to take over specified land without charge. The only stipulation made is that the land thus allotted must be utilised and improved within a year of taking possession. The prospective farmer must do what he can in the way of removing stones, fertilising the ground or providing drainage and fencing. If for three consecutive years he neglects to cultivate his parcel of land, he forfeits his rights. It may then be allotted to another family, or be used temporarily as a common.

Danish subjects who are not permanent residents in Greenland may receive grants of land under similar conditions—a concession to encourage pioneers in the field of agriculture.

At the moment, livestock is not numerous. There are about 100 Iceland ponies, a similar number of milch-cows and heifers, about fifty goats, 2,000 hens and some miscellaneous poultry. In the north attempts are being made to domesticate the eider-duck, but that is purely experimental.

Reindeer, once very numerous, have been greatly over-hunted, as many as 30,000 being killed in a single year. As a result, herds are thought to have been reduced to 20,000, and some experts put the present figure even lower. Hunting is still a primary pursuit in the northern districts, but in recent years the authorities have taken steps to safeguard stock—especially reindeer, foxes, walrus and eider-ducks—by applying stringent closed seasons. In general, the hunters, recognising the wisdom of these measures, have been found readily co-operative.

As reindeer meat constitutes a valuable contribution towards food supplies, a scheme is now being considered for introducing herds from Norway, though opinion is divided as to how far such an experiment would prove successful.

v

So far, sheep-breeding alone has proved of economic importance to the farmers in southern Greenland. Something like 250 families depend on it for their livelihood. Almost all the grass-grown lower mountain slopes around Julianehaab, Narssak, Frederikshaab and Igaliko are used as grazing grounds, and grass is also cultivated for winter feed. Most sheep-farmers also grow vegetables for their own consumption.

Stocks have increased from a mere 300 in 1915 to 20,000. Today's total might well have been higher but a very severe winter in the beginning of 1949, followed by a late spring and an exceptionally dry summer, reduced the then-existing flocks by half. The loss is only just being made good. To help the hard-hit sheep-farmers the Greenland Department shipped a large quantity of hay from Copenhagen and distributed it at cost price. In addition, an interest-free loan was made to sheep-farmers to enable them to meet current expenses and start building up their flocks anew.

As a result of the setback a comparative few gave up

sheep-farming and turned to fishing instead, but the majority have carried on with undiminished enthusiasm. Subsequent conditions have proved a little better. An earlier spring; milder weather; satisfactory hay-crops—all have combined to give the farmers heart. On the whole, present flocks are said to be hardy and of high quality, and this may well be because the severe season killed off the weakest animals, and only the fittest survived. In the year following the disaster flocks increased by 27 per cent.

Continuous experiments in all matters relating to sheep-breeding are conducted by the authorities at a sheep-breeding station and an experimental station where problems of agriculture and horticulture are investigated. Both these stations undertake consultative work by sending their experts to all sheep-farms and by arranging lectures and demonstrations. A trade paper is also published especially for the benefit of sheep-farmers.

It is proposed to move the sheep-breeding station from Julianehaab to a point higher up the fiord, where conditions for rational sheep-breeding are better. When this has been accomplished it will be possible to extend the scope of feeding and agricultural experiments, and a horticultural consultant will then be attached to the station, which will be organised as an actual agricultural institution.

At the moment no agricultural school exists in Greenland. When young people express a desire to enter sheep-farming they are apprenticed to the sheep-breeding station, where they receive practical and theoretical training for from three to four years. A few especially promising pupils are sent to Denmark to receive courses in practical agriculture with opportunities also of attending lessons at high schools and agricultural schools.

After young Greenlanders have served their time as apprentices at the sheep-breeding station in Julianehaab they are given every encouragement to start up on their own account. They may obtain a loan, free of interest, to enable them to build a house and pens. Their initial flock of sheep is also loaned. Once the beginner is on his feet, he returns an equivalent number of animals, which may be passed on to help some other new-comer. He is not expected to repay his cash loan until all the normal difficulties associated with starting up a farm have been successfully surmounted; then the debt is gradually liquidated by the deduction of one-third or one-fourth of any payments made to the sheep-farmer respecting products sold to the station.

In connection with the reorganisation of the station it has been suggested that the sheep-farmers might eventually take over the abattoir and cannery. For the time being, however, these are controlled by the Greenland Trading Company, though facilities are being provided for sheep-farmers to study the operation of both undertakings. As it is, net proceeds are applied for the benefit of farmers, partly by building up reserve funds and partly in the form of deferred payments to individuals in proportion to the quantities supplied by them. The eventual step to co-operative trading should, therefore, not be difficult. The greater part of production is sold to consumers in Greenland, but it is hoped one day to have an exportable surplus.

As agricultural experiments develop, attention will undoubtedly be directed to afforestation. Because of the rigorous climate, such trees as are to be found are stunted, but in some of the sheltered valleys of the southern fiords birch and willow attain a height of from 15 to 20 feet. Local people cut them for fuel, and some of the copses are quite extensive. Preliminary investigations seem to suggest that rational afforestation is possible on a small scale. The Greenland Department is now collecting material from experiments conducted in corresponding territories, particularly in Iceland. Again, there is considerable divergence of opinion between experts as to the prospect of success, but the possibility of augmenting fuel supplies, providing shelter plantations and perhaps timber, should make experiments worth while.

VI

The Greenlanders' natural manual dexterity, already referred to, finds an outlet throughout the long winter months in various forms of native craftsmanship which are not without economic importance. A traveller in Greenland sees many examples of this craftsmanship. Working in the simple materials to hand—skin, bone, wood, soapstone—the Greenlanders produce many articles of artistic value. The inhabitants of the settlement at Kangamiut, in the Sukkertoppen district, are particularly adept in carving, and farther north, in the region of Disko Bay, perfect model kayaks are offered for sale, complete with miniature sets of all the accessories—harpoons, paddles, darts and bladder-floats—all exquisitely fashioned to scale. In the north, too, are carved miniature sledges from walrus tusks, again with all the accessories and a span of huskies with harness of thongs.

Ornamental paper-knives, forks, strings of beads and the like are carved from ivory or bone; candlesticks, ashtrays, paper-weights and similar articles, often surmounted by a lifelike figure of a seal, are hewn from soapstone. Nearly everywhere along the entire west coast visitors may take their choice of sealskin bags, belts, shoes, footstools, cushions or fancy beadwork in the form of table mats, napkin rings or purses.

A special grass which grows near Cape Farewell is used by some Greenlanders in southern districts for wickerwork, and some beautiful examples of skilful plaiting are to be seen. And in the far north bird-skins, notably those of eider-duck and auk, are used for the production of cloaks, capes, rugs and tea-cosies and for a variety of other souvenirs.

In the old days Greenlanders used to bring such products to the Danish officials in their district, who would buy all they could to help the hunters through a difficult winter. Then the Society to Aid Greenland Children began to buy quantities of these home handicraft products, but it was not until 1938 that a Society for Greenland Domestic Industry came into being.

Formed with assistance from the Greenland Department, the Society's aim was to promote Greenland domestic industry and to help in the sale of the various products. At the same time, it was to provide guidance and training wherever they might be desired. The Society had barely been launched when war broke out, but in 1939 the value of novelties shipped to Denmark was more than treble the previous year's figure. The articles aroused much interest in Denmark and in other countries where the Society's products were shown at exhibitions.

From the outset the Society made it its policy to raise the quality of everything produced. All goods were specially marked in Greenland and subjected to careful scrutiny in Denmark. Detailed critical observations were compiled for the benefit of the craftsmen, calling their attention to any defects, or putting forward suggestions for improvements. The Greenlanders were further encouraged to develop their skill by a system of prize awards for especially artistic work. With the occupation of Denmark in 1940, however, this progressive programme became temporarily interrupted.

During the war, since goods could not be shipped to Denmark, the Society hit upon the idea of training Greenland men and women in the treatment of wool. At about that time sheep-farming was attaining some importance. Up to the outbreak of war increasing quantities of wool were being shipped to Denmark, but it had never been processed in Greenland, and all woollen yarns had been imported. Now it was decided to treat the home-grown wool on the spot and to introduce home weaving and knitting as already practised in the Faroe Islands.

But this, as it happened, did not involve abandonment

of existing home crafts. The coming of the Americans started a new demand for souvenirs of every kind. Before then little had been known of Greenland in the United States, and when they found that it was possible to acquire mementoes of their Arctic sojourn, the troops snapped up everything they could. Intensive production became necessary, and the Society for Greenland Domestic Industry was flooded with orders.

From its centre in the Julianehaab district it distributed products to the total value of several hundred thousand kroner. Between October 1943 and May 1944 alone its sales totalled 225,000 kroner. All the highly paid technicians and specialists employed on the construction of the big air-bases, exiled for years and with little on which to spend their money, jumped at the chance of sending back presents to the folks at home—presents of a kind never seen before from "somewhere near the North Pole".

Before this boom started there was a comparatively small stock of model kayaks, dolls and skin bags in hand. They were cleared in a flash, but, being of the highest quality, they provided their own publicity. Thereafter production, confined as it was to the winter months, could hardly keep pace with demand. The resourceful Greenlanders began to extend the range of their products. Some made excellent models of stone and earth dwellings in traditional style; and they made the roofs detachable to reveal an accurate Eskimo interior in miniature with blubber lamp and cooking utensils.

Within two years homecraft had developed into quite an industry. Quality improved with greater scope for practising skill, and a very considerable part of the population began to participate. There was a definite danger that the boom in souvenirs would tempt the hunters to neglect their hunting and fishing for the easier and bigger profits now open to them; but this was averted by confining the purchasing of homecraft products to a set season between October 1 and May 1. Goods then collected were distributed under a rationing scheme, so that the bases could be sure of stocks for the summer season.

Steps were also taken by the Society to ensure that no private person could make extra profit on the goods and that they reached the customers at the lowest possible price. A canteen operated at Julianehaab throughout the war by the U.S. Army bought the goods from the Society for cash, and then passed them on to the bases at fixed prices without profit.

Nevertheless, some active private trading did take place where some craftsmen dealt direct with ships' crews and casual visitors, or with Danes who had business links with some of the Americans.

Since the war a lot of output has been channelled through Copenhagen once more; but with a new generation of Americans taking turns of duty at the bases, a dual demand is assured. Combined totals, however, are very far below those of the boom years, the like of which will probably never be reached again.

Since the war wool-processing and working have been developed. When several Greenlanders had been given training in Denmark, some carding-machines similar to those used in Scotland were imported, with spinning-wheels, looms and knitting-machines. Greenlanders in the Julianehaab area now take courses in spinning, weaving and the production of knitted goods. Classes, which are organised by the management of the local sheep-breeding station, are always well attended, and it is more than likely that the versatile Greenlanders will prove as successful in these new fields of endeavour as they have in all the other varied enterprises they have tried.

CHAPTER XVII

THE £94,000,000 BASE

WHEN, in 1910, Dr. Knud Rasmussen founded the tiny settlement at North Star Bay and decided to christen it "Thule", it could be described quite literally as the world's end. But in that bleak solitude were men and women and children whose welfare the great explorer had at heart—the Arctic Highlanders, as they were sometimes called. In establishing an outpost of civilisation in the far north, Rasmussen was actuated by a twofold purpose. First of all he saw the need to provide a trading-post to which the Polar Greenlanders, who hunted bear, fox, narwhal and walrus in the Arctic wastes, could bring their wares for disposal. They were a forgotten few, outside the range of administration for the more populous settlements lower down the west coast. They formed the most northerly tribe in the world, with a distinctive culture of their own—a culture in which some archæologists trace the true basis of subsequent developments in other parts of Greenland. Rasmussen saw them as an important unit in the Greenlandic family, and sought to bring them into the family circle. But his vision went farther. He saw in Thule an ideal advance base from which to conduct future scientific expeditions. It was the region which lay closest to the great North American continent, whose Arctic fringe he longed to explore. And within that fringe, he felt sure, lay the key to many of the riddles propounded by the migratory Eskimos of old.

With the founding of Thule, Rasmussen became the first manager of the trading-post, assisted by Peter Freuchen, who had already accompanied him on former expeditions and who shared his enthusiasm for the new enterprise. He was answerable to a committee in Copen-

hagen, but as the man on the spot, and one who understood the Polar Greenlanders thoroughly, he had little
need to refer to anyone. Under his personal guidance
Thule developed into a flourishing outpost.

Today this little community, numbering just over 300,
thrives in its new setting. But Thule, already world-
famous for the many successful expeditions which its
celebrated founder launched from there, now finds itself
cast for an immeasurably greater fame. The establishment of Greenland's largest air-base beside the former
trading-post has transformed it, almost overnight, into a
focal point of world-wide importance.

It is said that Rasmussen himself was the first man to
realise that the vast amphitheatre in which Thule nestles
had possibilities as a site for an air-base. Not that he had
much sympathy with Arctic flyers. In his view the
coming of the aeroplane had taken much of the glamour
out of Polar discovery.

". . . from my heart," he once wrote, "I bless the fate
that allowed me to be born at a time when Arctic exploration by dog sleds was not yet a thing of the past."

As it happens, the dog-sledge is still far from being
outmoded, but in any case Rasmussen was too interested
in progress to hold back an opinion from personal pre-
judice. The story goes that the subject of Polar air-
routes cropped up in a conversation with Colonel Bernt
Balchen in 1927, and Rasmussen instantly suggested
Thule as an ideal site for an airfield.

This suggestion, apparently, stuck in Balchen's
memory. An airstrip was indeed established at Thule
during the Second World War, and subsequently, when
the development of Polar air-routes assumed new
urgency, he again remembered Thule, and knew that the
site was capable of infinitely greater exploitation.

In conferences with United States Air Secretary
Thomas Finletter and Lieutenant-General Lewis A. Pick,
Chief of the Corps of Engineers, and others, it was

decided that the Thule plan was not only feasible, but also desirable. The cold war was a reality that had to be faced; and no one could guarantee that it would not develop into a far more hideous reality. The best insurance seemed to be preparedness and strength—everywhere.

A great chain of Arctic air-bases had already been established, but there were gaps; and the biggest gap lay in North Greenland. A base at Thule would help to close it.

II

The story of how the dream of a base at Thule was translated into reality is as fantastic as any Eskimo legend. At the beginning of 1951 there was little to be found there apart from the small trading-post, a weather-station and a small one-way airstrip left over from the Second World War. Today there are miles of broad runways which are already being used by giant modern planes and the fastest jet-interceptors. There are steam-heated hangars, rows of administrative buildings and hutments, factories, workshops and most of the essential amenities associated with a modern airport.

The creation of such a base within the brief space of about eighteen months can justifiably be described as a miracle of achievement; yet during its construction it was treated as a secret operation, cloaked in all communications by the code-name "Blue Jay", and the precise site was not officially disclosed to the world until the autumn of 1952.

Perhaps the hush-hush atmosphere was unnecessary melodrama; but it must be remembered that world tension and the unending "cold war" tended to breed suspicion and caution. Rumours that Soviet Russia was busily occupied in building a similar sort of base in Franz Josef Land all helped to engender a mood of secrecy. Even now many details have not been divulged, though carefully screened Press delegates were permitted to visit the base for a conducted tour of inspection in September 1952.

Most of the delegates were astonished by what they were allowed to see, and all marvelled at the incredible amount of construction work that had been accomplished in so short a time and in the face of so many obstacles. Certainly the project could not have been tackled with greater despatch had it been an actual war operation. Indeed, from first to last it was organised and carried through with a determined massing of all possible resources, and backed by experience gained in establishing the war-time bases in Greenland. Lessons of amphibious campaigns and of the fabulous Berlin airlift were likewise of considerable value to the planners.

The Thule project opened in the spring of 1951 with the arrival of an airborne task force of about 600 picked men, whose miscellaneous gear and equipment included a 29,000-lb. mechanical excavator. This vanguard of "shock troops" had to start work immediately to clear the ground for the main body of 7,500 specially recruited workers who followed in a convoy of nearly fifty ships some three months later.

These workers had been recruited in secret at Rosemount, a suburb of St. Paul, Minnesota. Until they received definite sailing orders they were paid $4 a day as stand-by money to ensure that they would not sign on elsewhere. Full pay, in some cases as much as $1,500 a month, started once they were safely on board. The total stand-by bill was estimated at about £113,000, and something like £1,140,000 had been paid out in wages before any actual construction work had been done.

An immense amount of staff work had to be performed, and according to the pre-arranged time-table the main body should have arrived at Thule on June 23. But, as so many travellers to Greenland have found to their cost, local weather conditions can upset the most carefully calculated plans. The convoy ran into a belt of pack-ice which delayed it for seventeen days. Even when the ships got through and made anchorage in North Star Bay, the ice continued to take its toll. Damage was caused repeatedly to ships' propellers, entailing something like 250 replacements.

Still, the objective had been reached, and at least there were only the elements to be faced and no enemy forces to repel landing operations. A Beachmaster quickly set up his control post on the bleak shore; landing-craft nosed their way in; streams of ducks, trucks, jeeps, mobile cranes, bulldozers and giant rollers poured ashore in orderly columns, while armies of technicians, civilian workers of various construction firms, and naval, military and air-force personnel filed after them.

There was a great deal to be done and very little time in which to accomplish it before winter darkness and below-zero temperatures set in. It was absolutely essential to get the convoy out of North Star Bay by September, or it would be trapped in the ice. Those seventeen lost days were a nightmare to the planners.

The vanguard had literally moved mountains by this time, and the beginnings of a runway were being worked over by earth-movers preparatory to being covered with layers of crushed stones. An unexpected obstacle known as permafrost threatened to hold up work. Ground 4 feet below the surface which at first sight seemed rock-hard proved, on closer acquaintance, to be frozen earth, liable to thaw under the warmth of buildings erected over it, thus causing sinkage of foundations.

A solution to this problem was found by placing all the lighter buildings on wooden stilts, to provide insulation. Heavier buildings, such as machine-shops and hangars, called for other treatment, and it was found necessary, in addition to using wooden piles for the foundations, to insulate flooring from the ground with hollow 12-inch pipes. These had to be closed in summer to keep the warm air out, and opened in winter to let the cold air in.

As these and other difficulties were surmounted, many of the workers must have realised that the recruiting

GREENLAND'S BIG THREE.

Mr. Eske Brun, Chief of the Greenland Department, who remained at the helm through the war years when Greenland was cut off from Denmark.

Landshøvding P. H. Lundsteen, Governor of Greenland, assumed his present post in 1950, and has a firm faith in Greenland's future.

: Rear-Admiral F. A. H. Kjølsen, Royal Danish Navy, Chief of the Greenland mand under the North Atlantic Treaty agreement for the country's defence.

Vagn Hansen   *Jette Ban*

Godthaab Broadcasting Station was opened in 1942, and provides a complet
service of news, talks, plays, music and outside broadcasts. The printing-press ha
functioned since 1861 and has developed into an up-to-date and flourishin
enterprise.

Jette Bang   *Jette Ba*

Greenlanders are avid readers, and two students are here shown in the co
tinuation-school library at Egedesminde.
Right: A geography lesson for young Greenlanders in the school at Sukkertoppe

officials back in the States had not exaggerated in telling them that they were bound for a very remote spot, where conditions generally would be tougher than anything they were likely to have encountered elsewhere.

They must also have realised why they had been given such a careful screening, why their medical and dental overhaul had been so exacting, and why they had been given mental and aptitude tests before departure. Most of them were veterans from big construction jobs in many parts of the world. Rates of pay were as generous as the stand-by pay, to prevent them from signing on elsewhere while waiting for sailing orders.

In the early stages, before hutments had been erected, the men lived on the ships that had brought them to Thule. Some landing-craft were sunk to serve as piers in the first instance until a permanent jetty, 1,000 feet long, could be built.

Floating pipe-lines carried fuel ashore to temporary storage tanks until naval frogmen were able to install an underwater system. Dynamite was used to split the larger icebergs which threatened to block the anchorage, and some bergs were towed out to sea. Ice that packed round the branch piers, thus hindering the approach of small craft, was attacked successfully with a twin-jet steampipe.

By working ten hours a day for seven days a week, the construction teams made rapid progress—so rapid that workmen jestingly said that it took some moments each morning to get one's bearings because so many new structures seemed to spring up overnight.

When, in September, the bulk of the men had to be withdrawn, a great amount had been achieved. Four hundred maintenance men were left behind to man the base throughout the cheerless winter; but they remained with a good heart, sustained by the triumph of seeing the first plane—a big four-engined transport—take off from the virgin runway. The date of that epic event was

P

September 11—just six months after the arrival of the first airborne task force.

III

In the spring the main body was back again, and Thule roused from its winter calm to renewed activity. And now the airlift increased to support the developing battle of the build-up. More and more material poured in, until the vast amphitheatre, backed by the snow-streaked mountains, became crowded with dumps of stores and equipment of every conceivable kind. The derricks of mobile cranes rose up like masts among a sprawling sea of crates, barrels, girders, lengths of piping, and stacks of metal plates and corrugated iron. And ever plying backwards and forwards were fleets of miscellaneous vehicles: more trucks, rollers, jeeps; more bulldozers and automatic shovels; more tipping trucks and water-carts; big six-wheel lorries and humble station wagons—everything, in fact, ever devised to run on wheels or crawl on caterpillar tracks.

Through all this maze ran twin giant snakes—surface pipes carrying oil and steam—master weapons in the great construction war. In places, too, lesser snakes linked the new buildings as they sprang into being: cables to give hand-hold for workmen making for shelter in high winds —winds which sometimes reached 150 miles an hour.

Steadily, as the various construction teams went into action, the mixed mass of gear and equipment and material was transformed into huts and hangars and storehouses. To ensure a proper water supply, the largest saltwater distilling plant in the world was erected; but water could not be piped to individual huts because of the intense cold, so delivery by tank-trucks had to be arranged.

All the crews who flew on the intensified airlift were given special Arctic-survival drill back in America, being made to spend four consecutive days living under

Arctic conditions with nothing but the emergency equipment they would normally carry by plane.

By the end of the summer of 1952, when the new base was named officially for the first time, transport planes had flown more than 2,000 round trips. Between them they had delivered some 12,500 tons of cargo. Interviewed at that time, Major-General James W. Spry, commander of the Atlantic Division of the United States Air Force Military Transport Division, described that cargo as ranging from small packages to a ten-ton radar set, and added that 19,000 passengers had been carried to and from Thule since the project was first launched in March 1950. In all that time there were only two mishaps; no one was badly hurt and both aircraft involved had been repaired.

In addition, the Military Air Transport Service, flying by way of Westover, Massachusetts, Goose Bay, Labrador, and Bluie West 1, Greenland, or Frobisher, Baffin Island, carried 26,000 tons of supplies, equipment, food and other materials to Thule. To these gigantic airlifts must be added 280,000 tons of equipment brought by sea.

Finishing touches have still to be added, but already the new base, which covers 90,000 acres, presents a wonderful spectacle, and is a tribute to the zeal and skill of the men who created it. Some idea of that zeal is given by the fact that one construction team engaged in erecting huge fuel-storage tanks fixed a "one-tank-a-day" target for itself and actually hit this target, to the amazement even of some veteran contractors who declared them to be "supermen".

Two heavy maintenance hangars, capable of housing the largest planes while being serviced and repaired, were actually ready for use by the end of the first year. Four more are under construction, and will certainly be completed long before this book appears. All are steam-heated, as are the living quarters, where the workmen share two-bunk cubicles.

A 1,200-foot radio mast towers above the base, and there is now a port, capable of handling 11,000-ton ships. There are two 2-mile runways to replace the modest one-way strip of yesterday, and, of course, all the latest navigational devices have been installed.

IV

Although the construction of the Thule air-base has been described, with every justification, as one of the toughest engineering feats ever accomplished, and the men engaged upon the task had to endure conditions which, in the words of Lieutenant-General Lewis A. Pick, Chief of the Corps of Engineers, were "beyond anything ever encountered in construction", their health and morale were excellent.

Maintenance and construction teams left to carry on through the dark winter found it necessary to work in short spells of an hour or two because of the intense cold. Cold-storage lockers for meat had to be heated to their normal 10 degrees, and the motors of any vehicles in use had to be kept running continuously. But the cold and the wind and the darkness and isolation had to be faced, and there was surprisingly little sickness. Accidents, too, were not numerous, in view of the nature of the work.

One medical officer has been quoted as dubbing Thule "the healthiest place in the world", and it is recorded that nearly all the workers—no weaklings in the first place— registered a noticeable improvement in health there. Appetites increased enormously, making a liberal diet necessary.

Recreational facilities of varying kinds were provided as early as possible, and continue to develop. There are libraries, games rooms, hobbies rooms and a gymnasium; a bar known as "Guffey's Tavern", and facilities for learning arts and crafts or for studying. Numerous jazz bands have been formed by the musically inclined, and a cyclostyled newspaper, known as *Polar Post*, keeps the workers well informed on all that is happening in Thule.

Inevitably, the Americans working in the frozen fastness of Thule were not long in devising a local cocktail. Known as an "Ice Cap", it consists of a liberal four fingers of whisky blended with crushed glacial ice, which is said to effervesce on contact with the warm spirit. A taste for Nature's ready-made article is common to all the Greenland bases, and a legend over the bar at Narsarssuaq reads: "We serve million-year-old ice in our drinks!"

v

Long before the existence of the Thule air-base was officially disclosed, its broad runways were already proving their worth. Royal Air Force machines enjoy landing facilities while flying their special missions to drop supplies to men of the British North Greenland Expedition. Indeed, without these facilities their task would be doubly difficult. When a Hastings transport machine crashed in the middle of the Ice Cap in 1952, the rescue of her crew was made possible only by the existence of the Thule base, which enabled suitable rescue planes to be flown from America.

Throughout the summer of 1953, too, Hastings aircraft, flying from Britain, used Thule as a base for supply missions to both "Northice" and to points some 220 miles west.

Thule may still be literally the world's end, but thanks to the regular airlift, the exiled workers there have tangible contact with their homes. With planes coming and going all the time, it is even possible to send laundry back to the States regularly—a valuable consideration when every drop of water at the base has to be husbanded carefully.

But, notwithstanding the many unexpected amenities which have been provided in an attempt to lighten the lonely lot of the workers at Thule, nothing can disguise the fact that their assignment must rank as one of the toughest construction jobs ever undertaken.

Was it worth it? Worth it or not, the job is done. Thule air-base is an accomplished fact. Already the biggest modern passenger planes and the fastest jet-fighters have used its runways; and those who believe in the future of Polar air-routes in civil aviation say that Thule may well become one of the busiest air junctions in the world.

CHAPTER XVIII

TWO BRITISH EFFORTS

In the post-war resumption of scientific investigation in Greenland, two British expeditions have been launched. Though differing in character and purpose, their combined efforts form part of Greenland's story, and they merit a chapter to themselves.

The first, led by Dr. H. I. Drever, Lecturer in Geology at St. Andrew's University, was known as the British Expedition to West Greenland. Drever, who had conducted two previous expeditions before the war, conceived the idea of this new project in 1947, and, with backing from St. Andrew's University and the Carnegie Trust for the Universities of Scotland and from the Royal Society, London, he set off in June 1950 with a small party of five.

His companions included P. J. Wyllie, glaciologist; N. S. Tennent, photographer; T. J. Ransley, surveyor; W. S. Mackenzie and C. G. M. Slesser.

From Copenhagen they proceeded in the Greenland Trading Company's vessel, *Disko*, as far as Jacobshavn, where they transhipped to a new ice-ship *Tikerak*, which, in turn, took them as far as Umanak. There they boarded the coastal schooner, *Hvidfisken*, which bore them 80 miles northward to the little outstation of Nugatsiak, where they established their main base on July 23.

There was little in Nugatsiak but a handful of houses, a store and a jetty, and three rowing-boats. But they acquired the best of the three boats, a 16-footer, fitted an outboard motor, and prepared to explore two large glaciers, Umiamako and Rinks Glaciers, 20 and 40 miles to the east, respectively. Both glaciers were reported to be dispersing fast, so on-the-spot scientific investigations were planned.

Four Greenlanders, one with his kayak, were recruited to bring the party up to ten, and it was decided to tackle the more formidable Rinks Glacier first. They left their base camp at the end of July, and by August 2 were camping some 30 feet above sea level. Their rations were supplemented with fresh meat in the form of seals or gulls. Good progress was made, and by August 20 they had reached an altitude of 7,000 feet. By this time, however, Drever and Mackenzie had detached themselves from the party in order to keep a rendezvous with a Danish expedition under Professor Rosenkrantz, with whom it was hoped to co-operate on certain geological work.

Tennent, Slesser and Ransley, as mountaineers of the party, completed their glaciological work, and then tackled some peaks on Upernavik Island. Dr. Drever went on to Ubekendt Island to complete certain geological work he had commenced during earlier visits to Greenland; Wyllie carried out a geological survey on Qingussaq Island, and Mackenzie, working with Mr. Hans Pauli, second in command of the Danish expedition, surveyed some 320 miles of coastline.

Summing up the work of his party after their return in October, Dr. Drever declared that they had been "incredibly lucky", although the glaciological trip to Rinks Glacier had been seriously handicapped by thirteen days of bad weather—the only bad weather in a six weeks' programme. Tennent fractured his knee on his descent to the Rinks Glacier, but was nevertheless able to bring back a useful series of panoramic photographs, many of them in colour. Copies of these photographs were made available to the Danish geologists. All planned geological work was completed, but the outstanding feature, according to Drever, was "the amount and harmony of the co-operation between Danish and British personnel. Without such co-operation we should, indeed, have achieved much less".

This harmony and mutual regard have always existed

between Danish and British scientific explorers. Every-one who has ever participated in Greenland expeditions, small or large, speaks with feeling of the help and hospitality showered upon them by the Danes; while no less an authority than Count Eigil Knuth, writing of the British explorer, has this tribute to make: "We owe him a debt of gratitude as to Greenland." And he points out that the world is indebted to no fewer than three English-men for descriptions of first meetings between Eskimos and White men in three places in Greenland, thousands of miles apart—John Davis in 1585, Clavering in 1823 and Ross in 1829. John Ross, he also reminds us, was the first explorer to use dog-sledges and to employ Eskimo travel technique.

II

The second post-war effort by British explorers, the British North Greenland Expedition, is more familiarly known as the "Simpson Expedition" after its leader, Lieutenant-Commander C. J. W. Simpson, R.N. A bigger, more ambitious venture than the West Greenland Expedition, it is privately sponsored with the approval of the Royal Society, the Polar Institute and the Royal Geographical Society. It also enjoys the very considerable support of the Royal Navy and the Royal Air Force; and Simpson has paid high tribute to the great amount of kindly help, "official and unofficial", received from the Danes.

In a projected two-year sojourn upon the Ice Cap it is hoped to add very appreciably to the store of geological, glaciological, meteorological and biological knowledge already amassed by Greenland explorers of all nations. It is also intended to try out various new types of Arctic clothing and equipment and to carry out extensive experi-ments in the technique of dropping supplies and equip-ment from the air. In addition to making drops by para-chute in the traditional manner, a comparatively new technique of free-dropping, in which the French have already experimented, is being tried. For this latter manœuvre the transport planes fly as low as practicable and the supplies, specially crated, are tumbled out one after the other to be retrieved from the snow by the waiting explorers. This method is less costly than the old idea of employing multiple parachutes, but a certain amount of wastage is involved where articles are damaged on impact or become lost in snow-drifts. But it is only by practical experiment that ideas about the most suitable method of crating can be perfected. Early misadventures have already pointed to the folly of putting all eggs into one basket. For example, a lost crate of ball-bearings may render useless a dozen safely retrieved cases of windmill machinery for which the bearings are essential.

There are also attendant dangers in flying low over a vast snow-covered terrain. A phenomenon, known to Arctic flyers as a "white-out", can perplex even the most experienced pilots, who suddenly find that snow and sky have merged, with no visible horizon and no visible landmark. One reason why the Navy and the Royal Air Force have given support to the Simpson Expedition is that it presents them with an excellent opportunity for practical flying over Arctic terrain.

III

Nearly a year before the main expedition left Britain, Commander Simpson, with three colleagues—Captain M. E. B. Banks, R.M., Lieutenant F. R. Brooke, R.N., and Lieutenant Angus Erskine, R.N., flew to Greenland in a Coastal Command Sunderland flying-boat to carry out a preliminary survey.

Set down off the north-east coast, the advance guard of four ferried themselves ashore in a collapsible dinghy to keep a pre-arranged rendezvous with a Danish trapper. They then pushed inland over the rough ice, taking two days to cover the first 20 miles. Eventually they reached an unnamed lake which Simpson had spotted from the air when flying northwards with members of the Pearyland Expedition in the previous year. It had struck him then that it might yield a satisfactory anchorage for a flying-boat, and this was now confirmed.

The party struggled onwards and upwards to a point 6,000 feet above sea level. The ice stretched away to the west in a seemingly limitless expanse. There was no sign of life except for occasional polar-bear prints in the snow.

For four weeks Simpson and his companions dwelt in the icy wastes, gathering data and making plans for the main expedition that was to be launched in the following year. Then they made their way back to their original base, where they were picked up again by the Sunderland, piloted by Wing-Commander G. G. N. Barrett.

The return flight to England was accomplished without incident. Some plants and geological specimens were brought back for the benefit of the scientists at home, and it was announced that the advance guard had accomplished everything it had set out to do.

IV

In the following months preparations went forward for the main expedition. The first contribution towards the funds was £1,000 from Sir Winston Churchill out of the Sonning Prize that had recently been awarded to him in Denmark for furthering Anglo-Danish scientific interests. Twenty-five members were recruited, including five Army officers and N.C.Os., seven naval officers and petty officers, two Merchant Navy officers, ten scientists and a Captain from the Danish Army.

By July 2, 1952, all was ready, and on that day Her Majesty Queen Elizabeth inspected the men and their equipment on board the Norwegian sealer *Tottan* at Tower Pier, the men parading in their Arctic kit.

The Queen was received by Admiral of the Fleet Sir Algernon Willis, chairman of the Expedition committee, and by Lord Waverley, chairman of the Port of London Authority. The Bishop of Portsmouth conducted a short service of dedication, in which Her Majesty took part.

Commander Simpson finally sailed from Deptford on July 8 with an encouraging send-off in the following message from the Expedition's vice-patron, Sir Winston Churchill:

"I would not like you and the members of the British North Greenland Expedition to leave our shores without sending you my best wishes for your well-being and success in the adventures and experiences which you are facing in the Arctic. You and the young men who are with you have embarked on a daring mission. The conception and purpose of your enterprise will appeal to the hearts of your countrymen. My thoughts will be with you all and I shall follow your reports and deeds with the closest interest. As vice-patron of your Expedition I am proud to be associated with you all and to wish you God-speed and a safe and fruitful return."

After *Tottan* had called at Ivigtut, on the west coast of Greenland, to pick up three teams of sledge-dogs which had been trained during the winter, she visited Reykjavik, Iceland, to take on fresh provisions and some additional stores. Her cargo totalled about 260 tons, but even this did not include sufficient for the expedition's first-year requirements. Much additional material had to be shipped separately to Iceland to be picked up later by *Tottan* in a second trip.

The pack-ice was negotiated without undue difficulty, though sometimes members of the expedition were able to leave the ship and stretch their legs upon the ice. Young Sound was reached on July 27, and the ship anchored close inshore at Zackenberg, where the Danish Pearyland Expedition had established a temporary base two years before.

A camp site was now chosen, and unloading was soon

commenced with the aid of four Army pontoons and two small motor-boats. The "weasels"—amphibious track vehicles for use on the Ice Cap—waddled ashore under their own power. Everything was ashore within four days, stacked in orderly piles on the beach, two R.A.F. Sunderland flying-boats having arrived in the meantime with extra man-power to lend a hand.

On August 5 Commander Simpson flew to Britannia Lake with Squadron-Leader Higgins, commander of the Sunderland Squadron, and a few days later a Coastal Command Lancaster from a base in Cornwall flew over the lake and dropped a lifeboat by parachute. Unfortunately, one of the parachutes failed to open, and the boat was badly damaged by the impact. Commander Simpson and two companions set out at once in a small outboard motor-boat to retrieve the damaged lifeboat, but rough water capsized their own craft. They were able to swim to the wrecked lifeboat, and were finally rescued by a Sunderland captain, Flight-Lieutenant C. M. Stavert, who skilfully manœuvred his aircraft alongside. Lines were thrown to them, and with some difficulty the three men succeeded in hauling themselves aboard the flying-boat. This first mishap thus ended without disastrous consequences, though the lifeboat had to be written off.

A far more serious mishap occurred at the end of the following month when a four-engined Hastings aircraft of R.A.F. Transport Command crashed while dropping supplies to a unit of the expedition then established in a camp at 78·02° north and 37·50° west. Two members of the crew of twelve were injured, and as the machine was too badly damaged to be flown off, all took shelter within the fuselage. They had fuel and food calculated to last them for ten days, but rescue plans were made immediately news of the crash was received.

The Hastings had taken off from Topcliffe, Yorkshire, three weeks previously, and had been engaged in ferrying prefabricated huts and miscellaneous stores from the air-

base at Thule to the men on the Ice Cap. Now its crew
shared the plight of the men they had been sent to
succour.

Their adventure monopolised the headlines in the world
Press for many days, during which hypothetical rescue
plans were discussed. While it was possible to drop
comforts in the form of sleeping-bags, extra clothing and
food, the task of taking them off the Ice Cap presented
many difficulties. It was suggested that a big helicopter
might be flown from America; that an existing plan to
move "weasels" to that area might be speeded up; that
dog-sledge teams should be sent at once to bring the
marooned flyers to a point where a ski-plane could land.

They were 350 miles from the British base at Britannia
Lake and 480 miles from Thule. By September 23 bad
weather was still holding up rescue plans, though six
planes were now standing by at Thule. It was announced
that a Grumman Albatross amphibian machine with
rocket-assisted take-off would attempt to land on the Ice
Cap, as close to the stranded men as possible. Meanwhile,
the men themselves, who had been marooned for nearly a
week, prepared a short runway.

Then the weather cleared a little, and the big amphibian
made a daring bid to rescue the injured men. Put down
deliberately close to the scene, it lumbered crazily to a
stop, snow and ice spurting in showers in its wake. The
able survivors of the Hastings crew rushed their injured
comrades to the rescue plane, but though they were safely
installed within a matter of minutes, the amphibian was
already beginning to freeze fast to the Ice Cap. The nine
remaining men worked feverishly to free it; then, thanks
to the rocket-assisted take-off, the machine heaved itself
clear. For some breath-taking moments it floundered un-
steadily, then with increasing momentum it ploughed
forward and, to the relief of everyone, became airborne
once more.

While the problem of getting the nine remaining men

off the Ice Cap still awaited solution, efforts to sustain them were made successfully by a second Hastings aircraft, which, flying from Thule, dropped five consignments of supplies by parachute.

By a happy chance, that experienced Greenland flyer, Colonel Bernt Balchen, of the United States Air Force, happened to be in Thule, and, under his direction, a rescue plan was now organised. Three days after the wounded men had been brought back safely to Thule, a Dakota, specially fitted with skis and with jet take-off equipment, set off from this new base with two other machines—one to provide navigational aid, the other to act as path-finder and to give direction guidance from a point midway between Thule and the scene of the crash.

This aerial cavalcade took off from Thule at 8.35 a.m. on September 26, and the ski-plane touched down beside the wrecked Hastings three hours later. The Dakota remained on the Ice Cap for an hour and a half while preparations were made for the difficult take-off; then, with all nine men aboard, it skimmed along the improvised runway and took to the air again. The return flight to Thule was accomplished without incident, the rescued men being little the worse for their eleven-day ordeal.

In a message of thanks to General Vandenberg, Chief of Staff, United States Air Force, Sir John Slessor, Marshal of the Royal Air Force, said:

"I am most grateful for your whole-hearted co-operation in the rescue. All here are much relieved at the news and I would particularly like to thank the commanding General North-East Air Command and the Sixth Air Rescue Squadron for making this possible."

The pilot of the rescuing Dakota was Captain F. O. Burnett, and with his co-pilot, First-Lieutenant Hale, he spent three days studying and conferring before attempting the flight. Because of the limited range of their aircraft, they had to carry two fifty-gallon drums of high octane petrol for the return journey, besides the jet-assisted take-off equipment. Two of the aircraft used in the rescue had to be brought from a base in St. Johns, Newfoundland, 2,000 miles away from Thule.

Within a week of their rescue the Hastings crew flew back to Britain via Iceland, and the world came to learn something of their experiences on the Ice Cap; how they had made their home in the fuselage of the wrecked machine, insulating it with parachutes to render it habitable; how they had curtained off a part of the fuselage to make the three wounded men as comfortable as possible.

According to Flight-Lieutenant Michael Clancy, captain of the crashed plane, no one slept much the first night, for the temperature was 17 degrees below zero and there was a wind of 20 knots. But after the second day dropping of comforts and supplies helped considerably, and the fact that mail also reached the stranded men kept morale high. On the last day on the Ice Cap one man received a batch of eight letters.

Commander Simpson, whose advance camp was then about a mile away from the scene, was able to visit the men, and on their first Sunday conducted a simple service within the fuselage so that the injured men could participate. And long after all the men had been rescued that same fuselage came in useful as a storehouse and workshop for the expedition while a base hut was under construction.

v

The building of this hut took about three weeks, but during this time Commander Simpson and five companions who were with him on the Ice Cap were also kept busily occupied in collecting the miscellaneous stores which were being dropped daily by the R.A.F.

It was decided to christen this new station "Northice", to distinguish it from the "Eismitte" (Middle-Ice) station set up by Alfred Wegener. The hut was erected about 70 yards from the wrecked Hastings. It was furnished

Vagn Hansen

Thule folk still favour Eskimo-style turf-and-stone huts for winter dwellings, though they now line them with wood.

for the local store to open. Shopping for Thule's 133 inhabitants is confined to Wednesday and Saturday afternoons.

Vagn Hansen

Ships of America's Military Sea Transport Service nose their way through the ice near Thule with construction supplies for the Polar air-base. *Inset:* Lt.-General Lewis A. Pick (*right*), Chief of the Corps of Engineers, who supervised the construction of the base, and (*below*) Men of the U.S. Corps of Engineers prepare to unload vehicles needed for their mammoth task.

and equipped with bunks, benches, tables, an oil heater and a calor gas-cooker with the idea of providing a permanent crew of three or four scientists with essential needs.

Various setbacks were inevitably encountered. For instance, a petrol generator set was damaged by the drop. Fortunately, however, a spare had been provided, and this was retrieved safely from a snowdrift. For a time, too, the sledge-dogs were in poor condition, but a policy of allowing most of them to run free round the camp gradually brought them back into working trim.

On October 18, Graham Collitt, the meteorologist, was left in charge of "Northice" with two companions, while the others started on the 230-mile sledge journey back to Britannia Lake. After travelling for seven days and making about 20 miles a day, this sledge party, under Commander Simpson, sighted the mountain crests of Queen Louise Land, some 60 miles ahead. Two days later they reached a cache they had established on their outward journey on a small rocky outcrop on the fringe of the Ice Cap, 20 miles from land. Here they retrieved spare food and clothing before pushing on towards a prominent cliff to the north, where they now cached all spare food and fuel for the benefit of sledge parties due to start work in the following spring.

Now they found that ground which had been snow-covered on their outward trip had been stripped by fierce winds and had become a treacherous surface of hard blue ice. The area was also criss-crossed with crevasses, and a following gale made it difficult to control the sledges. So great was the strain on the brake-claws that the teeth broke, and the sledges often over-ran the dogs, who could gain little purchase on the slippery ice. But at last the Ice Cap was left behind; the wind dropped, and from a camp on smooth snow beside a glacier, radio contact was established with the base at Britannia Lake, 8 miles away. On the following morning men from the base came up to help in man-handling the sledges over the tongue of the

Q

glacier, and soon they were in the home stretch. In their absence the base hut had been completed. It was to be their "home" until work could be resumed in the following spring.

VI

In the last weeks of December another party of six, led by Captain J. D. Walker, R.E., set off with the "weasel" tractors for Danmarks Havn, where they were to be laid up for the winter under the care of two maintenance men, Sergeant S. Boardman and Sergeant J. Oakley. The problem of getting the party back to Britannia Lake after their mission had been fulfilled was aggravated by the lateness of the season, and it was decided that dog-sledge offered the best prospect.

Accordingly, Commander Simpson, with P. Wyllie, Surgeon-Lieutenant J. P. Masterson and Chief Officer E. O. Jones, Merchant Navy, set off with two sledges, each pulled by an eight-dog team. There was exceptionally difficult terrain ahead which, so far as they knew, had never before been crossed by dog-sledge at this time of year, and about five hours of twilight was all they could hope for each day.

That old enemy of all explorers, the wind from the Ice Cap, pinned them in their sleeping-bags on the second day out, but after this enforced inaction progress was made until they found themselves on the Storstrom glacier. This barrier between Queen Louise Land and the coast consists of ridges and hummocks, some 4 feet high and difficult to negotiate. It took them seven days to cross this frozen, irregular mass, an exhausting endurance test for both men and dogs. Even though, with forty degrees of frost, the natural inclination was to keep moving, it was necessary to make frequent pauses for rest. The weather, at least, was now clear and windless, but the going was so rough that it was only possible to average about 5 miles a day.

Time was lost, too, in stopping at intervals to repair one of the sledges which had suffered as a result of its severe buffetings. With much reluctance the party found themselves forced to jettison some of their stores and gear in order to lighten their loads. In this way they reached Seal Lake with the damaged sledge still in service, though so patched and spliced that, according to Commander Simpson, it looked "like a bosun's nightmare".

Now, in pleasing contrast, they were able to skim over the frozen surface of the lake, the dogs no less delighted than their masters by the easy going. On the eleventh day after their departure from their base they reached Walrus Point, where they enjoyed the shelter of a trapper's hut for three days while giving their sledges a more thorough overhaul than had been possible on the run. The Danes also provided them with a third sledge and dog-team, and Captain Walker and the three men who were due to return with them to Britannia Lake brought the party's strength up to ten.

For the first leg of the return journey they had the advantage of "weasel" tractors to carry all baggage, so the dogs, with only light sledges to pull for the initial 35 miles, were kept in fresh condition for the more formidable laps ahead. The party camped for the first night beside the Storstrom glacier, while Boardman and Oakley bade them farewell and departed in their tractors for Danmarks Havn.

In the opinion of Commander Simpson, the second crossing of the glacier was decidedly worse than the first. When they were about three-quarters of the way across, one of their sledges disintegrated beyond repair, while a second showed such signs of wear and tear as to leave little hope that it could survive much longer. As much as possible was loaded on to the one sound sledge, but, as on the outward journey, it was necessary to abandon a quantity of food and stores.

Then the sledgers found themselves in an area of ice

hummocks far worse than anything they had encountered before, with gullies 50 feet deep running across their path. Six men were required to man-handle each sledge up the icy slopes. After seven days of this sort of thing the going began to show signs of improvement, but suddenly they came to a steep cliff, to avoid which an uninvitingly long detour would have been necessary. A roped cliff descent had to be improvised, with all the ice-axes, tent-pegs and cordage that could be mustered. It took an hour or more to lower the dogs, sledges, baggage and men to the surface of the lake below.

After the lake had been crossed, most of the gear was cached, and the party completed the final stage of their return journey with light sledges, and without further trouble.

VII

It is too early to attempt to sum up the achievements of the British North Greenland Expedition, for some time must inevitably elapse before the full fruits of its scientific work at the "Northice" station, and elsewhere upon the vast face of the Ice Cap, become known.

Nevertheless, the volume of spade-work accomplished in the first year is impressive. Thanks to the airlift provided by the Services, a remarkable concentration of masses of complicated equipment and supplies of all kinds has been achieved in record time. Today, with a firmly established base and the Ice Cap station in service, the scientists of the party are free to pursue their researches under conditions never available before.

CHAPTER XIX

STRATEGIC ISLAND No. 1

GREENLAND's importance in global strategy has long been recognised, and in the Second World War the practical value of its bases and weather-stations was amply demonstrated. Germany, as we have seen, was very quick off the mark in securing a foothold at several points on the sparsely populated east coast, where her weather experts lost no time in setting up stations from which to transmit information calculated to be of value both to the Luftwaffe and to U-boat commanders. But they were no more than footholds, and the weather men were speedily ejected. The Allies were soon receiving their own meteorological information from Greenland stations which, in turn, were protected and serviced by the newly established west-coast bases, while bombers and fighters were ferried regularly to Europe by way of the base at Narsarssuaq.

Three factors combine to give Greenland its unique strategical importance—size, situation and weather.

Even during the presidency of Abraham Lincoln, the first two factors were noted by his Secretary of State, William Henry Seward, who, thinking globally, had far-seeing ideas about strategic defence. He was instrumental in bringing about the purchase of Alaska from Russia, and he also held that possession of Greenland was equally desirable. What Seward wanted was domination of both the Pacific and the North Atlantic by America; but today, under NATO, the defence of Greenland is the concern of all member nations. Moreover, the third factor, weather, is regarded as most important of all.

Those who know today's weather in Greenland are said to hold the key to tomorrow's weather in the North

Atlantic and in north-east Europe. In his report on the Pearyland Expedition of 1947–50, Count Eigil Knuth, the leader, placed meteorological research as first in practical importance in the scientists' programme.

"On April 22 and 23, 1950," he declared, "London experienced a heavy fall of snow which caused severe damage and traffic breakdown. The freak weather extended to the Mediterranean, where blossom on fruit trees was damaged. It was attributed to currents of cold air from north-east Greenland, and whether or not there was anything in this belief it is certain that to increase the reliability of European weather forecasts we must investigate the influence of the cold regions of the north, the Greenland Ice Cap and the Polar Basin. Our station at Bronlunds Fiord, close to the latter region, was able to look for the first causes at this unknown source. . . . Meteorological observations were now made from a permanent station over a period of two years, and the first documentary picture of Polar weather was built up stroke by stroke to provide scientific material altogether new."

II

As far back as 1921 the value of Arctic weather research was strikingly demonstrated by reports from Jan Mayern Island, between Iceland and Spitzbergen. An American engineer of Norwegian descent was instrumental in saving many lives in Norwegian waters alone by the accuracy of his storm warnings, yet, according to Vilhjalmur Stefansson, the Arctic expert, Greenland presents infinitely greater value as a centre for weather prediction.

That others were of the same mind is evidenced by the number of scientists of all nations who conducted meteorological research in Greenland just before the Second World War. Augustine Courtauld's work at the Ice Cap station set up by the British Arctic Air Route Expedition has been mentioned in an earlier chapter. While he was keeping his lone vigil in his snow-bound tent, a strong team of German experts, under the famous Arctic explorer Alfred Wegener, were established in an elaborate observatory they had constructed for themselves in the middle of the Ice Cap 300 miles north of the Arctic Circle. Living quarters and a store-room were scooped out beneath the surface of the ice, and a deep shaft was sunk between them for scientific study. An air-duct provided ventilation for the living quarters, and on the surface, immediately overhead, a tower of ice-blocks served as a mount for various instruments.

The three experts were Johannes Georgi, meteorologist from the German Naval Observatory; Fritz Lowe, from the Aviation Weather Bureau, and Ernst Sorge, who specialised in glaciological work. They manned their station throughout an entire winter, and the results of their labours are said to be among the most impressive ever achieved in Greenland. Unhappily, their expedition was marred by the death of its leader, Alfred Wegener, who perished on a return trip from the station which he had visited to ensure the welfare of his men.

Two years later the University of Michigan and Pan American Airways had a station at Peary Lodge, in the Upernavik District, from which Dr. Ralph Belknap made a journey inland for 180 miles to conduct a daily cycle of weather observations over a period of seven weeks.

At about the same time, Ernst Udet, Nazi Air Ace, spent several months flying in West Greenland with an expedition ostensibly engaged in making a film called "SOS Iceberg".

Following this, Pan American Airways appointed a Dane as aeronautical observer in Godthaab. He was Flight-Lieutenant Kurt Ramberg, and he was able to report that there was no day throughout the winter on which it would have been impossible for a flying-boat to find space for a touch-down in Godthaab Fiord. Meanwhile, the first successful Ice Cap landing had already been accomplished by Bert Hassell and Parker Cramer, members of Professor W. H. Hobb's University of Michigan Expedition, in the neighbourhood of Holsteins-borg.

More and more experience of flying over Greenland was being gained by international airmen. Wolfgang von Gronau crossed the Ice Cap north of Scoresby Sound three times in flights between Zeeland and Canada. Lauge Koch, the Danish explorer, made two non-stop flights from Spitzbergen to Pearyland, one with a German as co-pilot.

And all this time weather research went on. When war burst upon the world in 1939 there were six weather-stations in East Greenland and several on the west coast—all reporting meteorological forecasts by radio.

III

Three of the weather-stations on the north-east coast of Greenland at the outbreak of war were Norwegian; the rest were Danish. Early in the spring of 1940 one of the Norwegian stations intercepted a message from a German sealing-vessel then nosing her way through pack-ice between Spitzbergen and Greenland, and during the summer the Germans made many attempts to establish weather-posts on the east coast. Shortly afterwards their aircraft began to be seen over Greenland, and when, eventually, the Americans came to establish their bases by arrangement with the Danish Government, as narrated in Chapter X, their arrival was spotted by a reconnoitring Focke-Wulf Condor.

But Germany's prime consideration was still the establishment of worth-while weather-stations on the far-away east coast, and early in 1942 it gave a special command to a Lieutenant Ritter, who, as an ex-skipper of a whaler and the author of a number of books on the Arctic, was entrusted with the task of setting up a post on the east of Sabine Island.

Ritter succeeded, and settled down to transmit advanced weather forecasts for the benefit of the Luftwaffe and U-boats and German merchant ships. It was this base that was eventually bombed out of existence by Liberators after Ritter had captured the radio station at Eskimonaes.

In attacking this station the Germans fired a machine-gun into the air to give the impression that they were in force. The operators, who were armed only with sporting rifles, thus had sufficient warning in which to escape, taking with them a portable radio by which they were able to report events.

Ritter and his men meticulously sorted out the personal effects of the late occupants of the station and put them aside with the Danish flag and some fox-pelts before destroying the transmitting apparatus. Then the Lieutenant left the following note:

"The U.S.A. protects its defensive interests here in Greenland. We do the same also. We are not at war with Denmark. But the administration in Greenland gave orders to capture or shoot us, and, besides that you gave weather reports to the enemy. You are making Greenland into a place of war. We have stayed quietly at our posts without attacking you. Now you want war so you shall have war. But remember that if you shoot with illegal weapons [dum-dum bullets] which you have at hand here in the loft of the radio station, then you must take full responsibility for the consequences because you are placing yourselves outside the rules of war. Note we have put all personal effects of the hunters and all pelts in this hut, while we have destroyed the radio apparatus obtained from the U.S.A."

After leaving this note, which he signed as "Commandant of the Wehrmacht Detail in Eskimonaes", Lieutenant Ritter seized the soft-nosed cartridges, which were used for hunting game, and, taking three dog-teams and sledges, headed back for Sabine Island.

On the way the Germans encountered three men of the Danish sledge patrol. Their command to "halt" was either not heard or was misunderstood, so the Germans opened fire. A driver was shot, and after he had been buried beside the trail with a cross and the Danish flag to mark the grave, Ritter took the other two men with him to Sabine Island. There he released one, but retained the other, Captain Niels Jensen, to act as guide, as he wished personally to investigate a weather-station believed to be established at Mackenzie Bay.

The two men set off on this mission, but as soon as the German base had been left well behind them, the Dane, a powerful fellow, disarmed the Lieutenant and ordered him to march on. The tables turned, the astonished officer was forced to comply. Jensen marched his prisoner 350 miles to Scoresby Sound, where the headquarters of the Sledge Patrol were located.

For a month captor and captive lived together in the frozen wastes, taking their meals side by side, and even sharing the same sleeping-bag at night. Ritter was powerless, and had to accept the situation, for to have escaped would have availed him nothing; he could not have survived alone in that unknown wilderness of ice. The pair reached Scoresby Sound on May 1, and Jensen handed over his prisoner and resumed his command of the sledge patrol.

The war years provided the American airmen with extensive experience in Arctic flying. In *War Below Zero: The Battle for Greenland*, Colonel Bernt Balchen, Major Corey Ford and Major Oliver La Farge tell how new pilots were always carefully briefed by being shown series of aerial photographs of the territory over which they would have to fly, in addition to being given verbal instructions based on the experience of those who had gone before them.

"As the pilot approaches," runs the narrative, "he must be sharply alert for the landmarks which will guide him to the one safe landing place for hundreds of miles. There is no other place to put a plane down here; behind him lies the open ocean; beyond the dark coastal mountains the Ice Cap stretches like another sea. . . . You can sum this country up in one word—merciless."

On at least one occasion enemy radio men fooled the American flyers, luring them off course with false information and compelling one plane after another to make a forced landing on the Ice Cap. And almost until the end of the war attempts were made repeatedly to establish fresh weather-stations to replace those captured or destroyed.

IV

After the war came the urge to pursue weather research in peaceful conditions, not only for considerations of possible strategic defence in the future, but also for the purpose of planning commercial air routes. The prophecies of the aerial pioneers seemed near fulfilment. The day was approaching when Greenland would be a busy centre crossed by a network of Polar air-routes.

While the weather men of Count Eigil Knuth's Expedition were busy in Pearyland, others, from Canada and America, were active at other points on the northern extremities of Greenland. In collaboration with the Danes they established the first post-war weather-station at Thule in September 1946. A second was established at Eureka Sound in April 1947, and August of the same year saw a third spring into being at Resolute Bay. Two more were provided in the following year at Isachsen and Mould Bay, respectively, and in 1950 the most northerly of all, christened "Alert", was built on the northern fringe of Ellesmere Island, barely 450 miles from the North Pole. In the same year work was started upon yet another station on the north-east tip of Greenland. Since completed, and known as "Nord", it lies one hour by jet from similar installations which Russia has established 550 miles away on Franz Josef Land. It is furnished with an airstrip for re-supply, and is manned by Danes.

With the exception of the station at Thule, all the other weather-posts off the north-west coast of Greenland are in Canadian territory, but are jointly manned by Canadians and Americans. The task of keeping them supplied is fraught with difficulty, and twice a year—in the spring and autumn—American flyers from the base at Narsarssuaq lend a hand in dropping rations and other supplies by parachute. Apart from giving the airmen valuable practical experience in below-zero flying, it typifies the spirit of co-operation that exists in all these Arctic undertakings.

Service is reciprocal, of course. The work of the airmen stationed at the various Greenland bases is facilitated by the better and more comprehensive weather reports they are able to obtain from these far-flung outposts.

The construction of these weather- and radio-stations is a complex operation, beginning with aerial survey, and followed by careful pre-planning, the transportation of immense quantities of necessary equipment, and construction work under the kind of conditions endured by Polar explorers. Without the existence of the war-time bases in Greenland, and their counterparts on the opposite coasts of Baffin Island, Labrador and Newfoundland the sustained airlift necessary would hardly have been possible. The experience already gained in building those bases was, of course, invaluable, and many of the experts who had helped in those enterprises were available for peace-time planning.

Each station is now manned continuously by meteorologists, radio operators, radio mechanics, airstrip maintenance men and cooks. Eight surface readings are made daily, covering cloud ceiling, temperature, pressure, visibility and snow and ice phenomena. Met. men manufacture their own hydrogen for balloons, which are released twice daily to investigate upper air conditions at a height of 70,000 feet. Wind direction is obtained by radar, and a miniature radio transmitter attached to each balloon gives data on pressure, humidity and temperature. Smaller balloons give wind direction at lower levels.

Water supplies are a problem. At "Alert", for instance, a special tractor-drawn wagon with a built-in stove brings water from a frozen lake 5 miles away. A permanent metal pipe has been thrust through the 7-foot-thick ice, and is kept filled with petrol until water is wanted. The petrol is then ignited, and after it has burnt itself out a rubber pipe is lowered within the metal one and water pumped into the wagon. The built-in stove keeps it from freezing.

"Nord", the joint Danish–U.S. station, is just one example of what can be achieved by co-operation. Representatives of Denmark and America, who included Eske Brun, Director of the Greenland Department, and Lieutenant-Colonel R. B. Sykes, of the U.S. Weather Bureau, selected the site on a survey flight over the Princess Dagmar Peninsula. After a long period of preparation, the actual operation of establishing the station was launched in the spring of 1952. A preliminary party took off from one of the west-coast bases on April 4 in a plane equipped with skis, and were set down on the chosen site with tents and sufficient equipment to enable the members to prepare a runway. A strip of some 5,000 feet in length was marked out with red flags so that transport planes could soon follow with heavy material, consisting of ramps for unloading, tractors, sledges, and light track-vehicles such as weasels and snowmobiles, with stores of petrol and oil. In all about 600 tons of material was thus brought up by airlift.

Gradually the station sprang into being as eleven

specially designed prefabricated huts were assembled by
Danish workmen. These huts, manufactured in Denmark, were scientifically insulated with aluminium foil,
plywood, spun glass, wooden planks and tarpaulin. About
125 flights, mostly from the big new air-base at Thule,
were necessary to complete the whole operation.

The five weather-stations in Canadian territory are
now manned jointly by Canadians and Americans in equal
proportions, with a Canadian officer in charge and an
American executive officer. Those in Greenland are
manned by Danes and Americans. The complete chain,
stretching as it does across the top of the world, combines
to provide regular weather forecasts of incalculable value.

v

The pattern of air-bases, weather- and radio-stations
and Arctic airstrips has been largely shaped under an
agreement signed in Copenhagen on April 27, 1951,
between Denmark and the U.S.A. for the joint defence of
Greenland. Signatories were Mr. Ole Bjørn Kraft, the
Danish Foreign Minister, and Mrs. Eugenie Anderson,
the United States Ambassador, and the agreement was
ratified on June 1 in the same year by the Danish Folke-
ting by 80 votes to 7.

At the time of the actual signing a communique issued
simultaneously in Copenhagen and Washington made it
clear that the arrangement had been concluded within the
framework of the North Atlantic Treaty Organisation,
and that it replaced the provisional war-time agreement
under which American had first set up defence bases in
Greenland.

It was also explained that the development of communications had resulted in Greenland playing a vital part
in the defensive system built up by the North Atlantic
Treaty Organisation, the defence of the island being of
great importance not only to the immediate geographic
area of which it formed part, but also for the security of

all other member countries of the organisation, and especially that of Denmark.

In view of Danish sovereignty over Greenland, it was further decided by the appropriate organisation of NATO that the command for the local defence of Greenland should be given to a Danish officer. But as Denmark's own defence made very great demands upon her, it was only natural that she should seek aid from the other members of NATO in order to solve Greenland's defence problem. Against this background, then, the regional planning group suggested that Denmark and the U.S.A. should enter into negotiations with a view to agreeing on the necessary steps to be taken.

The terms of this new agreement are briefly as follows:

1. The American naval station at Gronnedal to be taken over by Denmark and operated as a purely Danish station, but the U.S.A. and other North Atlantic Treaty countries to have "certain rights of access" to the port. The status of bases and weather-stations handed back to Danish control in the summer of 1950 to be unchanged.

2. As need arises, defence areas to be established for joint operation by Denmark and the U.S.A., the flags of both countries to be flown over these areas. The nationality of the Commander to be decided periodically by agreement.

3. In those areas under American command the U.S.A. to enjoy certain rights with regard to the use of the area, but without impairing Danish sovereignty or the right of the Danish authorities to move freely throughout the island.

4. Denmark to be entitled to use such defence areas in co-operation with the U.S.A. in connection with the defence of Greenland, and the Danish military personnel, under a Danish officer to be attached to the staff of the American Commander, who must consult the Danish Commanding Officer upon all important matters affecting Danish interests.

5. Conversely, American military personnel might be sent to defence areas under Danish command, and the U.S.A. might use such areas in co-operation with Denmark.

6. For the North Atlantic zone, all defence areas in Greenland could be used by the ships, aircraft or armed forces of the other North Atlantic Treaty countries.

7. Present plans call for the setting up of only a few such defence areas, which, for the time being, would all be under American command, but which might be transferred by agreement to Danish command, if and when circumstances made such a change advisable.

8. Mutual assistance to be provided in various fields, such as movements by land, sea or air, on geodetic surveys and in meteorological research.

9. United States troops to be exempt from Customs duties and taxes, and jurisdiction over them to be specially arranged with the Danish authorities.

10. United States forces in the island to respect all Danish legislation concerning the native population, as well as Greenland's internal administration, and to avoid all contact with the civil population.

11. This new arrangement to remain in force for the duration of the North Atlantic Treaty. Meanwhile, should one of the countries wish to introduce any amendments, the other party must give consideration to such a request.

The North Atlantic Treaty, it should be noted, is of indefinite duration, though any member may withdraw after twenty years by giving one year's notice of its intention to do so.

In commenting upon the new agreement, after signature, Mr. Ole Bjørn Kraft described it as an expression of good co-operation within the Atlantic Pact. He added that it meant a strengthening of the defence of Greenland, and thereby of the whole North Atlantic area. "On the

cenes at
arsarssuaq—
"BluieWest 1".
The Control
Tower

Author

Danish Press Photographers' Assn.

modern airliner of Scandinavian Air Services on the runway, which skirts the
fiord where icebergs may be seen floating

Danish
and Ameri-
can flags
flying side
by side—as
on all the
American-
manned
bases in
Greenland.

Author

Danish side," he declared, "there is reason to be pleased with the understanding shown by the United States Government for the interests of the indigenous population of Greenland. The agreement is another proof that free sovereign nations are able by democratic means and through negotiations on equal terms to reach important results to their mutual satisfaction, based on mutual liberty and independence."

The former United States naval station at Gronnedal, mentioned in Clause 1 of the agreement, was built as a base for the U.S. Coastguard during the war, with a large oil depot where ships and planes could call for refuelling. It is equipped with permanent docking facilities where quite sizeable craft can load and unload, and with extensive barrack buildings and operation control-rooms. There is also a gently shelving beach on the fringe of the station which has been transformed into an airstrip for the use of amphibian machines which now link the various settlements along the coast.

Today Gronnedal serves as headquarters for the Danish Chief of the Greenland Command, Rear-Admiral F. A. H. Kjolsen. It is snugly sited, close to the thriving cryolite port of Ivigtut, and about 80 miles north-west of the big air-base at Narsarssuaq.

The possibility of developing the strategic advantages offered by Greenland seems limitless. The country's long coastline is riddled with fiords where submarines and other craft could hide or refuel in time of war. It has been estimated that the southern coast would be accessible to submarines and surface craft for at least a third of a normal year, and that troops and supplies could be landed at any time of the year along 50 per cent of the coast.

Writing on this subject in his book on Greenland, Vilhjalmur Stefansson indicates the possibility of unfriendly Powers being tempted by the necessity of securing weather-stations to drop units by air. It is perfectly feasible today, he argues, for complete meteorological

R

outfits and radio-transmitting apparatus to be dropped by parachute from an ordinary transport plane. Windmill generating plants, capable of sustaining a station for a full year, could also be dropped, with all necessary supplies and the technicians to man the station.

The very vastness of Greenland offers scope for a whole series of such operations, but Stefansson cites Pearyland in particular as affording exceptional facilities for setting up secret stations. The fact that the terrain there is not ice covered, but consists chiefly of rugged, broken rock with many ravines, makes observation by aerial patrols very difficult. "Almost anyone", he declares, "could establish and camouflage a base there."

This opinion was expressed eleven years ago, and though it probably holds true today in the main, the likelihood of "pirate" stations surviving undetected for long has been considerably lessened by all the defence measures which have been taken since.

The programme initiated by Denmark and the U.S.A., under NATO, may be said to contribute an insurance for world peace, and it is already beginning to pay valuable interim dividends in the development of civil aviation.

CHAPTER XX

WHAT OF TOMORROW?

CHANGING Greenland follows her path of progress with the inevitability of the great glaciers which sweep down from the Ice Cap through coastal valleys to keep their rendezvous with the sea. But, as we have seen, the tempo of her progress is a quickening one. She has come a long, long way in a very short time, and her people have survived all that a harsh, uncompromising climate could do to them and have adapted themselves to the shocks and stresses entailed by their ultra-rapid transition from Stone Age to the age of supersonics. What, then, of tomorrow?

The existence of the air-bases—particularly the monster base at Thule—ensures a growing contact of Greenlanders with the rest of the world, while the developing fifteen-year plan for implementing the recommendations of the Royal Commission ensures their preparation for such contact.

The list of Greenland's exports is ever growing and, apart from cryolite, now includes blubber, shark's liver, cod liver, train-oil, medicinal cod-liver oil, sperm oil, eiderdown and feathers, blue-fox furs, white-fox furs, polar-bear pelts, seal skins, wolf-fish skins, walrus hides, salted sea-trout, salted halibut, canned shrimps, salted fish, dried fish, wool and sheep and lamb fleeces.

All the time fresh experiments are being made. The scheme for introducing new reindeer herds has been mentioned; there are also fox farms and mink farms, and various other fields of endeavour are constantly being explored.

It is thought that the country could sustain a population nearly double its present figure of 22,078. There has been a steady rise throughout the years. In 1900 it stood at about 12,000. By 1938 it had reached 18,311; by 1944, 20,574. With the planned improvement of living conditions and the vigorous Health Service campaign, it seems certain that the rise must continue.

The development of a rational fishing industry presupposes the concentration of population in larger and fewer centres, and such a tendency has been manifest for a number of years, as more and more people have been drawn from the smaller to the larger settlements. The authorities, however, are alive to the danger of concentrating the entire population of western Greenland in a few places, even though it might minimise administrative problems in some ways. The fisheries, though highly important, must not, it is felt, be allowed to become all-important. The aim, therefore, is to maintain a balanced economic life by encouraging alternative industries in centres best adapted to them.

At the same time, the expansion of the fisheries has to be legislated for. As larger boats come into use the need to school Greenlanders in deep-sea technique will have to be met. It is proposed to acquire a 50-ton fishing cutter, with modern equipment, for use as a training vessel, and to establish a centre in Godthaab where would-be fishermen can be put through a theoretical course.

A scheme is already functioning under which Greenlanders attend courses at the Fishery High School at Esbjerg, Denmark, and afterwards spend a period of employment with Esbjerg fishermen to gain practical experience. It is likely to be extended. Again, Danish and Faroese fishing-boats are allowed in Greenland territorial waters only on condition that half their crews are Greenlanders employed upon equal terms.

Scientific investigations of all kinds are carried on continuously, with the result that fresh knowledge is being acquired all the time in geology, zoology, marine-biology, geodetical work, meteorology, glaciology, botany and mineralogy.

The Commission for Scientific Investigations in Greenland acts as a co-ordinating body to some extent, and new moves contemplated will bring the Arctic Station at Godhavn under the administration of the Copenhagen University. It is to be expanded, with sufficient laboratory space to enable foreign scientists to work there.

Geological survey work is also to be reorganised to ensure that any discoveries of economic importance are promptly assessed by technical and financial experts. To this end a committee of scientific experts is being set up with power to decide where geological research shall be conducted and to nominate the scientists who are to perform it. Supplementary to this there is to be an office for organising geological expeditions and for handling technical and financial problems which may arise concerning the exploitation of mineral deposits when discovered. The Danish Government, however, will be the final arbiter as to whether such exploitation can best be State-operated or left to free enterprise.

II

One effect of Greenland's emergence into the family of nations has been the fostering of a growing interest in the country and its people. The tendency to regard Greenland as remote, frozen and unfriendly—natural enough while it remained a closed country—is fast being dispelled. Soon the silence of her western fiords may be broken by the laughter of the first batch of summer tourists, and it is more than likely, now that barriers of distance lessen yearly, that travel offices of tomorrow will include Greenland in their holiday programmes as a matter of course. A start is being made by the United Shipping Company of Copenhagen, which hopes soon to offer a round trip at fares ranging approximately from £100 to £175. The Company has a long experience of sailing in Greenland waters, for it was one of its vessels that carried King Christian X on his tour of the west coast in 1921. The pleasure cruise now contemplated may be aboard M.S. *Dronning Alexandrine*, sailing from Copenhagen via the Faroes and Iceland.

As there are no hotels in Greenland so far, passengers will live on the ship, but the normal complement will be reduced from 130 to ninety for greater comfort, and there will be only one class. Passport and visa will be required only if these are necessary for entering Denmark, but passengers must have a clean bill of health and will be required to produce a certificate from their own doctors to this effect.

Various tours and functions are planned at ports of call. At Godthaab visitors may inspect the training college, the book-printing works and all the new municipal under-takings. There will be motor-boat trips in Godthaab Fiord, with salmon and halibut fishing, or walks to local beauty spots, with a typical Greenland Dance-and-coffee-mik ashore to round off the evening.

At Sukkertoppen, "the Venice of Greenland", visitors will see the fishing-station and freezing plant, and be given the opportunity of making gastronomical experi-ments by sampling local delicacies, including smoked halibut and "*matak*" made from the skin of a whale. The works of Greenland painters may also be on view.

A high light of the cruise is bound to be the crossing of the Arctic Circle, when traditional ceremonial, akin to that followed on crossing the Equator, but entailing some sur-prising variants, takes place on deck. If King Neptune's henchmen do their duty, no novice will escape this formality, and it is usually an occasion of great hilarity enjoyed by everyone. Initiates have bestowed upon them a Greenlandic title inscribed upon a Polar Diploma, which, signed by King Neptune and the ship's captain, certifies the time and place of their initiation. Possession of this document carries a certain privilege among sea-farers throughout the world, for, by old tradition, those who have rounded Cape Horn may place one foot on the table after dinner; but those who have crossed the Arctic Circle may put both feet up!

Even this will not exhaust the tour. At Egedesminde fully accredited Arctic voyagers will be entertained by dancing displays, dog-sledge races and kayak demonstrations. Watching some of the traditional Eskimo dance patterns, they will see, perhaps, the origins of the ever-popular square dance.

But at this point of the tour the scenery will command most attention. Between Egedesminde and Jakobshavn, the next port of call, the wonders of Disko Bay will unfold. It is the region of newly calved icebergs, towering monsters, starting on the first lap of their long journey towards the Atlantic. Sparkling in the Arctic sunshine, they float past in fantastic procession, no two alike, either in form or colour. Some are pierced by perfectly symmetrical Gothic arches; others sprout from the sea on thick stems in the semblance of gigantic mushrooms; others, again, rise in graceful pinnacles or float sullenly in rugged, crag-like masses. All move to keep the same appointment with Destiny; all are making for the broad Atlantic, ultimately to meet the Gulf Stream and melt and merge with the sea. Yet their variety is infinite. In colouring they range from virgin white to peacock green; some crystalline and ethereal in appearance; others seemingly solid and indestructible.

At Jakobshavn, birthplace of Rasmussen, wise tourists will take an after-dinner stroll across country to Holms Bakke, where they will be rewarded with one of the finest spectacles in Nature: a spectacle that should be reckoned as one of the wonders of the world. In the witchery of the Arctic twilight they will see the great glaciers thrusting purposefully down through the vast frozen valleys in an immaculate flow of virgin ice. It is here that the icebergs plunge into the waters of the fiord to begin their independent existence. As they elbow and jostle one another in their eagerness to reach the sea they seem like living things. Sixty feet a day is their measured progress. One can almost sense their petulant impatience.

Before leaving Disko Bay, tourists may visit Quervain's Havn (named after the Swiss explorer) and make an excursion to the fringe of the Inland Ice. For most of them this will be close enough acquaintance with the formidable Ice Cap. It will heighten their respect for the pioneers who traversed its unknown wastes and for modern adventurers like the men of the Simpson Expedition who, in the interests of science, deliberately maroon themselves in its merciless embrace.

By way of contrast, the suggested Greenland cruise will end with a visit to Julianehaab, in the more benign south. Founded in 1755, and beautifully sited, it has, somehow, a more mature air than many of the other settlements. It boasts the largest public hall in the country, built by the Greenlanders themselves, whose civic pride is also symbolised in an ornamental fountain in the square, commemorating, among other distinguished friends of Greenland, Dr. Knud Rasmussen and Dr. Hendrik Rink. New harbour works have lately been completed, and the community is a thriving one. Here the visitor may gain a glimpse of pastoral life, for sheep and cattle graze upon surrounding grass-grown slopes. It was hereabouts that the old Norse settlers waged their losing battle against an uncompromising climate; yet, seen in the serenity of summer sunshine, it is difficult to picture the severity of winter.

For the summer tourist of the future Greenland has much to offer. The amenities of hotels and cafés will come in time, and doubtless a thriving tourist industry will develop. Until then, however, ships will continue to serve as floating hotels, and their normal itinerary may be augmented by supplementary trips by motor-launch or flying-boat. To the novelty of background may be added scenic charm beyond peer; wild flowers in profusion for the Nature-lover; game in abundance for the sportsman; a paradise for fishermen; thrills of mountain climbing for the venturesome. Much of this, perhaps, lies in the future; but a start may be made very soon. Remembering how rapidly events are moving in Greenland today, a full-scale tourist industry may develop well within the next decade.

III

But it is in the air that the most far-reaching developments are to be noted. Existing air-bases already make Greenland potentially one of the most important world centres for aerial traffic; others will doubtless be added, just as the network of permanent weather-stations is certain to be extended.

It would be easy to be cynical about the strategic implications dealt with in the preceding chapter, but to do so would be to lose a sense of proportion. They are big bases, certainly, and a fortune has been expended upon them. Some were developed in war-time as a necessity, and the biggest of all was bred from the fear of war. The tendency to refer to them as "American Bases" persists, but we should remember that they exist today as part of the defensive partnership of the North Atlantic Treaty Organisation. We should keep it that way. Every NATO statesman needs to remember this.

Eske Brun has scouted once and for all the suggestion that Greenland is passing under American influence. "We shall never sell our last remaining colony," he has declared. "Americans are investing a great deal of money in Greenland, but that is all." And when international pressmen were permitted to inspect the new base at Thule, Brun impressed upon them: "You are here on Danish soil, and this base is a joint Danish–American base."

By the same token, the various scientific expeditions— the British North Greenland unit, or the French Victor party—operate in Greenland in co-operation with the

Danish Government. The fruits of their work are for the benefit of all, just as the work of Canadian, Danish or American weather experts who man the remote Polar stations combines to aid all NATO flyers.

That Greenland, by virtue of its great size, offers unique facilities for warlike experiments cannot be denied. The Ice Cap probably presents the most suitable field—next to the great Australian desert—for testing giant rockets and other atomic weapons. It also provides an excellent Arctic training-ground for military manœuvres. The United States Army, for instance, hopes to send a cavalcade of "weasels" across the northern fringe of the Ice Cap from Thule to the new weather-station at Nord—a gruelling test for men and machines, but one from which many useful lessons may be derived.

None of this, however, can be said to be aggressive. It all forms part of a policy of preparedness; an insurance, perhaps, for peace.

The most heartening thing is that, arising directly out of all these many endeavours, peaceful benefits have already resulted, with an immeasurable gain to civil aviation.

It was to further the interests of civil aviation that "Gino" Watkins led his First British Polar Air Route Expedition to Greenland, and it is significant, as Count Eigil Knuth has pointed out, that the site he chose for his base tallied with that subsequently chosen for the only east-coast air-base established in the war, Bluie East. Watkins had a prophetic vision, and Colonel Bernt Balchen, under whom the war-time bases were built, is equally far-sighted.

"Some day our whole conception of geography will be changed," he wrote in *War Below Zero*. "Then the Arctic will be the very centre of our new world, and across Greenland and Northern Canada and Alaska will run the commercial airways from New York to London, from San

Francisco to Moscow and Japan. Today's highway of war will be tomorrow's avenue of Peace."

And so it has proved. The sensational Atlantic crossing by two United States Air Force helicopters, "Hopalong" and "Whirlaway", in August 1952, would have been impossible had not touch-down and servicing facilities been available in Greenland. The machines, piloted by veterans of the Korean war, hopped 770 miles from Goose Bay, Labrador, to Narsarssuaq—a record for helicopters, though they eclipsed it themselves in their next hop of 840 miles to Iceland.

Although the development of the helicopter has many possibilities, an event of far greater importance to civil aviation followed within three months of this spectacular performance, with the first trans-Polar passenger flight from Los Angeles to Copenhagen, via Thule. This "Arctic Express", as it was termed, was a new DC-6B machine belonging to Scandinavian Airlines System, and the epoch-making flight was the result of months of careful planning. Nothing approaching it had ever been attempted before, and a host of new factors had to be taken into consideration.

Accumulated data on Arctic flying, gained by the United States Air Force in the course of hundreds of weather observation flights in Polar regions, was made available, and the Company also took full benefit of the knowledge of Arctic experts like General Hjalmar Riiser-Larsen and Colonel Bernt Balchen.

From a flying point of view the prevailing weather along the Polar route was considered to be extremely favourable. Winds above 25,000 feet were generally westerly, with a speed of from 20 to 25 knots, while at lesser altitudes they tended to be north-westerly with a speed of about 15 knots.

The flight was scheduled for November 19, and northwards of latitude 70° N. the mean wind during winter periods is a moderate easterly one. At higher levels it is zero. On Greenland's west coast and from the mountain range of Baffin Island easterly winds occur at altitudes below 10,000 feet.

A smooth flight was confidently forecast, and experience already gained in service flying showed that risks of icing are definitely less over the Polar route than over the North Atlantic route or over Europe. It was announced that passengers would be able to fly "in shirt-sleeve comfort".

On the other hand, navigation presented special problems, though here, again, a great amount of exploratory work in this direction had been carried out already by flyers of the Royal Air Force,* the Royal Canadian Air Force and the U.S. Army Air Corps.

The actual flight was scheduled as follows:

Depart Los Angeles	.	16.30 G.M.T.	08.30 Local Time	Nov. 19
Arrive Edmonton	.	23.00 ,,	16.00 ,,	,,
Depart ,,	.	01.00 ,,	18.00 ,,	Nov. 20
Arrive Thule	.	09.00 ,,	04.00 ,,	,,
Depart ,,	.	11.00 ,,	06.00 ,,	,,
Arrive Copenhagen	.	21.00 ,,	22.00 ,,	,,

As the magnetic compass cannot be relied upon in the area of the North Magnetic Pole, the flight between Edmonton and Thule, and Thule and the east coast of Greenland, had to be planned as a grid flight, changing to the conventional system of navigation from then onward.

Flying in the area of the Pole, any course taken, other than in a north–south direction, rapidly crosses the meridians at a constantly changing angle. To overcome this a special meridian was used as a standard, and the grid-net was drawn on this, enabling a course angle to be maintained at a constant value. Gyro-compasses were used in conjunction with astro-navigation to maintain direction.

On the Polar route, conditions for taking bearings of

---

* The *Aries* series of flights over the North Pole and the magnetic North Pole, carried out by the Empire Air Navigation School, have yielded immensely valuable data.

the position of sun, moon and stars are said to be excellent in summer and winter alike. A new instrument has been developed for use in winter, when the sun is below the horizon. Known as the Pfund Sky Compass, it uses the vertical polarisation of the sun's light. In addition, a system of radar navigation known as "Target timing" can be employed to check an aircraft's speed and direction. Yet another form of air navigation, developed by Colonel Balchen in a flight from Fairbanks, Alaska, to Oslo in 1949, uses air-pressure readings at known heights compared with those at take-off and landing points, expressed in millibars.

In command of the aircraft "Arild Viking", on the Scandinavian Airlines flight, was Senior Captain Paul Jensen, of Denmark, and two Norwegian navigators shared the heavy task of plotting the course. They were First Navigator Einar Pedersen, author of several works on Arctic navigation, and Navigator B. Heiberg Andersen. Both had considerable practical experience in Arctic flying.

In addition to a crew of ten, the "Arild Viking" carried twenty-four distinguished passengers, including Colonel and Mrs. Bernt Balchen, Mr. Eske Brun, Their Excellencies the Danish and Norwegian Ambassadors in U.S.A., and various Scandinavian, Canadian, American and Icelandic air officials.

Although the plane was delayed some ten minutes or so at the start, time was made up after leaving Edmonton, and Thule was reached ten minutes ahead of schedule. Visibility was excellent, and the flight was smooth and comfortable. The passengers celebrated the event by drinking champagne over the Polar regions. As they circled above Thule before coming in to land, Captain Jensen signalled a report via Godthaab Radio. Some of the passengers had travelled in shirt sleeves, but at Thule it was necessary to don fur coats as they emerged from their aircraft. Although it was dark, a tremendous welcome awaited them, and during a two-hour stop they

were fêted by the Danish colony and by the American
Officers' club.

On leaving Thule they flew over the Ice Cap at an
altitude of 15,000 feet, snug and secure, though the outside temperature was minus 35° Centigrade. Helped by
an 87 m.p.h. following wind, they made good progress,
and by 3 p.m. G.M.T., Captain Jensen was speaking
to Copenhagen by short-wave telephone. They had passed
Jan Mayen by then. The sky had been cloudless, and
below them they had seen the ocean crowded with ice-
floes.

Copenhagen was reached ahead of schedule in twenty-
eight hours, seven minutes. Waiting to greet the travellers on the tarmac at Kastrup Airport were three Greenland girls in full festival costume, with bouquets of red
and white carnations for the crew and for Mrs. Bernt
Balchen—the only woman on this epic flight.

"I think I prefer to fly over the Arctic than over the
Atlantic," was Captain Jensen's verdict, and he clinched
this barely a fortnight later by flying a second machine
over the same route!

IV

These two Polar flights have been described by Scandinavian Airlines System as "survey trips" preparatory to
establishing a regular passenger service over the same
route. It has twelve similar machines on order, and it may
well be that such a service will be in operation by the
time this book appears. The precise route planned will
run from Los Angeles, via San Francisco, Seattle, Van-
couver and Thule, and it is claimed that travel time from
the west coast of America to continental Europe along
the Northern Global Route will average approximately
thirteen hours less for the round trip than via New York.
Further schedules are being worked out for future trans-
Arctic flights which will cut travel time to Tokyo by

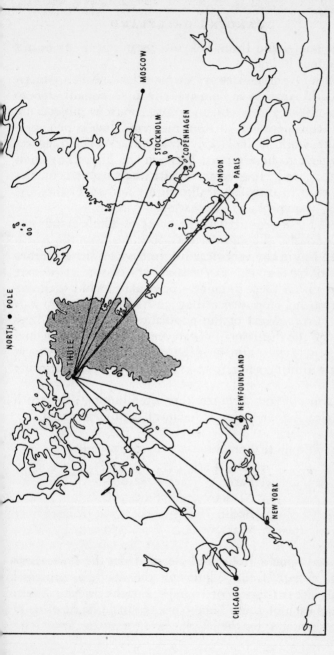

NORTH • POLE

MOSCOW

STOCKHOLM

COPENHAGEN

LONDON

PARIS

THULE

NEWFOUNDLAND

NEW YORK

CHICAGO

Knud Rasmussen, the famous Greenland explorer, is credited with having first visualised Thule as an aerial centre of trans-Polar routes of the future. Today this great air-base, barely 930 miles from the North Pole, is a reality, and airliners have made proving flights from Los Angeles to Copenhagen, and from Oslo to Tokyo, via Thule, thus effecting immense saving in time and distance. A glance at the accompanying map shows the obvious advantages of this Polar base, which is equidistant from most of the world's capitals.

sixteen hours, and from Tokyo to Scandinavia by nearly twenty-four hours.

British Overseas Airways Corporation and Pan American World Airways System are, of course, equally alive to the possibilities of Arctic air-routes. Various projects are under consideration at the moment, but much preliminary work is inevitably entailed. Working agreements have to be arranged between the big airline companies, as well as agreements with the various countries flown over to establish traffic rights and to fit into the existing framework of international aviation.

In all these negotiations the name of Thule stands out conspicuously. Though barely 930 miles from the North Pole, it will in the very near future have all the amenities of a modern airport. Air passengers of tomorrow may change planes there or enjoy a brief pause while their aircraft refuels before proceeding on its journey to *any part of the world*. Most of the population of the world lives north of the Equator. Whatever their nationality and whatever their ultimate destination a touch-down at Thule will bring them to the very hub of Arctic air-route traffic.

A table of flying distances serves to illuminate this truth more clearly than pages of technical argument could do.

Thule to London	.	. 2,470	miles
,, ,, New York	.	2,400	,,
,, ,, Paris	.	. 2,660	,,
,, ,, Moscow	.	. 2,780	,,
,, ,, Berlin	.	. 2,570	,,
,, ,, Warsaw	.	. 2,730	,,

Traced upon a globe, and viewed from the Pole, these routes radiate from Thule to the world's principal capitals like the spokes of a wheel. For the fastest modern airliners each of these "hops" represents a flight of from five to six hours; for the jet planes of tomorrow, even less!

v

Viewed from any angle, Greenland's future is full of portent. For her people, rising so rapidly to higher standards of social, cultural and economic development and a place of importance in world affairs, inspiring vistas must unfold themselves. For statesmen and strategists, envisaging the possible threat of future wars, the country may symbolise a bastion of defence, or a springboard for attack, according to the viewpoint, temperament or nationality of the individuals concerned. For the humble historian, striving to preserve a detached view as he chronicles the march of Greenland's progress, there is abundant hope of the ultimate fulfilment of the dreams of men like Hans Egede and Dr. Hendrik Rink—a Greenland happy and prosperous in the family of nations.

CHRONOLOGY

900	Greenland coast sighted by Gunnjborn, Norwegian navigator, driven off-course for Iceland.
982	Eric the Red flees from Iceland to Greenland.
986	Eric the Red leads Icelandic settlers to Greenland.
1000	Leif Ericsson brings Christianity to Greenland settlers.
1126	Norwegian bishop founds his See at Gardar, Igaliko Fiord.
1261	Greenland, hitherto a Republic, recognises sovereignty of King of Norway.
1360	Eskimo tribes from north destroy Norse settlements.
1410	Last vessel returns from Greenland to Norway.
1585	John Davis visits Greenland.
1607	Hudson sights north-east coast of Greenland.
1721	Hans Egede, Norwegian missionary, founds Godthaab.
1729	Royal Government in Copenhagen take over missionary work and trade in Greenland.
1730	Death of Frederik IV and accession of Christian VI.
1731	Royal Mandate for relinquishment of Greenland; Hans Egede elects to remain behind.
1732	King Christian VI unbends and sends supplies to Egede.
1733	Devastating smallpox epidemic sweeps the colony.
1734	End of epidemic. Christianshaab founded.
1741	Jakobshavn founded.
1742	Frederikshaab founded.
1751	Lars Dalager explores Ice Cap from Frederikshaab.
1755	Julianehaab, Sukkertoppen and Rittenbenk founded.
1758	Umanak founded.
1759	Holsteinsborg founded.
1771	Upernavik founded.
1773	Godhavn founded on Disko Island.
1774	Trade becomes Government monopoly.
1807	Greenland cut off from Europe by War.
1814	Union between Norway and Denmark dissolved; Denmark retains Greenland.
1822	Captain W. Scoresby, Junior, Scottish whaler, explores Greenland's north-east coast with his father, and produces the first accurate map.
1823	Captains E. Sabine and D. Clavering visit north-east coast and meet the only Eskimos seen in that part.
1829–30	Lt. W. A. Graah, a Dane, explores south-east coast.
1833	French Blossville Expedition to East Greenland.

1852   E. A. Inglefield sails into Smith Sound.

1853-5 E. K. Kane sails northward through Smith Sound to Kane Basin.

1857   Local Councils organised.

1864   Ivigtut, the cryolite centre, founded.

1867   E. Whymper and R. Brown fail in first attempt to penetrate interior.

1870   A. E. Nordenskiold and S. Berggren walk 35 miles inland from head of Aulatsiork Fiord to 2,200 feet.

        German expedition under C. Koldewey, reaches 77° N., Cape Bismarck.

1871   C. F. Hall explores Kennedy Strait and Robeson Channels.

1876   L. A. Beaumont, Nares Expedition.

1878   Jens Jensen reaches the Jensen Nunataks, 5,400 feet above sea level and 45 miles from western margin, latitude 62°.

1882   J. B. Lockwood, Greely Expedition.

1883-5 N. Nordenskiold penetrates 60 miles inland, latitude 68°, and two Laplanders in his party push on to 6,600 feet above sea level.

        G. Holm and T. V. Garde map coast between Cape Farewell and Angmagssalik.

1886   Peary and Maigaard push 100 miles inland, latitude 69°, and reach 7,500 feet above sea level.

1888   NANSEN, WITH FIVE COMPANIONS, MAKES FIRST COMPLETE CROSS-ING OF ICE CAP, LATITUDE 64°, REACHING 8,922 FEET ABOVE SEA LEVEL.

1891   Nansen publishes his account of the *First Crossing of Greenland*.

1892   Captain C. Ryder maps parts of Scoresby Sound.

        Peary and Astrup make northern crossing of Inland Ice, latitude 78°, and reach 8,000 feet above sea level.

1893   T. V. Garde penetrates 60 miles, latitude 61°, reaching 7,080 feet.

1894   Angmagssalik (pronounced Ammassalik) founded.

1895   Peary conducts big-scale sledging party in far north.

1899   H. G. Amdrup explores coast above Angmagssalik.

        Dr. A. G. Nathorst explores between Franz Josef Fiord and Scoresby Sound and discovers King Oscar Fiord.

1900   Amdrup explores east coast.

1902-4 Danish Literary Expedition to Cape York.

1905   Duke of Orleans proves Cape Bismarck an island.

1906-7 Danish Expedition under Mylius Erichsen and J. P. Koch dis-covers North-east Foreland.

1908   DISTRICT COUNCILS SET UP TO ADMINISTER PUBLIC ASSISTANCE, ETC.

1910   Einar Mikkelsen crosses north-east corner of Greenland.

        THULE FOUNDED AT NORTH STAR BAY BY KNUD RASMUSSEN.

1912   Rasmussen and Peter Freuchen cross from Inglefield Gulf to Dan-marks Fiord and back.

1913   Swiss explorer A. de Quervain crosses Ice Cap between Angmagssalik and Disko Bay.

      J. P. Koch and A. Wegener cross from Queen Louise Land to north-east coast, near Proven, reaching 9,500 feet above sea level.

      RASMUSSEN'S FIRST THULE EXPEDITION.

1917   RASMUSSEN'S SECOND THULE EXPEDITION.

1919   RASMUSSEN'S THIRD AND FOURTH THULE EXPEDITIONS.

1921   KING CHRISTIAN X VISITS GREENLAND.

1922–4 RASMUSSEN'S FIFTH THULE EXPEDITION.

1925   SCORESBY SOUND FOUNDED WITH NUCLEUS POPULATION TRANSFERRED FROM ANGMAGSSALIK.

      FIRST EFFECTIVE STEPS TOWARDS POLITICAL RE-ORGANISATION. DUTIES OF DISTRICT COUNCILS EXPANDED.

1926   Lauge Koch explores from Scoresby Sound to Danmarks Havn.

1927   W. H. Hobbs, University of Michigan, conducts meteorological experiments in Holsteinsborg area; J. M. Wordie adds details between Sabine Island and Day Sound.

1930   "GINO" WATKINS LEADS FIRST BRITISH ARCTIC AIR-ROUTE EXPEDITION AND CONDUCTS WEATHER OBSERVATIONS 40 MILES NORTH OF ARCTIC CIRCLE.

      GERMAN EXPEDITION, UNDER ALFRED WEGENER, WINTERS 300 MILES NORTH OF ARCTIC CIRCLE.

1931   RASMUSSEN'S SIXTH THULE EXPEDITION.

1932   "GINO" WATKINS DROWNED WHILE KAYAKING ALONE IN EAST GREENLAND.

1933   HAGUE COURT AWARDS GREENLAND TO DENMARK.

      University of Michigan and Pan American Airways carry out surveys.

      Charles Lindbergh flies to Greenland with his wife on surprise visit.

      DEATH OF RASMUSSEN, GREATEST OF GREENLAND EXPLORERS.

1934   Martin Lindsay Expedition crosses Ice Cap.

1935   Gunnbjörn Peak scaled by British-led party which included two Everest climbers, L. R. Wager and J. Longlands, and Augustine Courtauld and Ebbe Munck.

1938   Skjoldungen founded with nucleus population from Angmagssalik.

1940   DENMARK OCCUPIED BY NAZI WEATHER SPIES.

1941–5 U.S.A. assumes responsibility for Greenland's defence in agreement with Henrik de Kaufman, Danish Minister in Washington. Air-bases and weather-stations built.

1946   Denmark starts post-war development drive in Greenland.

1947   Danish Pearyland Expedition launched.

1948   FRENCH EXPEDITION UNDER PAUL EMILE VICTOR.

1949   Royal Commission set up.

1950   Commission issues report with many recommendations.

1951   Denmark passes many new Acts to implement Commission's re-
       commendations; also enters into new defence agreements with
       U.S.A. under NATO.
       Government monopoly ended.
       Work begun on new air-base at Thule.

1952   KING FREDERIK IX VISITS GREENLAND WITH QUEEN INGRID.
       British North Greenland Expedition, under Commander Simp-
       son, begins a two-year mission on the Ice Cap in far north.
       THULE, "BLUE JAY" AIR-BASE OFFICIALLY REVEALED AS AN
       ACCOMPLISHED FACT.
       SCANDINAVIAN AIRLINES SERVICE CARRY OUT FIRST POLAR-
       ROUTE PASSENGER FLIGHTS FROM LOS ANGELES TO COPENHAGEN
       VIA THULE.

1953   FIRST PASSENGER CRUISE TO GREENLAND PLANNED AS FORE-
       RUNNER OF REGULAR SUMMER HOLIDAY TRIPS.
       Copenhagen University takes over the Arctic Station at God-
       havn, and announces plan for extending accommodation to
       enable foreign scientists to make use of its laboratories.
       British North Greenland Expedition begins its second year's
       work on Ice Cap.
       Passenger flight from Oslo to Tokyo, via Thule.
       Changes in Danish Constitution make Greenland a part of the
       Kingdom, with two seats in the Danish Parliament.

ACKNOWLEDGMENTS AND BIBLIOGRAPHY

In the preparation of this book I have been especially fortunate in receiving much valuable co-operation from numerous Danish officials in London, Copenhagen and in Greenland. My thanks are due to all those who facilitated my on-the-spot inquiries and those who have rendered subsequent assistance in making available to me official reports and general material.

I am particularly grateful to Mr. Ebbe Munck, Counsellor-in-Charge of Press Affairs, and Mr. Tyge Kappel, Press Attaché at the Royal Danish Embassy in London, who have borne the brunt of my persistent questing for information; also to Mr. Sigvald Kristensen, Mr. Bengt Petersen and Mr. Sven Ebbesen of the Press Department, Ministry for Foreign Affairs, Copenhagen, and to Mr. K. Budde Lund of the Greenland Department, Copenhagen, for their kindly assistance and advice. Finally, I would add a word of thanks to the anonymous librarians at the British Museum Reading Room for their courteous and efficient help during my historical researches.

In addition to sources specifically mentioned in the text, the following works have been consulted with advantage, and due acknowledgment is here made to the respective authors and publishers.

A Description of Greenland, by Hans Egede.

"A New Era for Greenland," by Hans Henrik Koch. From *Danish Foreign Office Journal,* 1950.

"Americans Stand Guard in Greenland," by Andrew H. Brown. *National Geographic Magazine,* October 1946.

"Danish Defence," by Admiral E. J. C. Qvistgaard, Chief of Defence. Reprinted from *Berlingske Tidende.*

"Exploring Unknown Greenland," by Count Eigil Knuth. From Danish *Foreign Office Journal,* 1952.

The First Crossing of Greenland, by F. Nansen. 1892.

"Flying Around the North Atlantic," by Anne Morrow Lindbergh, with a foreword by Col. Charles A. Lindbergh. *National Geographic Magazine,* September 1934.

"Greenland and Denmark," by Knud Oldendow. From 1947 Handbook issued by Royal Danish Ministry for Foreign Affairs and the Danish Statistical Department.

Greenland, Its Nature, Inhabitants and History, by T. N. Krabbe. 1930.

"Greenland," lecture by P. V. Sveistrup, Head of Section of the Administration of Greenland. 1950.

Greenland (3 volumes). Issued by the Commission for the Direction of Geological and Geographical Investigation in Greenland. Oxford University Press, 1928.

"Greenland Turns to America," by James K. Penfield, First U.S. Consul in Greenland. *National Geographic Magazine*, September 1942.

Greenland by the Polar Sea, by Knud Rasmussen. 1921.

Greenland, by V. Stefansson. Harrap, 1943.

"Greenland—Denmark's Colony," by K. Borum. From Danish *Foreign Office Journal*, 1948.

History of Greenland, by David Cranz. 1820.

Northern Lights, by F. Spencer Chapman. Chatto & Windus, 1932.

Northward Over the Great Ice, by R. E. Peary. Methuen, 1898.

The Olaf Sagas, Snorre Sturlasson. Everyman's Library.

The Story of Hans Egede, by Jans Olaf. 1864.

"The Northernmost Country in the World," by Count Eigil Knuth. Issued by the Royal Danish Embassy, London, and reprinted from the *Geographical Magazine*.

Report on Greenland, 1950. Issued by the Greenland Department.

Report on Greenland, 1951. Issued by the Greenland Department.

To the Arctic, by Jeanette Mirsky. Allan Wingate, 1947.

Viking Settlers in Greenland, by Poul Nørlund. Cambridge University Press, 1936.

War Below Zero, by Colonel Bernt Balchen, Major Corey Ford and Major Oliver La Farge. Allen & Unwin, 1945.

Watkins' Last Expedition, by F. Spencer Chapman. Chatto & Windus, 1934.

1953   G. W.

INDEX